Christian Home Library

SERMONS AND TALKS
VOLUME 1

Ellen G. White

LS Company

ISBN: 978-1-0879-5768-5

Copyright 2021

Content:

Foreword 7

A Dream About the Value of Team Work 9

Called To The Wedding Feast 11

Diet and Health 15

Hearing and Doing 17

Preparation for the Judgement 24

Having Our Conversation in Heaven 33

Preach the Third Angel's Message—Avoid Trivial Topics 39

Remarks After Reading and Article—1888 Before the General Conference 42

The Minister's Relationship to God's Word 48

Religious Liberty 58

Picking Flaws 67

Behold Christ's Glory 70

Preparation for Christ's Coming 73

Christ and the Law 75

Responding to New Light	84
Who Will Accept the Light from Heaven?	90
The Spirit of Discernment	96
Cherishing Faith, Not Doubt	99
The Importance of Excerising Faith	104
The Danger of an I Spirit	108
Remarks by Ellen White at the Michigan Conference Campmeeting	113
Work and Baptism of the Holy Spirit Needed	119
Temperance	146
Keep the Commandments	155
Seeking Heavenly Treasures	170
"Walk in the Spirit"	183
Camp Meeting Message on True Education	187
The Ministry	196
The Will of God Concerning You	201
Talk Faith and Move Forward	204

Words to Students 209

The Christian Life 213

The Student's Privelege 220

Word to Students 223

The Foundation of Our Faith 227

Instruction to Sanitarium and Restaurant Workers 233

A Divine Prescription 234

How to Receive an Answer to Our Prayers 235

Light Reading 237

Light on Health Reform 238

Early Experience 239

Restaurant Work 240

Sanitarium Work in Southern California 242

A Reform Needed 243

Lessons from the Fifteenth of Romans 244

Lessons From the Visions of Ezekiel 259

Lessons From the Experiences of Pentecost 264

I Am the True Vine 268

Foreword

When Ellen Gould Harmon was in her early teens, no one would have predicted that eventually she would become one of the world's premier women public speakers. Yet, under the blessing of God, this frail teenager developed into a remarkably gifted and popular pulpiteer. It is estimated that during the seventy years of her prophetic ministry (1844-1915) she delivered at least 10,000 sermons and public addresses, on three continents. She spoke at Sabbath morning church services, camp meetings, ministerial councils, revivals, General Conference sessions, college chapel exercises, temperance rallies, conventions, church dedications, and wherever else there was need for public labor.

The range of Ellen White's interests, both in writing and in speaking, was as wide as human experience. The 465 Ellen White discourses analyzed by Horace J. Shaw in his doctoral dissertation (The Speaking of Ellen White, Michigan State University, 1959) reveal that she addressed topics such as health and temperance; issues affecting the ministerial, medical, educational, and publishing work of the church; and, especially, subjects encouraging Christian faith and living. In her public messages, as in her articles and books, Ellen White uplifted Jesus Christ with unparalleled conviction and skill. Christ was the center of her life and the focus of her preaching.

All the messages reproduced in this volume were delivered in public and stenographically reported, or were prepared with that purpose in view. Many of Ellen White's sermons may be found in the Review and Herald and Signs of the Times, but nearly all of those included in this series have been drawn from previously unpublished manuscripts, as they appear in our files. So, although there were no tape recorders in Ellen White's day, a person may get the true "feel" of Ellen White as a speaker by reading this book.

It will be noted that nearly all of these messages are from the latter half of Ellen White's ministry, a reflection of the fact that her sermons were more faithfully reported in that period than in her earlier years.

With the publication of this volume, we are beginning a new series entitled, Sermons and Talks. Additional volumes will be added as need and time require and permit. We trust that a deepening of spiritual insight and a closer fellowship with the Lord will reward all who read the messages in this book.

Chapter 1

A Dream About the Value of Team Work

While at Healdsburg I dreamed [of] seeing several span of horses harnessed to machinery which they were to draw. My husband stood looking on to see if the harness was of sufficient strength to hold in making the required effort. The horses started drawing the load.

Two horses from the number rushed out of their places and began to tug at the load, but could not start it one inch because they did not work in unison with the other horses. These looked back and seemed to think that the moving of the load depended upon them. They went first [to] one side and then [to] another, and became nervous and broke loose from the other horses and jumped in ahead of them all. In the act they were, they thought, taking the load when they were not stirring it. If these horses had kept their places they might have drawn their part of the load and been of important service, but when they rushed in ahead of the leading horses they were not drawing the load and were in the way, hindering the other horses from working.

I thought my husband struck these horses sharply with the whip. One turned to him, and said, "Don't strike so hard; you cut deep. We had zeal to start this load and we thought no one could start it but us. We see we have not moved it, but hindered its moving, but a check was all we needed, not to be cut on like balky horses. We will fall back on our traces and draw with the rest."

I awoke, and fell asleep the same night, and dreamed that my husband was trying to right matters in the church at Battle Creek. There was difficulty. There were two or three that thought they had wisdom to bring the church into good working order. They wished to rearrange the church, and then they said it would be free. These men and women had a machine of their own to work, but the machine of each was united with a larger machine. Every one must keep his or her hand employed on his or her own machine, and then the larger machinery worked beautifully and every revolution of the great wheel was exact and harmonious. If any neglected this machine which was connected with the great machinery, every revolution of the large wheel made a disagreeable noise which disturbed not only the building it was in, but the building across the road jarred and shook.

I saw two in particular leave their machines and [they] were watching the large wheel in the great machinery and were seeking to correct the great wheel, to have it more harmoniously and regularly. Instead of helping the difficulty, the machinery made a more disagreeable noise. I thought if all would stand by their own machines and diligently and faithfully do their own work correctly, there would be no trouble with the large machinery. But the noise of the large machine called the attention of several from their work. This difficulty was now to be settled. All wanted to know why the large machine ran so heavily, the wheel groaning at every revolution.

My husband spoke very decidedly and sharply. Said he, "You who left your own machine to correct the large wheel were out of your place. Had you kept by your own machines and worked them correctly, the large machine would have been all right." I thought my husband spoke very earnestly and reproved those who left their own work to attend to that which was not their work. Those that had been the most to blame said, "Do not be so severe. We thought we were carrying out your express directions in doing as we have done. But all we needed was a word and we would see our error. We thought everything was going to pieces, therefore left the very work we should have done, to save such a calamity, and sought to correct the large machinery, and so we made things very much worse.[1]

---

[1] Ms. 1, 1873; MR 900.14.

Chapter 2

Called To The Wedding Feast

[Sermon by Ellen G. White In Washington, Township, Iowa, Cir. 1874]

The words which I have selected as a foundation for a few remarks you will find in the 22nd chapter of Matthew, beginning at the first verse. (Verses 1-10, quoted)

The portion of Scripture presented before us, which I have referred to and have presented before your minds, is of intense meaning—much more than I am able to explain. It is of great interest to us, and we should consider it, and let it have due weight upon our minds. We find by perusing God's sacred Word of inspiration that when the promised Messiah, the Son of God, came into the world His own people, even His own nation—the Jews—would not and did not receive Him. As we are told in the first chapter of St. John, "He came unto His own, and His own received Him not." (John 1:11)

The provision was made, but they would not receive it. The Father Himself provided a ransom, even a sacrifice. His own dear Son submitted Himself to His Father's requirements, came into this sinful world, became a man of sorrow and acquainted with grief. He went about doing good, speaking in tones of tenderness, saying in the deepest and most fervent and sweetest accents ever uttered, "Come unto Me, all ye that labor and are heavy laden, and I will give you rest. Take My yoke upon you, and learn of Me; for I am meek and lowly in heart"; and He assures us we shall find rest to our souls.

"Again, he sent forth other servants, saying, Tell them which are bidden, Behold, I have prepared my dinner: my oxen and my fatlings are killed, and all things are ready: come unto the marriage. But they made light of it, and went their ways, one to his farm, another to his merchandise."

The great King Himself hath made a marriage for His Son. He hath sent forth His servants for many hundreds of years, saying, "Come, for all things are ready." But how little do the [people of the] world heed the invitation! They make light of it and go their ways to their worldly pursuits and worldly pleasures, the same as they have done for centuries. But the King sendeth forth His armies and destroys those murderers and burns up their city, and we are told in the ninth chapter of

Daniel, the 26th verse, that "the people of the Prince that shall come shall destroy the city; and the end thereof shall be with a flood."

"Then saith he to his servants, The wedding is ready, but they which were bidden were not worthy. Go ye therefore into the highways, and as many as ye shall find, bid to the marriage."

In the 14th chapter of Luke, verse 16, we find that there was made a great supper and many were bidden. Servants were sent forth to say to those that were bidden, "Come; for all things are now ready." (Verse 17) But they made excuses.

The King of the kingdom hath made a marriage supper for His Son. He hath sent forth His servants to say to those which are bidden, "Come to the marriage." The Lord is sending His servants, saying unto all who will hear, "Come, make ready for the great marriage supper of the Lamb; He is soon coming to receive all the faithful to the mansions prepared by Him, to partake of the feast which He hath prepared." He is sending, and hath been sending His servants for some thirty years past to say unto His people, "Come, make ready, put on your wedding garments; clothe yourselves with meekness, humility, and truth, and have yourselves clad in the righteousness of Christ, that you may be able to appear before Him, and enter into the guest chamber with those who shall sit with Me at the wedding of My Son."

All must be clothed with the wedding garment in order to be accepted, lest we be found speechless.

Is it not of the greatest importance that we be found having on the robe of righteousness, that we be ready when the Bridegroom cometh to enter in to the marriage supper? May we heed the invitation given and make ourselves ready that we may have admittance into the Master's house, that He say not unto us that none which were bidden shall taste of His supper. In the parable, those who were bidden heeded not its invitation, but continued excusing themselves, feasting upon the pleasures of this world as the masses do at the present time.

The servants of God are inviting and entreating them to come away from the alluring scenes of this vain and fleeting world, to make ready for the marriage supper, but they will not come. We hear them saying, There's no danger; tomorrow shall be as this day and much more abundant; no need of being disturbed. We must needs attend to farms and merchandise and the things of this life, lest we lose worldly interests, and become poor and suffer want. They forget that He who careth for the little sparrows and clotheth the lilies of the field, careth for the humble, trusting soul, and will guide and direct all those who are ready to do His will, and bestow upon His dear children such things as they need. To all who through patience and perseverance overcome, He hath promised to give a crown of never fading glory, a robe of righteousness, and an entrance into the beautiful city of our God.

This same King is sending forth His servants today. He is inviting His guests, saying, "Come, for all things are now ready." The Lord of the marriage is soon coming: behold, He is at the door. Delay not to open the door, lest He turn away from receiving you and you enter not into the marriage feast. Open the door and receive the Master, that you may enter into the mansions of everlasting rest and never fading glory prepared for all those that love Him. Who will make ready for the coming of Him who hath said, "Behold, I come quickly; and My reward is with Me, to give to every man according as his work shall be." (Revelation 22:12)

If we neglect our spiritual interests, neglect to offer up spiritual sacrifices acceptable unto God, which is our reasonable duty, we become entangled with the trifling cares of this life. If we even once omit our daily duty of calling upon God for His divine aid, His care and protection, we lose one day's enjoyment. We have not the sweet, melting influence of God's Holy Spirit attending us through the day, but we feel cast down and easily discouraged. The enemy of souls is ready to take advantage [of us] and often does, bringing us into captivity and sin.

We may sometimes be cumbered about much serving, like Martha; but how much more commendable was the act of Mary, who sat and listened to the teachings of Jesus. He says, "Martha, thou art careful and troubled about many things: but . ... Mary hath chosen that good part, which shall not be taken away from her." (Luke 10:41, 42)

How many times the things of this vain, deceitful world come between us and our eternal interests! Temporal things spring up within our hearts and choke those things which are spiritual. We permit the enemy of righteousness to persuade us that we should attend to the things of this life. We now and then neglect greater duties lest we suffer want. If we faithfully entreat God to give us strength and to perform temporal duties, and at the same time to give us grace and wisdom to overcome evil; if we have our hopes centered above and our conversation in heaven, whence we look for the Son of man who has bidden to the marriage all who will come: who has gone up on high to prepare mansions for all those who love and keep His sayings, and has told us He is coming to receive us, we may enter in to the wedding feast with Him, that where He is there we may be also. If we turn away from those calls and invitations, what will be the consequence?

In the 13th chapter of the Acts of the Apostles, 46th verse, we find that if we put

God's work from us, and judge ourselves unworthy of everlasting life, we have no reason to expect an entrance into the kingdom. The 24th verse of the 14th chapter of Luke informs us that "none of those men which were bidden shall taste of my supper."

The great eternal Father has prepared a marriage feast for His Son. Will we give heed to His servants who have been and are being sent forth to proclaim unto us the solemn invitation? Or shall we make light of it? Oh, why refuse to make ready for the marriage of the Son of God? There is room for all who will accept the invitation. None can say [that] those things were not duly represented. Remember, when the good man returns, those who are ready will go in to the feast and the door will be shut, and there will be no further entrance, for we read that when "the master of the house is risen up, and hath shut to the door" (Luke 13:25), then those who would find admittance will hear the answer, "I know you not...; depart from Me."

May we heed well the solemn warning and make ready to enter into the wedding, that His house may be filled. God's Word informs us, "Blessed are they that do His commandments, that they may have right to the tree of life, and may enter in through the gates into the city." (Revelation 22:14) May we be found faithful, and give diligence to our calling, and possess the promised reward of the faithful, is my prayer.[2]

---

[2] Ms 8, 1874; MR 900.56.

Chapter 3

Diet and Health

[Notes on Sermon Preached by Mrs. E. G. White at Los Angeles, California, May 16, 1884]

We are required, whether we eat or drink, to do all to the glory of God. One of the signs that we are in the last days is that this is not done. "As it was in the days of Lot." Luke 17:28. Minds are too largely occupied with thoughts of what to eat or drink or wear. Men have no time to think of what will fit them for eternal life. Shall we not act like rational beings? The greatest question that ever occupied the human mind is, What shall I do to be saved? If the thoughts take a low plane, the character will be correspondingly low. But if the thoughts are led to grapple with the difficult problems in the Bible, the mind and character will be strengthened. In the world much time is given to matters of eating and drinking and dressing. Shall we be like the world, or shall we show that we cannot spend our time as they do? Be careful not to go to extremes.

In regard to tea, coffee, tobacco, etc., we know that we have no use for any of these things. I have just seen a man who had sold his reason to drink. We don't want to be dependent on any of these things. As a people we are strictly temperate. We believe that using tobacco goes side by side with liquor drinking. We would present the pledge as much to the tobacco devotee as to the liquor drinker.

We should pay attention to diet. Three meals a day are as many as anyone requires, and in many cases two are better than three. But while you take the three meals do not encourage your children to eat at all times. Bring your fruit upon the table. As for preserves, they are not best for us. Some simple pies that are not injurious may be used. As to discarding salt absolutely, I do not think we should.

Some conscientious souls have dropped everything at once and have not used anything to supply the place of the meat, etc., which they have dropped. Persons become debilitated on account of such sudden changes. Could we have the assurance that the meat is healthful, there would not be so much objection to its use. But very much of it is diseased. Men have flocks and herds with disease; and they are sold for the market even when they are dying from disease. I once found a most disgusting scrofulous sore in a quarter of lamb that was apparently very healthy. You cannot tell that meat is healthy even when highly recommended. How much of this is eaten!

Animals are maltreated on the way to the slaughterhouse. There was one case of an animal that refused to go to the butcher. Its eyes were put out, it was pounded almost to a jelly, and finally dragged to slaughter and sold in market.

As for pork, I never have anything to do with it because God tells me not to touch it, and He knows best. It is a scavenger. Its only use is to gather up filth. God does not want us to become scavengers to the scavengers. Our safest position is to do as the Lord tells us.

We want to eat that which will give us the best quality of blood. Hadn't we better be studying the Bible than spending our time fixing up so many varieties of food? Have few kinds at a time and change often. Don't have the very same things right along all the time. Not many varieties at one meal, but varieties at different meals—this is the best plan. Food must be palatable in order to be nourishing.

[The secretary who was taking notes on Ellen White's sermon reports that Sister White "related experiences in experimenting on doing without salt or any seasoning whatever; also in doing without meat; and in coming down to two meals a day." The secretary recorded no details concerning these experiences.]

We don't make the health reform an iron bedstead, cutting people off or stretching them out to fit it. One person cannot be a standard for everybody else. What we want is a little sprinkling of good common sense. Don't be extremists. If you err, it would be better to err on the side of the people than on the side where you cannot reach them. Do not be peculiar for the sake of being peculiar. Away with cake. Persons may kill themselves with sweets. More harm is done to children by sweets than by anything else. The best food that I have obtained is the rolls.

Dry food is better than so much wet food. Eat what the system requires to produce good blood. Poverty of diet will produce disease of the blood. Be regular in your meals. Have wholesome food at all times, and make no difference for company.[3]

---

[3] Ms 5, 1884; MR 900.48.

Chapter 4

Hearing and Doing

[A Sermon at Santa Rosa, California Sabbath, March 7, 1885 Text: Matthew 7:22-28]

Here are brought before us two classes—the hearer and the doer. There is one that hears and does not; there is one that hears and does. This is he that not only hears but is a doer of the Word of the Lord: and this is the class that is building on the Rock. We want to be among the class that is riveted to the eternal Rock, and not of that class that is building upon the sand. For in these two classes of builders brought to view here, the one is laying his foundation in the sand, the other on the rocks. And the question comes home to us, How are we building?

How we are building is of great consequence. We want to know that the foundation is deep, so that the floods shall not move us. Our salvation cost something; it cost us the blood of the Son of God. While everything has been done that can be done to bring us into right relation with God, we want to think much of every privilege brought to us, and not to be always questioning God's dealings with us, whether this is right or that is right; but pursue a course that will stand the test of His law, a test that shall work out for us an eternal weight of glory.

God demands of us that we build a character that will stand that close test of the judgment. We will not have His protection in the time when the flood comes, if at that time it is found that we have wasted the hours of probation granted us now to build characters for eternity. For the character which we now build is not only for time, but for eternity. Those that are set forth in this parable as building on the sand are they that feel that they are all right. They come right up before the Lord and say, I have done this, I have done that. "Many will say unto me in that day, Lord, Lord, have we not prophesied in thy name? and in thy name have cast out devils? And in thy name done many wonderful works?" But this goes for nothing to the Lord. "Then will I profess unto them, I never knew you: depart from me, ye that work iniquity." (See Matthew 7:22, 23)

What is iniquity? Sin. And what is sin? Sin, says the beloved John, is the transgression of the law. Here is a class that is transgressing the law of God, and at the same time they come to Him boasting of what they have done, expecting His favor. And it is this class that is here represented as building on the sand. They have erected a standard of their own.

What is a perfect standard of character? The only standard ever given to man is the law of God, His holy commandments. If we have been building upon this rock, it will stand the test. If we have been erecting a standard of our own, and claim by that standard that we are perfect, and that we have reached perfect righteousness and holiness, we shall know in the day of God. No one will claim that they are perfect and holy if they tremble before the exalted standard of God. Is it safe to do this and cast aside the immutable law of God and then to claim to be holy?

Here is a mirror into which we are to look, and search out every defect of character. But suppose that you look into this mirror and see many defects in your character, and then go away and say, "I am righteous," will you be righteous? In your own eyes you will be righteous and holy. But how will it be at the bar of God? God has given us a rule, and we are to comply with its requirements and if we dare to do otherwise, to trample this under our feet, and then stand up before God and say, "I am holy, I am holy," we shall be lost in the great day of accounts.

What if we were to go out into the streets and soil our clothes with mud, and then come into the house and, beholding our filthy garments as we stand before the glass, we should say to the mirror, "Cleanse me from my filth," would it cleanse us from our filth? That is not the office of the looking glass. All that it can do is to reveal that our garments are defiled; it cannot take the defilement away.

So it is with the law of God. It points out the defects of character. It condemns us as sinners, but it offers no pardon to the transgressor. It cannot save him from his sins. But God has made a provision. Says John, "If any man sin we have an advocate with the Father, Jesus Christ the righteous," So we come to Him and there we find the character of Jesus, and the righteousness of His character saves the transgressor—if we have done on our part all that we could.

And yet while He saves the transgressor, He does not do away with the law of God, but He exalts the law. He exalts the law because it is the detector of sin. And it is Christ's cleansing blood that takes away our sins when we come to Him with contrition of soul seeking His pardon. He imputes His righteousness; He takes the guilt upon Himself.

Now, suppose that someone shall say, "Jesus has pardoned me and I have no need of the law any further. I will no longer live in obedience to the law." The question may be asked, "Shall we continue to sin that grace may abound"? No. If one should steal the money out of my purse, and then come, and confessing the crime, ask me to forgive him, and I shall pardon him, and then he goes and does the same thing again, does not this show that there is no change in his life? So it is with those who have asked God to forgive them and then gone right on transgressing His law. They say, "Lord, Lord," but He says, "Depart from Me." While I freely pardoned you, you were doing the same thing again. Your very course was leading others in the way of the transgressor. For this reason they were called the workers of iniquity. This very course of action was the means of leading others astray.

Christ offers a prayer to the Father, and He uses these words in this prayer, "Sanctify them through thy truth: thy word is truth" (John 17:17). I have sent them into the world as thou hast sent Me into the world, even so have I sent them into the world. And for their sakes I sanctify Myself, that they also might be sanctified through the truth. (See John 17:17-19) Mark these words, "I sanctify Myself." Thus He observes a life of perfect obedience, for He is the perfect pattern. Then He goes on and says, "That they may be sanctified"—by what? Through emotion? Through feeling? No. Through the truth. We cannot trust to feeling; we must know the truth.

Now, here is Christ praying to His Father that He will sanctify His followers through the truth. Then there is a truth that sanctifies, that has a sanctifying power upon the believer. And it becomes every one of us in this congregation to inquire what is the truth.

If we are to believe the truth and be sanctified by the truth, then we must search the Scriptures that we may know what is the truth. If we do this, we shall not build upon a false foundation. But if we do not, we shall find at last that we have made a great mistake and laid our foundation in the sand, to be swept away in the time of storm and tempest. I want eternal life if it takes out the right eye and if it takes off the right arm. The question with me is, am I right with God? Am I serving Him in humility and meekness of soul?

We are right amid the trials that shall try every soul of men that dwelleth upon the face of the earth. We may know what is the truth, and we may know what is error. We may know that we are laying our souls upon the foundation; we may know that we are not leading souls away from the truth. God help us that we may every one of us make sure of eternal life.

And here is another Scripture. (Deuteronomy 13:1-5 quoted) Here the commandments are set before them as a test of character. Said Christ, "I have kept My Father's commandments." And He is our pattern in all things. Now do we do the commandments from the heart? Are we studying to carry out in our lives the principle of the Sabbath commandment which God has put right in the bosom of His law?

We may go to the heathen and say to them that we love the truth and serve the true God; and they will tell you that they worship the true and living God. We have no other way to tell who the true and living God is, only as we turn to this commandment. That God who made the lofty trees and every thing that is lovely and beautiful under the heavens, He that weighs the hills in the balances—that God is the true and living God; He created the whole universe. And these commandments tell us who the true God is. If Satan can get this fourth commandment out of the Decalogue, then you will not be able to tell who the true and living God is.

Well, who is the true God? The God that created everything that is beautiful in nature. We are to look up through nature to nature's God. There we are to see the true God, the Maker of the heavens and the earth. The first four of these commandments show our duty to God, and the last six to our fellow men. We cannot break one of these first four and be in favor with God. Neither can we break one of the last six and be in favor with God. These we must urge upon the people.

Here are the words of David, "It is time for Thee, Lord, to work: for they have made void thy law." (Psalm 119:126) David refers to the last days, the very time when we are to know and be sanctified by the truth. We must cling to the truth. We must not let go the truth for friend or foe. There is a time coming when there will be great tribulation, such as never was or ever will be. Men will come claiming to be Christ. And here is a class that say, "I am sinless, I am holy." I have never heard one claim that who was not a sinner. They are not doers of the Word.

One man came to Oakland a short time ago, who at his own home was known to be a dishonest man. Here he falls into the hands of the holiness people, and now he is holy, he is sinless. He goes on step-by-step in this delusion until he claims to be a sinless man. Now for this class we have to be prepared; we must know what spirit they are of. There are some of these people that are deceived by these workers of iniquity. They accept the Lord, and they accept this holiness doctrine, with the Lord; but they are not the people that have power with God.

John saw the temple of God opened in heaven, and in that temple he saw the ark of His testimony. Says John, "Here are they that keep the commandments of God, and the faith of Jesus" (Revelation 14:12). The path of true obedience is found in the commandments of God. But Satan is going about as a roaring lion, seeking whom he may devour. He does not always appear like a lion; he has the power of clothing himself like a lamb, and he has a soft and a tender voice. And how shall we meet him? Shall we let him come in and take the control of our hearts? Shall we let him have the charge of our minds and lives? We cannot afford it.

Now here are those that come to us boasting that they are holy. There was one that claimed this in the city of Oswego. He was holding a revival meeting there. He worked so hard that he bled at the lungs, and they thought he would die. Yet while he was thus at work, and boasting of his holiness, the officers of the law were after him for stealing. While he was preaching, his wife saw the officer coming. She slipped out, and digging a little hole in the snow, buried the money and then came into the house. But she was seen to do this, and while they were protesting their innocence, here comes the officer into the room with the bag of money in his hands. Now, we meet this class everywhere we go.

There was a man, perhaps you know him. He claimed to be holy. "The idea of repentance," said he, "is not in the Bible." "If," said he, "a man comes to me and says that he believes in Jesus, I take him right into the church, whether he is baptized or not; I have done so with a good many." "And," said he, "I have not committed a sin in six years." "There are some on this boat," he said, "that believe that we are sanctified by the law. There is a woman on this boat by the name of White that teaches this."

I heard this, and I stepped up to him and said, "Elder Brown, you hold right on. I cannot permit that statement to go. Mrs. White has never said such a thing in any of her writings, nor has she ever spoken such a thing, for we do not believe that the law sanctifies anyone. We believe that we must keep that law or we will not be saved in the kingdom of heaven. The transgressor cannot be saved in the kingdom of glory. It is not the law that sanctifies anyone, nor saves us; that law stands and cries out, Repent that your sins may be blotted out. And then the sinner goes to Jesus, and as the sinner promises that he will obey the requirements of the law, He blots out their guilty stains and sets them free, and gives them power with God."

John saw a company standing around the throne of God, and the angel asked him, Who are these in white robes? He answered, thou knowest. And the angel said, "These are they who have washed their robes, and made them white in the blood of the Lamb." (See Revelation 7:13, 14) There is a fountain in which we may wash from every stain of impurity. And says the angel, "He shall lead them to fountains of living waters, and shall wipe away all tears from their eyes." (See V. 17) This will be the happy privilege of those that have kept the commandments of God in the earth.

Men will arise saying, Here is Christ, here, here, here; but is He there? While they are trampling the commandments under their feet, Christ says, "Whosoever shall break one of these least commandments, (MacNight) you shall be of no esteem in the reign of heaven. Not as long as the heavens remain, shall one jot or one tittle pass." And one said to me, why do you talk so much about the law, why not talk more about Jesus? We honor both the Father and the Son when we talk about the law. The Father gave us the law, and the Son died to magnify it and make it honorable.

But, says John, in speaking of the deceiver that doeth great wonders, He shall make an image to the beast, and shall cause all to receive his mark. (See Revelation 13:14-16) Will you please consider this matter? Search the Scriptures and see. There is a wonder-working power to appear, and it will be when men are claiming sanctification, and holiness, lifting themselves up higher and higher and boasting of themselves.

Look at Moses and the prophets; look at Daniel and Joseph and Elijah. Look at these men and find one sentence where they ever claimed to be sinless. The very soul that is in close relation to Christ, beholding His purity and excellence, will fall before Him with shamefacedness. Daniel was a man to whom God had given great skill and learning, and when he fasted the angel came to him and said, "Thou art greatly beloved." And he fell prostrate before the angel. He did not say, Lord, I have been very faithful to you and I have done everything to honor you and defend Your Word and name. Lord, You know how faithful I was at the king's table, and how I maintained my integrity when they cast me into the den of lions." Was that the way Daniel prayed to God? No; he prayed and confessed his sins. He said, "Hear O Lord, and deliver; we have departed from Thy Word and sinned." (See Daniel 9:5) And when he saw the angel, he said, "My comeliness was turned in me into corruption." (Daniel 10:8) He could not look upon the angel's face, and he had no strength; it was all gone. So the angel came to him and set him upon his knees, but he could not behold him. And then the angel came to him with the appearance of a man. Then he could bear the sight.

Why is it that so many claim to be holy and sinless? It is because they are so far from Christ. I have never dared to claim any such thing. From the time I was fourteen years old, if I knew what the will of God was, I was willing to do it. You never have heard me say I am sinless. Those that get sight of the loveliness and the exalted character of Jesus Christ, who was holy and lifted up, and His train fills the temple, will never say it. Yet we are to meet with those that will say such things more and more, every year.

A lady came to me in the city of Oakland, threw her arms around my neck, and said, "You are a child of God, but I am sanctified, I am holy; and we want you to come in with us." I turned to the Bible and showed her what is said. Then I said to her, "Suppose you should go to your children and say to them, 'You need not keep the commandments of God, you are holy. All you need do is to say that you love Christ; you need not think you have anything to do, but simply say I love my father and mother.' What would be the results? Just as surely as you stand opposed to the law of God, you have no investigation to make. If your character is not in harmony with the law of God, it is not in harmony with heaven, however you may profess to be holy and sinless."

In the days of Martin Luther, there were those that came to him and said, "We do not want your Bible, we want the Spirit." Martin Luther said to them, "I will rap your spirit on the snoot." However great their pretences, they are not the children of God. I remember thirty-six years ago, I was in New York, in the house of Brother Abbey. A man came in there with an umbrella in his hands, and there he stood and said, "I am Christ." I had looked upon Christ, and I said to him, "Sir, you have no part with Christ. If you were Christ you would never have uttered that sentence." He raised his umbrella to strike me, but my husband stepped in between him and me, and said to him, "What are you going to do sir?" He said, "I am Christ, and will execute His will upon those that dispute His claims."

I met a man at St. Helena that boasted that he had not committed a sin for six years. And one of his own party said to me, "I will not have him in my house again; he is a tyrant. He will come into my house and say, 'I have just as much right in this house as you,' and order my wife around, and demand her to wait upon him." And this is the man that had not committed a sin for six years.

I want you to understand that pretences are not the evidences of true character. Now I speak these words to you because wherever there is a little company raised up, Satan is constantly trying to annoy and distract them. When one of the people turns away from his sins, do you suppose that he will let him alone? No, indeed. We want you to look well to the foundation of your hope. We want you to let your life and your actions testify of you that you are the children of God. Let there be that littleness, that humbleness of soul, that they may know that you have been taught in the school of Christ. And when He shall appear in the clouds of heaven, we shall exclaim, "Lo, this is our God; we have waited for him, and he will save us." (Isaiah 25:9) Then it is that the crown of life will be placed upon the brow of the faithful ones. Then will come the voice of the Saviour saying, "Well done thou good and faithful servant; ... enter thou into the joy of thy Lord." (Matthew 25:21-23) What, faithful in putting their feet upon the law of God? No, No. These have not the mark of the beast upon them. I want that peace that comes through an obedience to all of the commandments of God. Amen.[4]

---
[4] Ms. 5, 1885; MR 900.8.

Chapter 5

Preparation for the Judgement

[Sermon by Mrs. E. G. White June 27, 1886, Orebro, Sweden]

(Revelation 20:11-15) Here is presented before us the great and solemn day when the judgment is to set and the books be opened, and the dead are to be judged according to the things that are written in the books. I have questioned in my mind, as I have seen the people in our cities hurrying to and fro with business, whether they ever thought of the day of God that is just upon us. Every one of us should be living with reference to that great day which is soon to come upon us.

The inhabitants of the old world had the message of warning sent to them 120 years, but it did not suit their inclination to heed that warning, therefore they turned away from the message of truth which God sent to them. It was for their interest to heed that message and find a refuge from the coming storm of God's wrath.

Do we consider from day to day that a record is going up to heaven of all our actions here? If we would take heed to our ways, and if we would have the fear of God before us, our lives would be far better than they are today. We are here as probationers, on trial. God is testing us; God is proving us to see what characters we shall build up. Angels of God in heaven are sent to our earth to weigh moral worth. And our heavenly Father has sent us the message of warning, that we shall get ready for that day of final reckoning. He has bid us to watch and pray lest we enter into temptation that surrounds us. He has bid us to "search the Scriptures; for in them ye think ye have eternal life: and they are they which testify of me." (John 5:39)

It is our privilege to understand the great responsibilities that God has placed upon us, so that we shall not be in darkness as to what is coming upon our world. We cannot afford to meet that day without a preparation. But when we think of this great and solemn event of Christ's coming in the clouds of heaven with power and great glory, we should live in great humiliation before God lest we fail of the grace of God and prove ourselves unworthy of eternal life. When we see that the world is given up to the seeking of pleasure and the indulgence of appetite, we should weep between the porch and the altar, crying "Spare thy people, O Lord, and give not thine heritage to reproach." (Joel 2:17)

We see that the world at large have no thoughts of this great day, and many of them do not care to hear anything about it. But we must meet the record of our lives. We must remember that there is a witness to all our works. An eye like a flame of fire beholds us in all our actions of life. Our very thoughts and the intents and purposes of our hearts are laid bare to God's inspection. As the features are produced upon the polished plate of the artist, so are our characters upon the books of record in heaven.

We ask you, "How stands your character in the sight of God today? Are you preparing your souls for the grand review, that you may have the white robe of character in that day?" You cannot afford to indulge in sin and iniquity; you cannot afford to be found a transgressor of God's great moral rule of righteousness.

If God had no law as a moral standard, whereby every case must be judged, there could be no judgment, and the cases of men and women could not be tried. If we have not been found in harmony with God's requirements in this life, we will not be in harmony with His requirements in the future life.

What excuses have we today that we are not in harmony with the laws of God's government? And what excuse can we render in the day of God for the disobedience of His requirements? Will you say "The whole world was in disobedience to the law of God, and I thought I would not be singular"? In that day, this excuse will not be accepted. You may present excuses now, but you will not venture to present them before the judge of all the earth, for just as soon as the books are opened and the characters that are written there are brought out, every mouth will be stopped, for the guilt of all stands as plainly revealed to themselves as to God. Everyone then will see just where he departed from the right way. Everyone will then discern the influence he had upon his fellow-men by his own departure from God's righteousness, to turn them away from the ways of truth and right. Everyone then will understand just what he did to dishonor the God of heaven by breaking His law.

Everyone who comes forth from the dead when Christ comes in the clouds of heaven, and those who are living, will stand before the judgment seat of Christ. The deeds and acts which we have thought to have been done in secret where no eye could see, are made known. There was an eye that saw and registered the deeds done by man.

When Belshazzar had his great sacrificial feast, there was a witness present which he did not discern. They were drinking their wine and having their luxurious feast, and praising the gods of silver and gold, extolling their own wisdom, but right over against the wall facing the king a bloodless hand traced the terrible characters testifying of his true condition. The message came, "Thou art weighed in the balances and art found wanting." Now the Lord is weighing characters in the sanctuary, and the deeds of those who are careless and indifferent, rushing on in the paths of sin and iniquity, are being registered in the books of heaven.

The God of heaven has given us reasoning powers and intellect, and He wants us to use them. He has given us this body which He wishes us to preserve in perfect health so that we can give Him perfect service. The Lord God is an ever present witness to the deeds of wickedness done among the children of men upon this earth. How does He look upon men and women for whom He has paid an infinite price but who yet refuse to obey His laws? They refuse to be saved in His appointed way, which is entire obedience to His commandments.

Here are youth right here in our midst in this large city, but do these youth appreciate the powers that God has given them, that they should return Him service for all that He has done for them? The future of society is indexed by the youth of today. Some of the youth are making their aim high, as did Joseph. They have aimed to keep themselves unspotted from the world. The Lord God of heaven is looking upon the children of men with intense interest, and what are we doing? Are we keeping, as did Abraham, the ways of the Lord? Are we teaching our children to love and obey God? We want to be in such a position that we can educate these young men brought within the reach of our influence, and leave them a good example. We should be in such a position here that the notes of counsel and warning will be given them as from God, and that what God has given them through His messengers, may come back to Him in souls saved.

But suppose these youth frequent the saloon, and take their drink of beer and wine and strong drink? Nadab and Abihu were in holy office and they drank wine and strong drink. The influence upon them beclouded their perceptive powers so that they could not discern sacred things. Those who are forming habits of intemperance are beclouding their reasoning powers so that they cannot discern between truth and error. It is the great work of Satan for this time to tempt the appetite so that error shall be placed on a level with truth. We want all the sharp powers of our intellect to be engaged in the work of conflict against the deception of Satan, and we must keep the spiritual and moral powers unperverted, so we will know what is truth. God asks for all the entrusted capabilities and talents He has lent us. Will you give them to Him?

Our sisters cannot afford to use their God-given time on unimportant things which will give them no spiritual strength, but will, if they continue, separate them from God. It is a solemn thing to die, but it is a far more solemn thing to live. Here is a world that is lying in wickedness around us, and what are we, as men and women who claim to be sons and daughters of God, doing to save the souls of those around us? God requires that we shall give back to Him in willing service all the powers that He has given to us. Let us look forward to the day of final reckoning. How will our case stand in that day. Will it make us unhappy then that we have served God and kept His commandments? God has given us rules to regulate our lives so that we shall have His care and protection in this life.

The lawyer came to Christ and asked Him, "What shall I do to inherit eternal life?" (Luke 10:25) This was a positive question, and was just as decidedly answered. "What is written in the law? How readest Thou? And he answering said, Thou shalt love the Lord thy God, with all thy heart and with all thy soul and with all thy strength, and with all thy mind, and thy neighbor as thyself. And He said unto him, Thou hast answered right; this do, and thou shalt live." (Verses 26-28) This means to keep the first four commandments, which show the duty of man to his God, and the last six which show the duty of man to his fellowmen.

Here is the work that is before us. The soul anxiously inquiring, "What shall I do to be saved?" is answered. The way is laid open. It is to love God above all things, and our neighbor as ourself. We ask you, Are you doing this? Are we who profess to be followers of Jesus Christ, imitating His life? Are we following His example? If we are, we are in such a position that we can have a living connection with heaven. We are channels of light to the world.

Christ said to His disciples, "Ye are the light of the world. ... Let your light so shine before men, that they may see your good works, and glorify your Father which is in heaven." (Matthew 5:14-16) It may seem to you that you have shown great self-denial and self-sacrifice in obeying God's law. Does He require more self-denial on your part than He has shown for you, that you should not perish but have eternal life? He has led the way, will you follow? He says, "I have kept my Father's commandments." (John 15:10) Will you keep the commandments of God? He left the royal throne in heaven, and changed the crown of glory for one of thorns. He placed His feet in the blood-stained path which led the way to Calvary. He has told us that those who will be partakers with Him in His sufferings, will be made partakers with Him in His glory also.

We may never have to suffer as He did; but we should ever keep before us the Author of our salvation, and never exalt self, never be lifted up in pride or self-sufficiency.

He was despised and rejected of men. Those He came to save could not see in Him anything that they should desire in Him. Should He come into our world today without earthly honor or princely power, who would receive Him as the king of glory, the majesty of heaven? How many proud church members would be so ashamed of Jesus and the reproach that would be likely to be attached to them should they accept Him, that they would refuse to follow Him? Oh what love, what matchless love, has been displayed by the Son of man! And all this the Son of God endured that He might bring many sons and daughters to glory. Who is willing today to be on the Lord's side?

We cannot wait until the judgment before we consent to deny self and to lift the cross. We cannot then form characters for heaven. It is here in this life that we must take sides with the humble, self-denying Redeemer. It is here that we must overcome envy, strife, selfishness, love of money, and love of the world. It is here that we must enter the school of Christ, and learn of the Master the precious lessons of meekness and lowliness of mind. And here it must be our aim and earnest effort to be loyal and true to the God of heaven by obeying all of His commandments and thus be fitting up for the mansions that Christ has gone to prepare for all who love God. Christ says, "Let not your heart be troubled; ye believe in God, believe also in me: In my Father's house are many mansions: if it were not so, I would have told you. I go to prepare a place for you ... that where I am, there ye may be also." (John 14:1-3) Now the mansions are being fitted up in heaven. Are we being fitted with pure elevated holy characters for those mansions?

All heaven is interested in our salvation. God's angels are in this very congregation. Could your eyes be opened, you would see not only good angels who are trying to impress hearts, but you would see also evil angels who are seeking to make of none effect the message of truth God has in mercy sent.

While we are in this world we are not safe unless our petitions are continually ascending to the God of heaven that He will keep us unspotted from the corruptions of the world. Our Saviour has told us what would be in these last days. Iniquity will abound, but the souls that are open to the influence of the Spirit of God will receive strength to withstand the corruptions of this degenerate age.

Enoch walked with God three hundred years previous to his translation to heaven, and the state of the world was not then more favorable for the perfection of Christian character than it is today. And how did Enoch walk with God? He educated his mind and heart to ever feel that he was in the presence of God, and when in perplexity his prayers would ascend to God to keep him. He refused to take any course that would offend His God. He kept the Lord continually before Him. He would pray, "Teach me Thy way, that I may not err. What is thy pleasure concerning me? What shall I do to honor Thee, my God?" Thus he was constantly shaping his way and course in accordance with God's commandments, and he had perfect confidence and trust in his heavenly Father, that He would help him. He had no thought or will of his own; it was all submerged in the will of his Father.

Now, Enoch was a representative of those who will be upon the earth when Christ shall come, who will be translated to heaven without seeing death. But be sure that if your hearts are inclined not to do God's will, not to keep the way of the Lord but to follow your own way, then you are not in harmony with the God of heaven. We want to pray with David, "Open Thou mine eyes, that I may behold wondrous things out of Thy law" (Psalm 119:18) Many close their eyes lest they shall see the truth. They do not want to see the defects in their life and character, and they are disturbed if you mention anything about God's law. In this they show that they have a human standard of their own; that their will is not the will of God. We want that you should not be deceived by Satan, the first great adversary of God's law. We want to bear in mind that God's law is the only standard by which He will judge man.

If we are to enter heaven at last, we must bring all of heaven into this life that we can. The religion of Christ never degrades the receivers; it never brings them down upon a low level. Truth is ever elevating in its influence, lifting them up on the high platform of truth. The religion of Jesus Christ has a refining influence upon men and women. When the truth of God finds access to the heart, it commences its refining process upon the character. Men who are coarse and rough become humble, teachable, learning, ever learning, in the school of Christ. The mighty cleaver of truth has taken them out of the world. Then there is the work to be done for them to fit them for God's temple. They are hewed and squared and chiseled and fitted for the mansions in heaven. Those who are naturally full of self-esteem become meek and lowly; they have a change in character. In the beginning, God said, "Let us make man in our image, after our likeness." But sin has almost obliterated the moral image of God in man. Jesus came down to our world that He might give man a living example, that he might know how to live and how to keep the way of the Lord. He was the image of the Father. His beautiful and spotless character is before man as an example for him to imitate. We must study the copy and follow Jesus Christ, then we shall bring His loveliness and beauty into our character. In doing this we are standing before God through faith, winning back by conflict with the powers of darkness the power of self-control, the love of God that

Adam lost. We are through Jesus Christ living and keeping the laws of God.

When the judgment shall set, and the books be opened, and every one be judged according to the deeds done in the body, those who have imitated Christ in obedience to God's commandments, will be blessed. "And another book was opened, which is the Book of Life: and the dead were judged according to their works." (see Revelation 20:12)

John also saw the holy city, the new Jerusalem, with its twelve gates and twelve foundations, coming down from God out of heaven. He was shown that city and saw the streets of transparent gold clear as crystal. Every one that goes into that city is changed and sanctified in character here in this life. The nations that have kept the truth enter in to the city of God, and a voice is heard, clear and distinct, "Blessed are they that do His commandments, that they may have right to the tree of life, and may enter in through the gates into the city." (Revelation 22:14)

There the crown of immortal glory is placed upon the head of the overcomer. Then how earnest should be our work here that we may win souls to Jesus Christ. We cannot afford to devote our God-given powers to our own pleasure, for one moment. We must devote our lives to our Master. You must expect to carry on this battle with self-denial and self-sacrifice. The Word of God says through His apostles, "Ye are laborers together with God." (See 1 Corinthians 3:9)

Our work may seem at times to be very discouraging, but if one soul is turned from the error of his way to righteousness, there is joy in heaven. The Father and the Son rejoice in the presence of the angels. The song of triumph and victory is sung and echoed and re-echoed through the courts of heaven. Then why should we not be wise in this life, and work for the glory of God? "They that be wise shall shine as the brightness of the firmament; and they that turn many to righteousness as the stars forever and ever." (Daniel 12:3) We want that our lives here shall be refined, ennobled, elevated, like Jesus Christ's. When Christ is formed in you the hope of glory, you will begin to lay aside your favorite sins. You will fear to offend God, and you will love His law.

I see before me today the purchase of the blood of Christ. There is value in every soul. Said the Lord through His prophet, "I will make a man more precious than fine gold; even a man than the golden wedge of Ophir." (Isaiah 13:12)

It is the truth of God received in the heart and practiced in the life that makes man thus precious in the sight of God. As John sees this precious company refined and purified around the throne of God, the angel inquires, "What are these which are arrayed in white robes? And whence came they?" And John answers, "Sir, thou knowest." And the angel answers, "These are they which came out of great tribulation, and have washed their robes, and made them white in the blood of the Lamb. Therefore are they before the throne of God, and serve Him day and night in his temple: and he that sitteth on the throne shall dwell among them." (Revelation 7:13-15)

Now is the opportunity for us through repentance toward God, to wash our robes of character and make them white in the blood of the Lamb that we may stand in white raiment before the throne of God. We are to wash our robes of character, and have our names registered in the Lamb's Book of Life; and He says, "They shall hunger no more, neither thirst any more; neither shall the sun light on them, nor any heat. For the Lamb which is in the midst of the throne shall feed them, and shall lead them unto living fountains of waters; and God shall wipe away all tears from their eyes." (Verses 16, 17)

We want you to live for the future immortal life, and we want you to decide, "As for me and my house, we will serve the Lord." Now is the time for you to give yourselves without reserve to Jesus. Be determined that you will have Christ at the loss of everything else. The very obstacles and difficulties you meet here are to strengthen your faith by overcoming these obstacles, and every victory gained is registered in the books of heaven. Every good deed you do, leading souls to walk in the way of God's commandments, is also registered in the books of heaven.

Let not the enemy deceive you. He has filled the world with his heresies. You want to plant your feet upon the Word of God; then you will be all ready to come under His rules and commandments in the kingdom of bliss. If you ever sing the song of triumph and redemption in the kingdom of God, you must first learn that song here. Is Jesus abiding in your heart? If he is, you will talk about Him. You will reveal Him in life and character. You will talk of His power and make melody to God in your heart. The sweet spirit of meekness will be cherished; self will be crucified. Purity and holiness will be developed in the character.

I speak because I know what I am talking about. For more than forty years I have stood in the desk proclaiming salvation to sinners, and my heart has yearned over them. God has opened before me the glory of heaven, and I have obtained a sight of the majesty and glory of my Redeemer. I have obtained a sight of the angels in glory. I was very young when the physicians said, "You must die, you cannot live more than three months." It was then that God gave me a sight of His glory, and said, "Go proclaim the message I give you, to the people." I started out in my weakness. I could hardly stand. I had not spoken aloud for weeks, but when I stood before the people, God's power came upon me. Voice was given me and I talked from two to three hours with clearness. But when I had finished, my voice again was gone. I traveled for three months in this way and then the pain of the lungs ceased, and ever since I have been doing the work which the Master has given me to do. I have traveled and labored and God has given me strength to continue unto this day.

I want to say to whomsoever the glory of God has been revealed, "You will never have the least inclination to say, 'I am holy, I am sanctified.'" After my first vision of glory, I could not discern the brightest light. It was thought that my eyesight was gone, but when I again became accustomed to the things of this world I could see again. This is why I tell you never to boast, saying, "I am holy, I am sanctified," for it is the surest evidence that you know not the Scriptures or the power of God. Let God write it in His books if He will, but you should never utter it.

I have never dared to say, "I am holy, I am sinless," but whatever I have thought was the will of God, I have tried to do it with all my heart, and I have the sweet peace of God in my soul. I can commit the keeping of my soul to God as unto a faithful Creator, and know that He will keep that which is committed to His trust. It is my meat and drink to do my Master's will.

And now I present before you the cross of Calvary. If you will come to that cross in penitence, in faith, in obedience to God's commandments, you will come in the only appointed way. If you lose heaven, you lose everything. If I can only see the King in His beauty, it is all I desire. Let me listen to the sweet music of His voice, saying "Come, ye blessed of My Father, inherit the kingdom prepared for you from the foundation of the world." (Matthew 25:34) Who of you in this congregation shall we meet there? We want to see you crowned in the city of God. We want to see when the judgment shall sit and the books be opened, that you can stand with the glory of God shining in your countenance. If we can only have that life in the city of God we shall be eternally blessed.

I warn you, Do not place your influence against God's commandments. That law is just as Jehovah wrote it in the temple of heaven. Man may trample upon its copy here below; but the original is kept in the ark of God in heaven; and on the cover of this ark, right above that law, is the mercy seat. Jesus stands right there before that ark to mediate for man. We want you to keep God's commandments and live. Seek for immortality, and the crown of life, and then you will have heaven at last.[5]

---

[5] Ms 6a, 1886; MR 900.5.

Chapter 6

Having Our Conversation in Heaven

[Sermon by Ellen G. White in Copenhagen, Denmark, July 24, 1886]

(1 Peter 1:13-16) The apostle Peter here gives instruction for believers to gird up the loins of their minds. We are to have special care over the thoughts of the mind. We are not to allow our minds to be diverted and allured by different things, because there is something more important for us. If we would allow the mind to take its natural turn, it might dwell upon unimportant things and we receive no benefit thereby.

Here is presented before us the one great event—the coming of our Lord and Saviour Jesus Christ, when the graves are to be opened and the dead be raised, and we are to be changed. This event should fill our mind and crowd out everything else. We want to make the most of the privileges and opportunities we have to prepare for the future immortal life.

The truth of God has taken us out of the quarry of the world to fit us up for the heavenly temple of God. We may look upon one another and think, "There is a great work to be done for that brother and for that sister," but we may not take into consideration the work that is to be done for ourselves. And if Satan can get in among the people [and produce] a spirit of criticism, then he is satisfied, for a root of bitterness springs up in these [members] wherewith he will be satisfied. We are not all of the same character, but we are brought together in church capacity and we count ourselves as children of God, and we talk of having a home in the city of God.

Our faith is that if we perfect a Christian character we shall be numbered as the family of God in the mansions that He has gone to prepare for us. Now, our heavenly father brings us together in church capacity that we may gain in knowledge and be fitting up for the community of heaven. "Well," some may say, "All I want is that everyone should see eye to eye." But there are those who want everyone to see just as they do. They do not consider that they have traits of character that must be changed. Then, what is the work before us in order to be ready to be among those who are waiting for their Lord to come in the clouds of heaven? It is for us to be in a position of humility before God. "Gird up the loins of your mind, be sober, and hope to the end for the grace that is to be brought unto you at the revelation of Jesus Christ."

The Lord has not placed before one individual the trade of becoming a church tinker, but we want individually to feel that we have a responsibility before God to be a blessing to everyone with whom we associate. And we are to consider that every brother and sister is the purchase of the blood of Christ. Here we are, living stones out of the quarry, and we are to be chiseled and fitted for the new Jerusalem. Do not let any of us think that we are all right. As soon as we are taken out of the quarry, we have a work to do for ourselves. "The flesh lusteth against the Spirit, and the Spirit against the flesh," and we want to be considering those things that will give us solidity of character. We do not want to have a high estimate of ourselves, but we want to esteem others better than ourselves. We want that our souls shall be uplifted to God every moment for help, for fear we shall fall. And while some are so diligent to look after others, they will forget the work there is for their own soul.

We are to heed the exhortation of the apostle, that we are to be holy in all manner of conversation. And as we separate those things from us which will be a hindrance to our advancement, the Holy Spirit will come in. We want to be filled with the spirit of Jesus, and if you are not closely connected with Christ, then the thoughts of your mind will be upon unimportant things; but if you are connected with Jesus, you will just as surely be a channel of light as Jesus is light, for Jesus has said to His followers, "Ye are the light of the world."

Now, we are by living faith to keep our eyes fixed upon the Author and Finisher of our faith. "As obedient children, not fashioning yourselves according to the former lusts in your ignorance: but as He which hath called you is holy, so be ye holy in all manner of conversation."

Before we become acquainted with Jesus, the conversation is upon the dress, and what shall we eat, and what shall we drink, and what shall we wear? And we find fault with one another. But as soon as we become acquainted with Christ, our conversation changes.

Here we are, objects of His love. Has the change taken place in us? Namely, have we passed from death unto life? Have we died indeed to self? Have we fastened our hearts and affections upon the great God? He is all light and power.

Every provision has been made for us that can be made by our precious Saviour, that we may have that abundant grace so that we may overcome every defect in our character. And we cannot afford to satisfy ourselves in this life, but we want the fullness that is in Jesus, and we must train ourselves to talk of those things which will bring to us peace and light. As we have our conversation upon heaven and heavenly things, the angels of God are all around us; and when we are, in our thoughts and with our hearts, drawing near to God, then He is drawing nigh to us. His love is in our hearts, and then we speak it from our lips.

It is not only our duty to train our minds upon heavenly things, but we are to talk of these things, for it is our duty to bind about our mind, to gird up the loins of our mind, and say, "I will not think of these things." Then it is our duty to guard our conversation.

We would think, from the shadow that many walk in, that they had no Saviour. But I want to speak to those, and say "Christ is risen! He is not in Joseph's new tomb, but He has arisen and has ascended up on high to make intercession for us!" We have a risen Saviour interceding for us, and we must walk in harmony with God. He is seeking to "purify unto Himself a peculiar people, zealous of good works." If we seek with all our hearts to be obedient children, conforming our will to the will of God, then the work can go forward in us without interruption. Let us not forget for one moment that we are living for the future immortal life, and let us put away from us everything like complaint and faultfinding. Let our words, our conversation, reveal to the world that we have a hope that is big with immortality.

We want that His will shall be our will. We do not want that our will shall be such that it will control all that [are] around us. One brother said to me, "Sister White, we must see eye to eye. Now, I view matters in this light and my brethren in another light, and I cannot make them see everything as I do. Their habits and ways are altogether different from mine."

"Thank God, Brother," said I, "that there is only one like you in the world, for if we were all like you we could not live in the world long, for there would be no harmony. Your brother's ways are just as precious to him as yours are to you."

God wants us to go through the mill. Here this man's sharp character must be burnished off, and here is one who has taken hold of the truth who has always been coarse in his conversation, and he must overcome that. This is the very thing the apostle means when he says, "You must overcome in order to have a home in heaven." Jesus must be in my whole work to transform my character. We must accept the truth as it is in Jesus, and then how kind will we be to one another, how courteous, for this was the work of my Master. We shall see the precious mold of Jesus upon the character, and when we learn the precious lessons He has for us to learn, we will be like Jesus. "Come unto Me," says He, "all ye that labor and are heavy laden, and I will give you rest. Take My yoke upon you, and learn of Me; for I am meek and lowly in heart: and ye shall find rest unto your souls."

Here you are with your variances and differences. Now, "Come to Me," says He, "and learn of Me." Nine-tenths of all our trouble comes from our esteeming ourselves too highly. But just as soon as we begin to look and see how many virtues we can find in others with whom we associate, then we will not be so ready to see their defects, and we will dwell upon the good in their character in place of their faults. In doing this, we bind them closer to our hearts by the firm cords of love.

The question was asked me, "Sister White, why is it you have such control over your children and those you bring up?" The answer was given, "Gain their confidence and love, and you can have perfect control." Let every member in the church be working in such a manner that he can gain the confidence of his brethren and sisters, then the precious light that emanates from Jesus will be reflected upon his life and character. There is something meant in this expression, "Building up yourselves in the most holy faith." And whenever you shall have the consolation of the Spirit of God, you should feel an earnest desire to give that consolation to others.

If you have the precious light from heaven, talk about it. And have we not everything from Jesus to talk about? I could give you subjects that would put to the stretch your thoughts and mind, and yet there is a great deal more. The great plan of redemption is not half comprehended. If we could only understand the plan of salvation, we would be the happiest people upon the face of the earth. The truth that God has given us would so fill our minds that we could not talk of earthly things. And then it is almost impossible for you to explain to others the greatness of salvation that you feel in your own heart. Jesus wants you to dwell upon this salvation.

Our precious Saviour has died to bring us to God. He has suffered as our Sacrifice, and all this was that we could stand freed from sin, cleansed from all iniquities. The cleansing blood of Christ is enough for us to talk about from morning until night, if you will only let your minds run in this direction. We want an intelligent faith. We want to understand how much of the blessing of God we can claim. Hear the word of God on this point. And if He has given us His Son, "How shall He not also with Him freely give us all things?"

It is through the Son of God that we claim the promises that He has left on record for us. Here we have come out, and are keeping His commandments, because we see it is His requirement. We make ourselves peculiar from the world in this respect; and as we follow the best light we have in keeping His commandments, it is our privilege to claim His blessing, and then lay your whole burden upon Jesus Christ and claim by faith His rich salvation. While Satan will press upon your soul his darkness and tell you [that] you cannot be saved, tell him, "Jesus died for me; it was a whole sacrifice that was made in my behalf, and I claim a whole salvation. The Master would have me joyful, for He has said it (John 15). The Word of God declares plainly and positively, 'Herein is My Father glorified, that ye bear much fruit; so shall ye be My disciples. ... These things have I spoken unto you, that My joy might remain in you, and that your joy might be full.'"

Not that they should feel that they were under bondage to the law. "This is My commandment, That ye love one another as I have loved you." We want to believe the words of Christ, for they are spirit, they are life. We want to take Him at His word. We want to walk right out upon the narrow plank of faith. We want to serve God with all the heart, might, mind, and strength, and then it is our privilege to claim to be children of God.

God wants to pour into your souls the light and glory of His presence. He wants that His joy shall remain in you and that your joy may be full, that when you meet with your brethren and sisters you can say, "Hear what the Lord has done for me. He has given me a rich experience, and if I seek Him for His blessing it will come." Then you begin to talk of Christ's coming, and the end of all things at hand, and how we are getting ready for His appearing. Then you talk of that heavenly city; you talk of the tree of life in the midst of the paradise of God, and you talk of the King in His beauty, with His kingly crown, and of the riches that are to be given to the children of God; you talk of that stream that goeth out from the throne of God; and then you say "Praise the Lord, O my soul, and all that is within me give Him glory."

Why, if we were such a people today, what impressions would we make upon the world! They would say that we have something that they have not, and they would begin to inquire, "What can I do to be as happy as that man?" My brethren and sisters, God is your strength, and He does not want you to go crippling along in this life. And when you enter the gate of the New Jerusalem you will read over the gate, "Blessed are they that do His commandments."

Jesus will welcome you, and with His own hand place the crown upon the brow of all those who enter there. Then they sing the song of Moses and the Lamb in the kingdom of glory. Well, now, is there not inducement enough that God has set before us so that we should think upon heavenly things? And the best of it is, we do not enter the city as convicts, but as sons and daughters of the Most High God. The Father stands at the gate and welcomes everyone to His bosom. There we shall show forth the matchless charms of our Redeemer. And the song will echo and re-echo through the courts of heaven, "Blessing, and honor, and glory, and power, be unto Him that sitteth upon the throne, and unto the Lamb for ever and ever."

I ask you, is not this enough to talk about? Shall we go mourning, just as though God's wrath was about to break upon us, or shall we talk of that infinite love that has been brought to us by the infinite sacrifice of the Son of God? When you think of these things, and of the love of Jesus, you will love one another, and you cannot help it.

Christ has manifested His interest in humanity. He says, "Inasmuch as ye have done it unto one of the least of these My brethren, ye have done it unto Me." We are dealing with Jesus in the person of His saints. Then be very careful how you wound the hearts of your brethren and sisters. We are almost home, pilgrims and strangers only a little longer. All heaven is interested in the salvation of men, and, in harmony with them, we should be interested for those around us. We should be getting ready for the heavenly city.

Oh, I praise God with all my soul, because Jesus has died for us, and He has wrought out for us a far more exceeding and eternal weight of glory that we shall have in that day! Then, brethren and sisters, be getting ready to move. Keep your mind upon the better country, even the heavenly. Learn to sing the song here upon this earth. The best song you can learn is to speak kindly to one another, for in heaven the business of the inhabitants is to please one another. Bring all of heaven that you can into this life. We have a living Jesus, and let us triumph in a living Saviour. He saves us with an everlasting salvation.[6]

---

[6] Ms 9, 1886; MR 900.54.

Chapter 7

Preach the Third Angel's Message—Avoid Trivial Topics

[A morning talk given at Grimsby, England, Sept. 21, 1886]

However much we know of the Scriptures it is important that we know still more. "Let him that thinketh he standeth take heed lest he fall." (1 Corinthians 10:12) One man may think he understands the Scriptures and go out to present the truth, and yet he may be lacking on some points. We may get the heart and mind fixed upon something that has no special bearing upon the true point.

A brother came to me and asked me what I thought about the salvation of infants, whether they would be saved. I said, "That does not concern you or me." There are points on which we must be careful not to mar present truth. All those who are to engage in the work of God must bind about their minds. There are those whose imagination is large, and they will be ever reaching out for something original. They will even fasten upon some word in a sermon and think upon that until the whole truth is covered with mist.

Now, we want to know what is essential for our work here. What is essential for our work now? If any of you should be asked to give your opinion on some point and you should not know just how to answer it, do not be ashamed to say you do not know, but you do know what we must do to be saved. When one came to Christ and asked what he must do to be saved, Jesus told him he must love God with all his heart, and with all his might, and with all his mind, and with all his soul, and his neighbor as himself. And these are the points we must keep before us—to love God supremely and our neighbor as ourselves. There is a great work before us.

Now, there may be those who will inquire what will be the sign of the coming of the Son of Man, and we may know what this is. We read that there will be signs in the sun, in the moon, and in the stars, and trouble in the nations. All these tell us that the end is near. The coming of the Lord is at the door. Well, we understand what being at the door means. When one stands at the door, all that remains for one to do is to enter.

Now, in regard to the coming of the Son of man, this will not take place until after the mighty earthquake shakes the earth. After the people have heard the voice of God they are in despair and trouble such as never was since there was a nation, and in this the people of God will suffer affliction. The clouds of heaven will clash, and there will be darkness. Then that voice comes from heaven, and the clouds begin to roll back like a scroll, and there is the bright, clear sign of the Son of man. The children of God know what that cloud means.

The sound of music is heard, and as the cloud nears, the graves are opened and the dead are raised, and there are thousands of thousands and ten thousand times ten thousand of angels that compose that glory and encircle the Son of man. Those who have acted the most prominent part in the rejection and crucifixion of Christ come forth to see Him as He is, and those who have rejected Christ come up and see the saints glorified, and it is at that time that the saints are changed in a moment, in the twinkling of an eye, and are caught up to meet their Lord in the air.

The very ones who placed the purple robe upon Him, and put the crown of thorns upon His brow, and those who put the nails through His hands and feet, look upon Him and bewail. And this is the very sign of the coming of the Son of man.

Now, I want to tell you, brethren, you must be careful not to fasten upon vagaries. We had a good brother whose mind was destroyed because of this. He would read page after page that would turn his mind off from the right point. The third angel's message is the all-important point. Do not let your mind turn to vagaries, but keep your eyes fixed upon the truth. What we want is to give a certain sound. The angel is giving a definite message, "Sound the warning." And what does this mean? Why, it is the angel giving this message to men, and they are to take up this message and proclaim it to warn others.

You want to open your minds, to gird up the loins of your mind, and hope to the end. You do not want to get many things upon the mind to take it away from the truth the angel is proclaiming. When the latter rain comes upon the people of God, you must have a preparation to press right on, because those whose vessels are clean, whose hands are free just when that latter rain comes, get the light that comes from on high, and their voices are lifted, every one, to proclaim the commandments of God and the testimony of Jesus Christ.

Now, there are many signs that will take place before the coming of the Son of man, but when the white cloud is seen, this will be the sign of the coming of the Son of man. There will be signs in the sun, moon, and stars, and the nations in perplexity. These all testify that Christ is coming, and He is revealed in the clouds with power and great glory.

The sign seen in the setting sun and rising sun has nothing to do with the sign of the coming of the Son of man.

Now brethren, you want to get hold of the pillars of your faith. Here is Christ in the great antitypical Day of Atonement, and you must understand that you need a special preparation for the Day of Atonement. We want our sins taken away; we want to confess them that they may go beforehand to judgment. Do not go away in discouragement, but believe that Christ is able to cleanse you from all unrighteousness. We must cease to sin, because sin is the transgression of the law. Put away sin, and then cling to the Mighty One who is able to wash away every stain of sin. Now, this is a work of humility at this time, and we must confess our sins and get nearer to God so He can write "Pardon" against our names.

And be sure, when you go out to teach others, not to get your minds upon little things, but keep your mind upon the great work of God, for Satan will surely turn you off if possible. Do not try to be original and get up something you have not heard your brethren speak of, for many have been shipwrecked in this way. Keep the mind upon the third angel's message. When you keep this before the minds of the people, they will see wisdom in it. But when you get a great many little trifling things before them, they become confused just like the Jews.

What we want to do is to get the truth before the people.[7]

---

[7] Ms 81, 1886; MR 900.55.

Chapter 8

Remarks After Reading and Article—1888 Before the General Conference

[Copied from WCW Letterbook #G pp. 27-36] Mrs. E. G. White, Minneapolis, Minn.,

Now, brethren, I have felt one of the most solemn burdens ever since I have returned from Europe. I have felt one of the most solemn burdens resting upon me. And I have been unable to rest nights, and have been trying to labor for this one and that one and the other [one], and do what I could for the souls of others; and I tell you, as I told my friends in Oakland, I feel horribly afraid to come into our conference.

The Lord has revealed to me the position our people should take in regard to speculations in lands and so forth, but they do not heed it. It was the same with our institutions; the temptations have been hard, for our brethren have drawn their money from these places of usefulness and invested them in lands and in mines; and there have been individuals who have drifted out there to engage in these worldly prospects. The devil has a snare laid for their feet.

Well, I have labored there this summer some. I tried to labor in Fresno but could not stay there on account of malaria, so we went to Burrough Valley and tried from there to help the Fresno brethren. Time after time we would go to Fresno, but could not ride in the daytime on account of heat and dust, so we had to ride by moonlight. Night after night we traveled over those sandy deserts by the light of the moon, and would get there in the early morning and no place to stay. [The city was] all full of men to get property. Even the hotels were full. Now, God is not in that at all, but it is one of Satan's snares.

Another way is to break up the union that is existing among our people. There are those who profess to stand by our side; we work right together and all seems to be in harmony. Now, said I, if you professing to stand by my side and then get into the snare of the enemy in your investment and I bear my testimony, you go right on as though it had no application. You believe the testimony. You believe, but when it comes to you, then you go to someone who has not been affected and open your soul to them and say, You better look out for such a person; he is going just like Canright did. Now there is no comfort in it, no consolation in it.

There are those here who will do the very same thing. If anything comes that does not strike their ideas, they go to someone who knows nothing of the affair, and pour out their soul to them and say, Now such and such a thing was said. Those things will not bear repeating, and it is strange why they tell them. They try to swell the differences and cover [conceal and minimize] points of agreement as much as possible. I don't care if you have been ministers for years; I don't care who it is; 'tis the work of the devil. When you find men covering these truths up, it is your duty to go to that person and try to fasten his mind on God.

Now, cannot you be sensible? Can you not be men of God? We want knowledge and we want every soul to be in union, and we want every power of our being to be brought to the altar of God. Don't tell any hearsay. If I should [have] taken for granted what I heard, I should have taken it that Brother Lane had the given up truth. But I knew better; but I did wish that [about 8 words are missing] and let us know how he was getting along.

Another letter comes from Battle Creek saying that such and such a thing has taken place and so and so has not done right. I have not seen the parties to talk with them. No, they had not seen the parties, but they could converse with me clear across the Rocky Mountains, which took some eight days. Now, I would like to know why we cannot be Christians when we have the Bible and the testimony which God has given us; why we cannot act upon it. It is discouraging to the very life and soul; and the very time when I should have been writing letters to Europe and persons in different places, I have been so oppressed and burdened that I could not write a word even to my own friends. I would use all my strength so that I could not write: I could only think of them and pray for them, and they have not had a line.

Brother Geymet, the Brother from Italy, and Brother Conradi should both have received letters from me, but I have not written to them. I thought surely I would write, but I did not have the time, and my whole time was taken up [by problems] this side of the Atlantic. No time for missionary work. Is this doing as God would have us do? Should we not guard the interests of one another, and live out the truth? And when you see someone doing wrong, in the place of going to others and thus strengthening him in the wrong way, why not go right to him in the meekness of Christ and tell him what it is to be a Christian? Now we are to labor as those who have to give an account.

I do not measure a man by his work in the desk, but by his work in his home, among his brethren, in his daily life, that he may present every man perfect in

Christ Jesus. May God help us, brethren and sisters, to seek him at this meeting. Is heaven closed that we cannot have access to God, that the power of His grace cannot be bestowed upon us? Why, He wants us to be filled with all the fullness of His love. Why, every face here should shine with the glory of God. It ought to reflect the divine rays of light on the countenance of everyone here. It is to be talking of heaven and heavenly things and of the redemption through Christ.

Why, is it possible that we believe that we are to leave these earthly scenes of sin and sorrow? Then why not reveal it to the world? Why not show to the world that the power of the truth is with you, and then be as a shining light to the world. I want to know if there are not those who will rise up in the judgment to condemn you who profess the truth, because you have not represented the truth as it is in Jesus, and thus help to pave the way to heaven.

I have been awake night after night with a sense of agony for the people of God, that the sweat would roll off from me. Some things fearfully impressive were presented to me. I was in an assembly when a man of noble majestic stature came in and took his position on the platform and unrolled [something] which looked like several long leaves fastened together. And as he turned the pages his hand ran down the page and his eyes swept over the congregation. As he turned them from right to left I could see what was on them. I saw there different names and characters and sins that were written down. There were sins of every description—selfishness, envy, pride, jealousy, evil-surmising, hypocrisy and licentiousness, hatred and murder in the heart, because of this envy and jealousy. These sins were right among the ministers and people. Page after page was turned.

Well, how was this? And a voice said [that] the time had come when the work in heaven is all activity for the inhabitants of this world. The time had come when the temple and its worshipers had to be measured. These were worshipers that were consecrated. Then there were other names that were to be blotted out of the book of life. They had had light and knowledge, and precept upon precept, and appeal upon appeal, but they had never had the transforming grace of Christ in their hearts. They had never had a living connection with Jesus Christ, therefore the light that would come to them through His word they did not bring into their lives and character.

This is what I saw, and I woke up and found myself sitting up in bed with great drops of perspiration on my brow. I felt paralyzed. After this some things happened which caused me great sadness, and it was there I sunk under the burden. I do not care for myself; I would as leave lay down my life now as at any future time, but I believe that God will spare me just as long as He has a work for me to do. The worst thing—the most grievous—is the want of love and the want of compassion one for another. That is what God presented in such a light before me, and I wanted to say to you that if ever there was time when we should humble ourselves before God, it is now.

I have not as much strength now as I have had in the past. God helps, lives, and reigns, and you can seek Him individually. What souls are there here who will have their sins unforgiven and their names blotted out of the book of life? We do not know what we are doing. If we have unclean hands we cannot enter heaven. Is it so that we are being fitted for the society of angels? Is it so that we are to come in the presence of a holy God? Do we sense it? Do we sense that we are to make characters every day, that God is watching the development of character and weighing moral worth, and that our lives are daguerreotyped on the books of heaven as your face is stamped on the polished plate of the artist? I cannot see how you can be so lazy and so indolent and so easy and contented.

I went to a meeting in Oakland and told them I could stay only a little while and I must say what I had to and then go home. There was a brother there who wanted to confess to his brethren that he had become mixed up in worldly affairs and now he could see his wrong. But the burden rolled on me and I stayed till three o'clock in the morning; but we agonized with God in prayer till we got the victory.

We do not half know [how] to pray. We do not know how to get the victory. If only we [would] come to Him and knew how to pray, our hearts would be melted and we would see the blessing of God, and our hearts would become softened by the love of Christ. And when the love of Christ is there, why, then you can do anything. But it has been Satan's studied work to keep the love of Christ out of our hearts. But the trouble is, there is a great lot of ceremony and form. What we want is the love of Christ, to love God supremely and our neighbor as ourselves. When we have this, there will be a breaking down as with the walls of Jericho before the children of Israel. But there is such an amount of selfishness and desire of supremacy in our ranks. Why, it is most painful. We see it everywhere.

I want to say to my brethren, Shall we humble our hearts before God and be converted? Shall we put off all of the self-sufficiency and the lifting up of ourselves, and come down at the foot of the cross? The lower we lie at the foot of the cross the more clear will be our view of Christ. For just as soon as we begin to lift ourselves up and to think that we are something, the view of Christ grows dimmer and dimmer and Satan steps in so that we cannot see Him at all. But what we want is to come and dwell in view of the cross.

Is there no power that can take hold of our sensibilities and show us that we are near the verge of the eternal world? Can we not get our minds on the other side? What can be done to arouse our people? Why, these light afflictions, how we talk about them. Hear what Paul says about them: "For our light affliction, which is but for a moment, worketh for us a far more exceeding and eternal weight of glory; while we look not at the things which are seen, but at the things which are not seen." Etc. (2 Corinthians 4:17, 18) Would you consider that to be beaten with rods, to be a night and a day in the deep, suffer with hunger, cold, nakedness, and all these things—and worst of all from false brethren—were light afflictions? But he says, These light afflictions.

Now brethren, I am thoroughly disgusted and indignant for my Saviour, that those who profess to be Christians are babies. They are indignant if anyone does anything that does not suit them. And if anyone crosses their path, they are discouraged and want to give up. Well, let them give up if they cannot do what is right. They must be hewed and fitted for the heavenly building. Now there is too much self. We want self to die and be hid in Christ Jesus, then we will not talk of discouragement and difficulties and all these small things, but we will talk of the great plan of redemption and the matchless power of Jesus Christ to come to our world and take upon Him human nature that we through Him might be elevated and have a seat at His right hand. What could be more pleasant than that?

If this is not enough, what more could heaven do for the fallen race than has been done? What more, says Christ, "could I do for My sheep than that I have done"? What more? Will He have to let us go? He will unless you change your attitude before God, for He has done all He could to save us. According to the light that we have received, so is our accountability before God. Walk in the light as He is in the light. There is no darkness in Him at all.

Well, suppose you are walking in the light, what then? Why, your testimonies will be light. You will talk light, and all this evil surmising and evil speaking will be put away. You will talk and we will not be thinking of ourselves and what others are doing, but what God and Jesus are doing. Well, what are they doing? They are cleansing the sanctuary. Well, we should be with Him in this work and be cleansing the sanctuary of our souls of all unrighteousness, that our names may be written in the Lamb's book of life, that our sins may be blotted out when the times of refreshing shall come from the presence of the Lord. It is the most solemn work that was ever given to mortals.

You have no time to be exalting self, but [only to] lift Jesus up. Oh, lift Him up! How can we do this? How can we [be] seeking all the time to be saving ourselves, and exalting ourselves? May the God of heaven let his power come upon your hearts that we may have right characters and pure hearts and know how to labor for the sick [and] suffering. Says the shepherd of the flock, [quotation missing]. Who does He mean—ministers? No. Everyone who has named the name of Christ, who has tasted and knows that the Lord is good.

Go to work for those who are around you with brokenness of spirit, with hearts all melted by the love of Christ. Christ can work with you, but He will never work without the cooperation of man. Get in the right place and God will put His power on you, and combine His divine with our human efforts, and we can work out our salvation with fear and trembling. That is a power that Satan cannot resist or overthrow. It is when you have a right hold from above that Satan cannot tempt you. We want you to be reconverted, and [have] the grace of Christ in the heart.

It is high time that we were awake out of sleep, that we seek the Lord with all the heart, and I know He will be found of us. I know that all heaven is at our command. Just as soon as we love God with all our hearts and our neighbor as ourselves, God will work through us. How shall we stand in the time of the latter rain? Who expects to have a part in the first resurrection? You who have been cherishing sin and iniquity in the heart? You will fail in that day.

Well, now, there is a class who will come off conquerors. Is it those who cherish sin and iniquity in the heart? No; these cannot stand in that day. There are many temptations coming from Satan, and if we are not deceived it will be because we have a knowledge of the truth. If they do not fall under the miracles of Satan, if they are not led astray by Satan's miracles, they will fall by the wrath of God. Do not be discouraged and think that He will never pardon, because He says that though your sins are as scarlet He will make them as snow. The God of heaven offers every inducement for you to come and submit to the refining process. Shall we not come?

The love of Christ in the heart will do more to convert sinners than all the sermons you can preach. What we need is to get the love of Christ, that we may study the Bible and know what sayeth the scriptures. The word will be unfolded through the ceaseless ages of eternity. Now, brethren, we might as well tear away the rubbish from the doors of our hearts now, just now, and let us be getting ready for the judgment, for we have no time to waste.[8]

---

[8] MR 900.39.

Chapter 9

The Minister's Relationship to God's Word

[A sermon preached in the Seventh-day Adventist Church in Des Moines, Iowa, December 1, 1888]

Text: (2 Timothy 4:1-11)

Here we have presented before us the work of him who shall open the Scriptures to others. It is a most solemn work, and all who engage in it should be men of prayer. It is not enough for the minister to stand up in the desk and give an exposition of the Scriptures. His work has but just begun. There is pastoral work to do, and this means to reprove and exhort with all longsuffering and doctrine; that is, he should present the Word of God, to show wherein there is a deficiency. If there is anything in the character of the professed followers of Christ, the burden should certainly be felt by the minister, and not that he should lord it over God's heritage. To deal with human minds is the nicest job that was ever committed to mortal man.

There will be human prejudices and many other things that will bar his way. He will have to meet hearts that have never been subdued in their childhood. They have never been brought into order and into line; they have never been brought under control. Therefore, in dealing with these minds, where reproof is necessary, to rebuke with all longsuffering, to be successful in this work, the servant of God will have to arm himself with the same mind that was in Christ Jesus; and if he walks humbly with his God, he will recognize in every soul for whom he has labored that they are the purchase of the blood of Christ; that our precious Saviour considered them of such value that He did not withhold Himself, but gave up His life in order that they might have a provision, a trial, a time when they should consider the things of eternal interest, and that they should weigh them carefully, attentively, and see if they do not consider whether or not it is to their advantage and profit to build into eternal life.

Here the apostle presents a solemn charge to every minister of the Gospel. He arrays them before God and the Lord Jesus Christ, who shall judge the quick and the dead, to preach the Word, and they are not to show a partiality for merely the prophecies and the argumentative portions of the Scriptures, but the greatest and most important lessons that are given us are those given us by Jesus Christ Himself. If we become thoroughly acquainted with the doctrines of Jesus Christ, then we shall be able to win souls to Christ. We shall have the love of Christ in our hearts, for we will see that we can do nothing without it. Why, Christ says, "If ye abide in Me, and My words abide in you, ye shall ask what ye will, and it shall be done unto you." (John 15:7)

It is not enough that we merely give an exposition of the Scriptures, but we must have the Word of God abiding in us; and Christ has said that unless "ye eat of My flesh and drink of My blood, ye shall have no part with Me. None but those who eat of My flesh and drink of my blood shall have eternal life." (See John 6:53-56) Then He goes on to explain what it means. Why, he says, "the flesh profiteth nothing; it is the spirit that quickeneth" (see Verse 63), and He says that His flesh is meat indeed and drink indeed. Therefore, we are not to merely open the Bible and read something to the people and then go away out of the desk and carry no burden of souls with us.

God designs that every minister of the gospel shall increase in efficiency. He designs that they shall have more power in prayer, that they shall become more intelligent in handling the Word of God, continually growing in grace and in the knowledge of our Lord and Saviour Jesus Christ; and the more that they think and talk of Christ, the more they will meditate upon the blessed Saviour and the Word He has given them to obey, the more they will reflect the image of Jesus Christ; and by so doing they will become partakers of the divine nature, having escaped the corruption that is in the world through lust.

Remember this point—"having escaped the corruption that is in the world through lust." If we are in that position where we shall speak the truth in the demonstration of the Spirit and of power, we shall be men and women of prayer. We shall seek God earnestly, and as ministers of God preaching the gospel, we should carry these great truths into our daily lives, and show that we are living examples of what we preach—that we are carrying into our everyday life practical godliness—then wherever we go we will be a power.

There are some who have power just while they are in the desk, and it goes no further, therefore their influence is like the morning dew which the sun shines upon and drinks up; there is nothing to it; but if he carries the Word into his life, if he is eating and drinking of the blood and flesh of the Son of God, then he is a party with Christ, he is a partaker of the divine nature. Like the branch connected with the living vine, he has been drinking sap and nourishment from the True Vine, and it will be seen wherever he is.

Let us see what [the Word says] further: "For I am now ready to be offered, and the time of my departure is at hand. I have fought a good fight, I have finished my course, I have kept the faith: Henceforth there is laid up for me a crown of righteousness, which the Lord the righteous judge, shall give me at that day: and not to me only, but unto all them also that love His appearing" (2 Timothy 4:6-8)

Well, there is an incentive before us constantly to be faithful. As to those [to] whom God has committed sacred trusts, we are to be faithful, and if we are faithful, then the God of heaven will pronounce us worthy of eternal life, and [will bestow] that crown of righteousness that is laid up for the faithful who shall be overcomers at last.

Now, there are some that may think they are fully capable with their finite judgment to take the Word of God, and to state what are the words of inspiration and what are not the words of inspiration. I want to warn you off that ground, my brethren in the ministry. "Put off thy shoes from off thy feet, for the place whereon thou standest is holy ground." There is no finite man that lives, I care not who he is or whatever is his position, that God has authorized to pick and choose in His Word.

It is true that the apostle has said that there are some things hard to be understood in the Scriptures. So there are. And if it were not that there are subjects that are difficult and hard to be understood, well might the skeptic who now pleads that God has given a revelation that cannot be understood—well might he, I say—have something else to plead. God's infinity is so much higher than we are, that it is impossible for man to comprehend the mystery of godliness.

Angels of God looked with amazement upon Christ, who took upon Himself the form of man and humbly united His divinity with humanity in order that He might minister to fallen man. It is a marvel among the heavenly angels. God has told us that He did do it, and we are to accept the Word of God just as it reads.

And although we may try to reason in regard to our Creator, how long He has had existence, where evil first entered into our world, and all these things, we may reason about them until we fall down faint and exhausted with the research when there is yet an infinity beyond. We cannot grasp it, so what man is there that dares to take that Bible and say this part is inspired and that part is not inspired? I would have both my arms taken off at my shoulders before I would ever make the statement or set my judgment upon the Word of God as to what is inspired and what is not inspired.

How would finite man know anything about that matter? He is to take the Word of God as it reads, and then to appreciate it as it is, and to bring it into the life and to weave it into the character. There is everything plainly revealed in God's Word which concerns the salvation of men, and if we will take that Word and comprehend it to the very best of our ability, God will help us in its comprehension.

Human minds without the special assistance of the Spirit of God will see many things in the Bible very difficult to be understood, because they lack a divine enlightenment. It is not that men should come to the Word of God by setting up their own way, or their own will or their own ideas, but it is to come with a meek and humble and holy spirit.

Never attempt to search the Scriptures unless you are ready to listen, unless you are ready to be a learner, unless you are ready to listen to the Word of God as though His voice were speaking directly to you from the living oracles. Never let mortal man sit in judgment upon the Word of God or pass sentence as to how much of this is inspired and how much is not inspired, and that this is more inspired than some other sources. God warns him off that ground. God has not given him any such work to do.

We want to keep close to the truth that is for our times—present truth. We want to know what is the truth now. We claim to believe the third angel's message; we claim that the angel was flying through the midst of heaven proclaiming the commandments of God and the faith of Jesus. This was the proclamation. Did you hear his voice? Did he speak so you could hear that message? Did the world hear it? Did the world hear any note? Did they want to hear? Will anyone hear it? Yes, those who have been walking out step by step as Jesus leads the way, and when the position of Christ changed from the holy to the most holy place in the Sanctuary, it is by faith to enter with Him, understand His work, and then to present to the world the last message of mercy that is to be given to the world. And what is it? It is a message to prepare a people for the second coming of the Son of Man. It is God's great day of preparation, and therefore every minister of Jesus Christ should have in his course of action, in the burden of his labor, a zeal and living interest, and intensity in his efforts which is appropriate to the truth that is for this time, which is claimed to be the last message of mercy to our world. Well, then, we cannot sleep, we cannot be indifferent; we must labor for the precious souls around us, of men and women; we must work with all our might, for the Lord is coming.

The real laborers will be careworn, oppressed in spirit, and they will feel as did Christ when He wept over Jerusalem. When they see crookedness and impenitence, and when they see people who will not listen to the Word of the Lord, why they will feel as He felt when He exclaimed, "O, Jerusalem, Jerusalem, thou that killest the prophets, and stonest them which are sent unto thee, how often would I have gathered thy children together, even as a hen gathereth her chickens under her wings, and ye would not." (Matthew 23:37) Here are precious invitations of mercy, and while we carry them and try to let the light be reflected upon the world in darkness, we cannot see, perhaps, that the rays of light are penetrating everywhere. We may not see this, but it is so, if we carry the light and have the right spirit—and we want the right spirit—and we want to labor in Christ and have Christ with us constantly.

Here in Second Timothy, the second chapter, beginning with the eleventh verse, we read: "It is a faithful saying: For if we be dead with Him, we shall also live with Him: If we suffer, we shall also reign with Him: if we deny Him, He also will deny us: If we believe not, yet He abideth faithful; He cannot deny Himself. Of these things put them in remembrance, charging them before the Lord that they strive not about words to no profit, but to the subverting of the hearers" (Verses 11-14)

What does that mean? It means that there may be contentions over words and over ideas, but they should be to some purpose, they should be to break down the stubbornness and the opposition that is in human hearts in order that their spirits may be softened and subdued, so that when the seeds of truth are dropped into the soil of the heart, they may take root there. We do not know which shall prosper, this or that; it is God alone that giveth the increase. Therefore we must labor in discouragements, but we want to labor in Christ. The life must be hid with Christ in God, and as the minister's labor is to watch over the flock of God as overseers, there are cautions that they are to heed: "Study to show thyself approved unto God, a workman that needeth not to be ashamed, rightly dividing the Word." (Verse 15) This is a great labor; it is a great burden. It is not to obtain the praise of men, it is not to look to any living mortal on the earth, but to God we are to look, with an eye single to His glory.

If we look to Him, He will certainly help us. He will give us His grace to help to labor on; He will give us strength to go forth weeping, if need be, bearing precious seed, and doubtless we shall come again with rejoicing, bringing our sheaves with us. That is what we want. We want to bring sheaves to the Master. We want to consider that we are missionaries, wherever we are, in the highest sense of the word, and there is a great work before us. We want a sharpened intellect, growing in grace and in the knowledge of our Lord and Saviour Jesus Christ, growing up to the full stature of men and women in Christ Jesus.

What then? Why, we are to present every man approved in Christ Jesus. That is our work; and when men and women accept the truth, we are not to go away and leave them, and have no further burden for them. They are to be looked after. They are to be carried as a burden upon the soul, and we must watch over them as stewards who must render an account. Then as you speak to the people, give to every man his portion of meat in due season, but you want to be in that position where you can give this food.

The Word of God is rich. Here are the precious mines of truth, and we can dig for the truth as for precious treasures hidden away. We buy a field. After we buy it, we hear that there is buried in it a vast amount of wealth; so we begin to plow and turn over every portion of that field carefully, till we have found the precious jewels.

Here is the garden of God. Here is the precious Word, and we should take that Word and study it carefully; study its pages thoroughly and be in a position where we can gather the divine rays of light from glory, and reflect them on those around us. God wants us to be fruitful in the Scriptures. And when you may go forth to your fields of labor, you may indeed feel that you are weak men, but you are not handling weak subjects. You are handling subjects of eternal moment, and you are to study and search the Scriptures for yourselves. You are to dig in this mine all the time, and the "entrance of Thy words giveth light; it giveth understanding unto the simple" (Psalm 119:130)

Whereas [people merely with] human nature might search the Bible, study its pages, be able to see its beauty, yet the searching would profit them nothing, but when they come with a humble heart, with a prayerful spirit, when they take hold of that Word with reverence, and open its pages with a prayerful heart, why the enterings of that Word—the Word must enter into the heart. It is not enough to read it merely, but it must enter, it must take right hold of the soul, and bring your spirits into subjection to the Spirit of God.

And when this transforming process has been accomplished—and we know that you are men mighty in the Scriptures when you can stand up before the people and can present Christ to them crucified—we know you have been to the Living Fountain; we know that you have been drinking of that Fountain, which is Christ in you springing up into everlasting life, so the words that you shall utter will be right words. They will not be vain words, coming together with a jingling sound, just to please the people. No, all this is to be shunned. You are to shun everything of that character. You want to be in a position where the blessed truth of heavenly origin shall have a transforming influence upon the life and upon the character.

Now let us see what it saith in Philippians, second chapter, commencing at the twelfth verse: "Wherefore, my beloved, as ye have always obeyed, not as in my presence only, but now much more in my absence, work out your own salvation with fear and trembling."

There is no carelessness allowed here; there is no indolence; there is no indifference; but we are to work out, each of us, our own salvation with fear and trembling. Why? Let us see: "Wherefore, my beloved, ... work out your own salvation with fear and trembling." Well, then, you say, am I to go around fearing and trembling all the way? Yes, in one sense, but not in another sense.

You have the fear of God before you, and you will have a trembling lest you will depart from the counsels of God. There will be that trembling. You will be working out your own salvation all the time with fear and trembling. Does it rest here? No, let us hear how the divine power comes in: "For it is God that worketh in you both to will and to do of His good pleasure." (Verse 13) Here are man's works, and here are God's works. They both cooperate. Man cannot accomplish this work without the help of the divine power.

God does not take man with his own natural feelings and deficiencies and place him right in the light of the countenance of God. No, man must do his part; and while man works out his own salvation, with fear and trembling, it is God that worketh in him to will and to do of His own good pleasure. With these two combined powers, man will be victorious and receive a crown of life at last. He stands in view of the haven of bliss and the eternal weight of glory before him, and he fears lest he will lose it, lest a promise being left, he shall come short of it. He cannot afford to lose it. He wants that haven of bliss, and strains every energy of his being to secure it. He taxes his abilities to the utmost. He puts to the stretch every spiritual nerve and muscle that he may be a successful overcomer in this work, and that he may obtain the precious boon of eternal life.

What will I do? When the world sees that we have an intensity of desire, some object that is out of sight, which by faith is to us a living reality, then it puts an incentive to investigate, and they see that there is certainly something worth having, for they see that this faith has made a wonderful change in our life and character.

A transformation has taken place, and you are a different man. You are not the same passionate man that you used to be. You are not the same worldly man that you were. You are not the man that was giving way to lust and evil passions, evil surmisings and evil speakings. You are not this man at all, because a transformation has taken place. What is it? The image of Christ reflected in you. Then you are bearing in view that there is a company to stand by and by on Mount Zion, and you want to be one of that company, and you are determined that you will form a part of that company. Let me read: (Revelation 14:1-3, quoted)

Why were they [the 144,000] so specially singled out? Because they had to stand with a wonderful truth right before the whole world, and receive their opposition, and while receiving this opposition they were to remember that they were sons and daughters of God, that they must have Christ formed within them the hope of glory. They were ever keeping in view the great and blessed hope that is before them. What is it? It is an eternal weight of glory. Nothing could surpass it.

Paul had a view of heaven, and in discoursing on the glories there, the very best thing he could do was to not try to describe them. He tells us that eye had not seen nor ear heard, neither hath it entered into the heart of man the things which God hath prepared for those that love Him. So you may put your imagination to the stretch, you may try to the very best of your abilities to take in and consider the eternal weight of glory, and yet your finite senses, faint and weary with the effort, cannot grasp it, for there is an infinity beyond. It takes all of eternity to unfold the glories and bring out the precious treasures of the Word of God.

Do not let any living man come to you and begin to dissect God's Word, telling what is revelation, what is inspiration and what is not, without a rebuke. Tell all such they simply do not know. They simply are not able to comprehend the things of the mystery of God. What we want is to inspire faith. We want no one to say, "This I will reject, and this will I receive," but we want to have implicit faith in the Bible as a whole and as it is.

We call on you to take your Bible, but do not put a sacrilegious hand upon it, and say, "That is not inspired," simply because somebody else has said so. Not a jot or tittle is ever to be taken from that Word. Hands off, brethren! Do not touch the ark. Do not lay your hand upon it, but let God move. It is with His own power, and He will work in such a manner that He will compass our salvation. We want God to have some room to work. We do not want man's ideas to bind Him about.

I know something of the glory of the future life. Once a sister wrote to me and asked if I would not tell her something about the city of our God, further than we have in the Word. She asked me if I could not draw something of its plans. I wrote her that I would have to say to her, "Put off thy shoes from off thy feet, for the place whereon thou standest is holy ground." "No," said I, "you cannot paint, you cannot picture, and the martyr tongue cannot begin to give any description of the glory of the future life; but I will tell you what you can do: You can 'press toward the mark for the prize of the high calling of God in Christ Jesus.' You can die to self; you can seek to grow up to the perfection of Christian character in Christ Jesus." That is our work, but when men begin to meddle with God's Word, I want to tell them to take their hands off, for they do not know what they are doing.

But here is the company. John sees it and wonders what means the scene. The account goes back in the chapter previous. I will not read it, but it shows where Heaven sends a message to the children of men, and they begin to embrace it, and follow the Lamb step by step until they enter into the sanctuary, and on till they are redeemed and stand with the Lamb on Mount Zion. And then it is explained why their song was so different from any other song. It was a new song. And he goes on to state that "in their mouth was found no guile: for they are without fault before the throne of God."

Now, brethren, we see just what is before us. If we have unruly tongues, and they will talk, we want to have them cured. How shall we get them cured? Follow the Lamb. Follow the footsteps of Christ. We want our conversation to be sanctified. We want no impurities on our lips; we want none in our hearts; we want nothing that will defile. We want clean hands and pure hearts, and we want to keep our minds constantly awake.

We are altogether too well satisfied. Many of our ministers are as weak as babes. They understand the theory of the truth—can present that well enough—but when it comes to working out their own salvation with fear and trembling, if they meet with a little obstacle, they begin to talk doubt and discouragement, and in a despairing tone, and you will find they will stumble over little mites of obstacles that they should not notice at all. That is terrible.

What we want is to be armed with the same mind that was in Christ Jesus our Lord. And when we are armed with His mind, we can say with the apostle, that we are not to look at the things that are seen, but we are to look away from these things. These things which are seen are temporal, but the things which are unseen are eternal, therefore we are to keep our minds fixed upon heavenly things, the eternal weight of glory. That is what we are to think about and what we are to talk about.

If we would only consider like rational beings that there is a heaven before us to gain and a hell to shun; if we should keep that in mind, do you think that we would let the things of this earth sap away all our religious fervor? We shall not handle these things long. We are passing through this world as pilgrims and strangers, and in a little while we shall lay off our armor at the feet of our

Redeemer, and we must be getting ready for that event. We want our actions, and our words and our thoughts to be right, for we all have an influence for good or for evil.

Here is my family that will be sanctified because of my right course of action. If I have spoken defiling words, if guile has passed my lips, if I have been peevish and cross, then I shall lie against the truth which I claim to believe. Therefore I will not be on that side of the question at all. I will have my mouth clean and my tongue sanctified. I will have my heart sanctified that I shall not take up a rumor against my brother, because I am told in the Word of God that he that taketh up a reproach against his neighbor shall not dwell in the hill of the Lord. (Psalm 15:3) Therefore, I must have clean hands and a pure heart, for it is they that shall stand in the hill of the Lord. Now, I want to be of that number that shall stand in the hill of the Lord. It does not make one whit of difference with my character whether anyone shall think ill of me or think good of me. It does not affect me, but it will affect them. May God help us that we may come up to that very place where we can appreciate these things.

We want to see the family altar established, and we want there to bring our children right before God with earnest prayer, just as the minister labors for his congregation when he is before them. Every father should feel that he is placed at the head of his household to offer up a sacrifice of thanksgiving to God and of praise to Him, and to present these children to God and seek His blessing to rest upon them, and never rest until he knows that they are accepted of God—until he knows that they are children of the Most High. Here is a work for the mother. What a responsibility rests upon her! Do we consider and realize that the greatest influence to recommend Christianity to our world is a well-ordered and well-disciplined Christian family? The world sees that they believe God's Word.[9]

---

[9] Reported by W. E. Cornell. Portions of this manuscript appear in Evangelism, 7BC, This Day With God, Our High Calling, and Manuscript Releases 347 and 749, Manuscript 13, 1888; MR 900.26.

Chapter 10

Religious Liberty

[First page missing.] ready to contend for man's right to worship God according to the dictates of his own conscience. The minds of the people of God have been bewildered, and they have not discerned that Satan was stealing a march upon them, exulting that he could employ their voice and pen upon matters of minor importance, and so keep them from warning the people of their danger. There are many who, if they understood the spirit and the result of religious legislation, would not do anything to forward in the least the movement for Sunday enforcement.

But while Satan has been making a success of his plans, the people of God have failed at their post. God had an earnest work for them to do, for the honor of His law and the religious liberty of the people are at stake. Yet the watchmen failed to discern the deceptions of the enemy that they might give the trumpet a certain sound in season to have some decided influence.

At the time of the trouble in the church and college at Battle Creek, in 1882, I was in Healdsburg, California, and my soul was in agony as I pleaded with God to arouse His people that they might not be ignorant of Satan's devices. God would have us see and realize the weakness and depravity of men, and put our entire trust in Him. "For we wrestle not against flesh and blood, but against principalities, against powers, against the rulers of the darkness of this world, against spiritual wickedness in high places. Wherefore take unto you the whole armour of God, that ye may be able to withstand in the evil day, and having done all, to stand." (Ephesians 6:12, 13)

There are many who are at ease, who are, as it were, asleep. They say, "If prophecy has foretold the enforcement of Sunday observance, the law will surely be enacted," and having come to this conclusion they sit down in calm expectation of the event, comforting themselves with the thought that God will protect His people in the day of trouble. But God will not save us if we make no effort to do the work He has committed to our charge. We must be found faithfully [doing our duty as] vigilant soldiers, lest Satan shall gain an advantage which it is our duty to prevent.

We should diligently study the Word of God, and pray in faith that God will restrain the powers of darkness, for as yet the message has gone to comparatively few, and the world is to be lightened with its glory. The present truth—the commandments of God and the faith of Jesus—has not yet been sounded as it must be. There are many almost within the shadow of our own doors for whose salvation no personal effort has ever been made.

We are not prepared for the time when our work must close. We must take a firm stand that we will not reverence the first day of the week as the Sabbath, for it is not the day that was blessed and sanctified by Jehovah, and in reverencing Sunday we should place ourselves on the side of the great deceiver. The controversy for the Sabbath will open the subject to the people, and an opportunity will be given that the claims of the genuine Sabbath may be presented. Blindness and disloyalty to God so prevail that His law is made void, but the psalmist says of such a condition, "It is time for Thee, Lord, to work; for they have made void Thy law."

It is time for God's people to work as never before, because of the increase of wickedness. The God-fearing, commandment-keeping people should be diligent, not only in prayer, but in action; and this will bring the truth before those who have never heard it. The world is overborne with falsehood and iniquity, and those whom God has made the depositaries of His law and of the pure religion of Jesus must be determined to let their light shine. If they do nothing to disabuse the minds of the people, and through ignorance of the truth our legislators should abjure the principles of Protestantism, and give countenance and support to the Roman fallacy, the spurious sabbath, God will hold His people, who have had great light, responsible for their lack of diligence and faithfulness. But if the subject of religious legislation is judiciously and intelligently laid before the people, and they see that through Sunday enforcement the Roman apostasy would be reenacted by the Christian world, and that the tyranny of past ages would be repeated, then whatever comes, we shall have done our duty.

The man of sin thinks to change times and laws. He is exalting himself above God, in trying to compel the conscience. But God's people should work with persevering energy to let their light shine upon the people in regard to the law, and thus to withstand the enemies of God and His truth. When the law of God has been made void, and apostasy becomes a national sin, the Lord will work in behalf of His people. Their extremity will be His opportunity. He will manifest His power in behalf of His church.

When in Healdsburg the Lord wrought upon me mightily; I could not rest, and I asked the Lord to give me strength to meet my brethren again in General Conference, and I would set these things plainly before them. I would not shun to declare to them the whole counsel of God. While you have been allowing your minds to be diverted from the very work that God would have you do, and have been doing that which He has not called you to do, Satan has exulted, and has carried on his work with all diligence. You have neglected the testimonies that the Lord in mercy sent to incline your feet in the right path. Some of you have utterly refused these words of warning. You have been strong in your own ideas, set in your own ways, and you would not heed reproof or receive correction. The powers of darkness were mustering their forces. Satan was stirring men with a power from beneath that he might outgeneral the armies of Israel and take the field. We have lost much time and many precious opportunities, and Satan has had things his own way.

I promised the Lord that if He would give me His presence I would attend the next General Conference and would speak the words He should give me. I felt that if I was permitted to stand before you again I must have the presence of God with me as Moses had when he led the children of Israel through the wilderness, that my words might have power with you who have been partially blind to the importance of our time and work. I felt that I would make every effort in my power to urge our brethren to seek the Lord while He is to be found, to call upon Him while He is near. I would show them that unless they were imbued with the Spirit of God they could do no good in their work. Their coldness, their lukewarmness, was an offense to God. They must walk in Christ's light or Satan would put his blinder before their eyes and they would call light darkness and darkness light.

I tell you now that you must have divine enlightenment. If you do not seek this, Satan will set up his hellish banner right in your homes, and you will be so blinded to the real nature of his deceptions that you reverence it as the banner of Christ. If you seek God with contrition of soul, His angels will be round about you, and will minister to you, helping you to discern between the sacred and the common. But a nominal faith, a nominal religion, will find no favor with God.

It has been clearly presented before me that many who now preach the truth have never been converted. They need to have Christ the hope of glory formed within them. They need pure, undefiled religion, then they will not glorify poor, erring mortal man to his injury and with loss of their own souls. We need, oh so much we need, the deep movings of the Spirit of God in all our hearts.

My brethren, we must have Jesus enthroned within, and self must die. We must be baptized with the Holy Spirit, and then we shall not sit down, saying unconcernedly, "What is to be will be. Prophecy must be fulfilled." Oh, awake, I pray you, awake! For you bear the most sacred responsibilities. As faithful watchmen you should see the sword coming, and give the warning, that men and women may not pursue a course through ignorance that they would avoid if they knew the truth. The Lord has enlightened us in regard to what is coming upon the earth that we may enlighten others, and we shall not be held guiltless if we are content to sit at ease, with folded hands, and quibble over matters of minor importance. The minds of many have been engrossed with contentions, and they have rejected the light given through the Testimonies because it did not agree with their own opinions. God will not work a miracle to convince these rebellious ones of the truth of the Testimonies, and compel them to acknowledge His message. He has given sufficient evidence for their faith, and it is only the stubbornness of the natural heart that prevents them from acknowledging the light.

God does not force any man into His service. Every soul must decide for himself whether or not he will fall on the Rock and be broken. Heaven has been amazed to see the spiritual stupidity that has prevailed. You need individually to open your proud hearts to the Spirit of God. You need to have your intellectual ability sanctified to the service of God. The transforming power of God must be upon you, that your minds may be renewed by the Holy Spirit, that you may have the mind that was in Christ.

If the watchmen sleep under an opiate of Satan's, and do not recognize the voice of the true Shepherd, and do not take up the warning, I tell you in the fear of God they will be charged with the blood of souls. The watchmen must be wide-awake, men who will not slumber at their post of duty, day nor night. They must give the trumpet a certain sound, that the people may shun the evil and choose the good. Stupidity and careless indifference cannot be excused. On every side of us there are breakers and hidden rocks which will dash our bark in pieces and leave us helpless wrecks, unless we make God our refuge and help. Every soul should now be distrustful of self. Our own ways, our own plans and ideas, may not be such as God can approve. We must keep the way of the Lord to do His will, making Him our counselor, and then in faith work away from self.

Light must come to the people through agents whom God shall choose, who will give the note of warning, that none may be in ignorance of the purposes of God or the devices of Satan. At the great heart of the work Satan will use his hellish arts to the utmost. He will seek in every possible way to interpose himself between the people and God, and shut away the light that God would have come to His children. It is his design to keep them in ignorance of what shall come upon the earth.

All should be prepared to hear the signal trumpet of the watchman, and be ready to pass the word along the walls of Zion, that the people may prepare themselves for the conflict. The people must not be left to stumble their way along in darkness, not knowing what is before them and unprepared for the great issues that are coming. There is a work to be done for this time in fitting a people to stand in the day of trouble, and all must act their part in this work. They must be clothed with the righteousness of Christ, and be so fortified by the truth that the delusions of Satan shall not be accepted by them as genuine manifestations of the power of God.

Brethren, years have passed in which every professed follower of Christ should have been engaged in most earnest work to press back the armies of the powers of darkness. Years have been lost because the people of God were not closely connected with the source of all power. For years past every soldier of Christ should have been equipped for the warfare, prepared to meet and avert the dangers that threaten our liberties. The Word of God is to be our defense. We are to search the Scriptures as never before. We are to contend for the faith once delivered to the saints, and turn from our dependence upon man. We are to idolize no man, exalt no man, but let God be our fear and our dread.

I call upon you as Christ's ambassadors to take your feet out of the path they are now in, for it is not the path of duty or of safety. Repent before God that you have not been faithful watchmen, standing unitedly in the work for the salvation of souls. Tell the people the time of night. Tell the faithful and true that the morning cometh; tell the slothful and ease-loving, and those who are working on the enemy's side, that the night cometh. Years have been lost, but will you now awake? Will those in responsible positions take in the situation, or will they, by their indifference and inactivity, say to the people, "Peace and safety"? May God help every one to come up to the help of the Lord now.

The watchmen have been asleep, but may God grant that they may not sleep the sleep of death. Let all who are standing upon the walls of Zion give the trumpet a certain sound. It is a solemn time for God's people, but if they stand close by the bleeding side of Jesus. He will be their defense. He will open ways that the message of light may come to the great men, to authors and lawmakers. They will have opportunities of which you do not now dream, and some of them will boldly advocate the claims of God's downtrodden law.

The word of the Lord has come to us in positive notes. Will you hear and obey? Says the prophet Isaiah, "Cry aloud, spare not, lift up thy voice like a trumpet, and show My people their transgression, and the house of Jacob their sins." (Isaiah

58:1) Who is doing this at this time? Because of the backslidings of God's people, living faith has become almost extinct. The deep movings of the Spirit of God are not manifested among us as God would be pleased to manifest His grace. How long will this state of things continue?

Instead of increased power as we enter the perils of the last days, weakness, dissension, and strife for supremacy, are apparent. But if we had a connection with the God of heaven we should be mighty in Him, and yet we would walk with all lowliness of mind, having self hid in Jesus. But now both spiritual and natural feebleness and death are depriving us of workers. God alone, by His Holy Spirit, can arouse us from the slumber of death. There is now need of earnest working men and women who will seek for the salvation of souls; for Satan as a powerful general has taken the field, and in this last remnant of time he is working through all conceivable methods to close the door against light that God would have come to His people. He is sweeping the whole world into his ranks, and the few who are faithful to God's requirements are the only ones who can ever withstand him; and even these he is trying to overcome. Much upon these things has been shown to me, but I can present only a few ideas to you.

Go to God for yourselves; pray for divine enlightenment that you may know that you do know what is truth, that when the wonderful miracle-working power of Satan shall be displayed, and the enemy shall come as an angel of light, you may distinguish between the genuine work of God and the imitative work of the powers of darkness.

Ministers may do a great work for God if Jesus abides in the heart by faith. "Without me," says Christ, "ye can do nothing." I would that I had the power to present before you your sacred, solemn responsibility. Unless you fall upon the Rock and are broken, unless Christ shall put His mold upon you, these words will not be heeded. You are too self-sufficient, too self-satisfied to feel that such words are needed. But they are truth. Has not God made you the depositaries of His message? And has He not additional truth to reveal to His people, if they will carefully search for it as for hid treasure?

The ministers of God should be able to bring forth from the treasure house of His Word things new and old. "Educate, educate, educate," said the angel. "Give the people the truth. Lift up Jesus before them. Lead them in the path cast up for the ransomed of the Lord to walk in. Give them line upon line, and precept upon precept, here a little, and there a little. Never cease to study the Bible for yourselves, that you may in an intelligent manner present to the understanding of the people that which is to be."

The word was spoken to me, "Speak to the people all the words that I shall give thee. Wake up the mighty men. Let them become fully aroused, that they may with pen and voice stir up the people to whom God has given great light, that they may let their light shine forth in clear, steady rays to the world. A world is to be warned; and when the third angel's message goes forth with a loud cry, minds will be fully prepared to make decisions for or against the truth.

"The great charge is to be made by Satan and his evil angels, united with evil men who will fix their destiny by making void the law of God in the face of convincing evidence from His Word that it is unchangeable and eternal." The very time of which the prophet has written will come, and the mighty cry of the third angel will be heard in the earth, His glory will lighten the world, and the message will triumph; but those who do not walk in its light will not triumph with it.

It is now too late in the day for men to please and glorify themselves. Ministers of God, it is too late to be contending for the supremacy. The solemn time has come when ministers should be weeping between the porch and the altar, crying, "Spare Thy people, O Lord, and give not Thine heritage to reproach." It is a day when, instead of lifting up their souls in self-sufficiency, ministers and people should be confessing their sins before God and one another. The law of God is made void, and even among those who advocate its binding claims are some who break its sacred precepts. The Bible will be opened from house to house, and men and women will find access to these homes, and minds will be opened to receive the Word of God; and when the crisis comes, many will be prepared to make right decisions even in the face of the formidable difficulties that will be brought about through the deceptive miracles of Satan. Although these will confess the truth and become workers with Christ at the eleventh hour, they will receive equal wages with those who have wrought through the whole day.

There will be an army of steadfast believers who will stand as firm as a rock through the last test. But where in that army are those who have been standard-bearers? Where are those whose voices have sounded in proclaiming the truth to the sinning? Some of them are not there. We look for them; but in the time of shaking they have been unable to stand, and have passed over to the enemy's ranks. Christ says to him who feels his weakness, "Let him take hold of My strength, that he may make peace with Me, and he shall make peace with Me."

The power of God is waiting the demand of earnest faith. The Lord Jesus has been coming near to us in this conference. I thank God for the heartbreaking I have seen in the ministers' prayer meetings. The Lord has been moving upon the hearts of ministers that they might lay hold of His strength. But for some reason, the very ones who most need the influence of these meetings have not been present. The very ones who most need to drink at the fountain of life, who ought to stand in the forefront in our ranks, have not received the power that God has been willing to bestow upon them. The future will tell the results of failing to improve these precious morning meetings. Day after day has passed, and some have not humbled their souls before God. Oh, will the Lord pass them by? They are the ones most in need of hearing every word the Lord has for them.

Those who would now help souls destitute of wisdom, sanctification, and righteousness, must themselves have on the whole armor of Christ's righteousness; for we can never lead the people to an experience of which we are not partakers. Those who have not tasted of the rich blessing of God will make little of the blessings that others have received. The light which God is giving to His people may be slighted, refused, rejected, but it is thus treated at great peril to men's souls. Brethren, God is working for us, and I feel deeply in earnest that not one ray of heaven-sent light may be regarded with indifference. God's communication to man is to be appreciated and cherished. If we do not appreciate the light of heaven, it will be our condemnation; our position will be similar to that of the Jews when they rejected the Lord of life and glory.

I hope the words I have spoken will not go out of your hearts, like water out of a leaky vessel. I have not spoken to you my own words. I promised the Lord that if I were permitted to meet with you again I would not withhold the truth, although it might not please you all. I know there are some that will be benefited, and in the day of reward the faithful overseer, the faithful shepherd of the flock, will receive a crown of glory. I entreat you, for Christ's sake, do not let the spirit of the enemy take possession of you, and the work be marred in consequence in your hands.

We very much desire the help of Elder Littlejohn. God has not released him from the work. We very much desire that Elder Smith shall have the power of the grace of Christ with him at every step, that he shall have Christ as his counselor; for Satan will surely seek to leave upon his mind impressions that will be detrimental not only to his own soul but to the flock of God. He has had a part in the work almost from its very beginning. The third angel's message will triumph. [Oh] that Elder Smith may triumph with it, and may have the full assurance of God's approval in all his work. He is in danger of making wrong moves, and it will be, with his temperament, exceedingly hard for him to acknowledge that he has erred.

The work of God is precious in every particular, and it is to go forth to the churches in all its divine fullness. Elder Smith and Elder Littlejohn can communicate the reasons of our faith in a clear and understanding manner which will interest and instruct minds, and if they have a living connection with Jesus, power will attend their labors. God has entrusted to Brother Smith the treasures of His truth, but he has naught wherein to boast because of this. He must walk humbly with God, and God will work with him and for him. He needs to drink deep draughts of the living water, not occasionally but continually, that he may present the fulfillment of prophecy with power and fervency. Increased light will shine upon all the grand truths of prophecy, and they will be seen in freshness and brilliancy because the bright beams of the Sun of Righteousness will illuminate the whole.

Do we believe that we are coming to the crisis, that we are living in the very last scenes of the earth's history? Will we now awaken and do the work which this time calls for, or will we wait till the things which I have presented come upon us? God will make Brother Smith strong in His strength if he will walk not in the counsel of men but in the counsel of the Holy One of Israel. My husband, myself, and Brother Smith have been united in the work for many years. From his youth, Brother Smith has been engaged in the work, and it has become a part of his being. He knows our labor, and is acquainted with the work that God has given me to do, and, like John, he can speak of the things which he has seen, and the things that he has heard, and the experience he has had in relation to the work God has given me to do. And this witness Satan will strive most earnestly to silence, that he may better obtain access to minds by making of none effect the testimonies of the Spirit of God. Brethren and sisters, the Lord wants to impart to us increased light. He desires that we shall have distinct revealings of His glory, that ministers and people shall become strong in His strength. When the angel was about to unfold to Daniel the intensely interesting prophecies to be recorded for us who are to witness their fulfillment, the angel said, "Be strong, yea, be strong." We are to receive the very same glory that was revealed to Daniel, because it is for God's people in these last days, that they may give the trumpet a certain sound.

God help us to work unitedly and as we never have worked before, is my prayer. There is need now of faithful Calebs, whose voices will be heard in clear, ringing notes, saying of the immortal inheritance, "Let us go up at once and possess it; for we are well able." We need now the courage of God's faithful servant of old. Not one wavering, uncertain note should come from the watchers' trumpets. They must be true to the sacred, solemn work that has been entrusted to them, and lead the flock of God in right pathways onward and upward to victory.[10]

---

[10] Manuscript 18, 1888. See The Review and Herald Extra, December 24, 1889, Art. B, par. 13.

Chapter 11

Picking Flaws

[Morning Talk by Mrs. E. G. White Ottawa, Kansas, May 12, 1889]

The enemy is at work with those who have placed themselves in doubt and unbelief; and they are not satisfied only to be there themselves, but all the time they are strengthening others in the same line, and they want others to believe just as they do. From the light God has given me, there never was any new light that came from heaven but that Satan could find something in it to pick at. And so it is with some of the people of today—they will pick at little things. They want the light, but there comes along the enemy just as he did to the men of Nazareth, and although the Spirit of God told them that Jesus was the anointed one and Christ told them what His work was—to break the power of the enemy and let the oppressed go free, to loose the bands of wickedness and to preach the gospel to the poor. (See Luke 4:18)[11]

But it seems to me that we do not take these things and learn the lessons from them that we should. Now the unbelieving came up and the devil took advantage of it and began to work, and they began to say among themselves, Who is this? Is not this the son of Joseph and Mary? And just the minute this thought came into their minds they began to work it out. And you know how it worked. They arose right up and laid hold of Christ and led Him to the brow of the hill and were going to destroy Him. Now, there has not been any improvement made in human nature since that time. Human nature is human nature still. If there is any little point where they can divert the mind, they make the most of it. You see it in the counsels. It has been presented to me again and again. They [church leaders] are laying plans for the work of God, trying to make arrangements whereby they can advance the work of God, and there stands someone trying to trig [block] the wheels. As I said to one of our brethren not long since, "You have done more to set back the work of God than ten or twenty of our enemies, because you construe some point into something wonderful, and you have held the committee for hours over nothing, only to throw in a block to trig the wheel, and the time wasted and the good resolutions that should have been carried have been lost. You come in

---
[11] They remained in doubt and unbelief.

and they think you are a good man, a moral man, and what you say is all right, but every time you have a chunk to throw in, and they are worried out in their counsels and nothing is accomplished which should have been done, on account of this hindrance."

Now brethren I want to tell you, when the Spirit of God comes into our midst, it will strike the minds that are ready to receive it. But if their minds are not open to receive it, they are all ready to pass judgment upon the messenger and the words spoken. In the place of coming to God and asking Him to give them a new heart and a new mind, that the transforming influence of the grace of God shall be upon them, they commence to find fault and pick flaws. It doesn't strike them, and it must harmonize with their ideas and they will stand right there until these things are culled out of the way, and they place themselves right there to judge. This is the way it was at Minneapolis.

It is because I know the very same spirit is here, and that we should not give place to it for a moment that I say these things. I know that while the Spirit of God will make impressions upon human minds, the enemy will come in and make the most of any little thing that it is possible to make and the leaven will begin to work because the devil wants it so. Now brethren and sisters I want to place you on your guard. I want to ask you if you are satisfied with your coldness, your unbelief, your backslidings. Have you not had enough of it? If not, the devil will give you all you desire. We don't want any more.

We see that we are in no better condition than the Jewish people. God gave them the clear light that they might stand as His holy, peculiar people. He had given them the prophets, and then Christ Himself came in order that He might present the truth to them. But when His own nation rejected Him, He turned away. He told them, "Ye have ears, but ye hear not, eyes have ye but ye see not." (cf. Jeremiah 5:21) Then they inquired, "Are we blind also?" Christ said, "If ye were blind no sin would be attached, but it is because light has come and ye choose darkness rather than light." (See John 9:14) Was it a real darkness? No, it was not. The light of truth had shone upon them, but Satan was throwing his blinder before their eyes, and they received it not.

Now brethren, there is a blessing here for you. You may think it strange that I speak to you about these things, but it is my duty. We never want this thing acted over again on God's earth; and if God gives me strength I will do it. I want you to inquire, How is it with my soul? Will you take the light, or will you stand complaining? It is time we should know where we are. We should have a chance to pray and talk and seek God. What we want is the Lord, and we don't want anything else. But we have it here in these words of Zechariah. Joshua stood before the Lord, and Satan stood there at His right hand to resist him. "The Lord rebuke thee," He said, "is not this a brand plucked out of the fire?" (Zechariah 3:2)

Now here are the people of God and God wants you to be getting ready for the great day of salvation, that you may be getting others ready. He wants you to have a fitting-up, that you may have a message for the people that will cut its way through the fleshy heart, and that you may go crying through the porch and the altar, "Spare thy people, O Lord, and give not thine heritage to reproach." (Joel 2:17) Now open your ears to the truth you have had and put away your doubts, unbelief, and Christless surmisings.

God wants you to come and drink of the clear waters of the streams of Lebanon, and when you have drunk yourselves you will want to call others to drink. Convert after convert is presented to me who does not know what it is to have faith in Christ. It seems they are ready to die; there is no light in them; they are dying for the want of God.

I went to a meeting where I could stay only three days, and in that time I spoke to them seven times. They begged of me to stay longer; they seemed starved, and they would get up and talk of how they wanted this truth and this light, but the devil was ready to bring in something to shut out the light, and many are ready to have it so. They don't know what the pure atmosphere is, but may the Lord help us that the clear light of His glory may surround us. May God help us to stand on vantage ground before the enemy that we shall have our minds broken off from things below and get hold from above.

Christ, when talking to the people of His time, told them that they had blinded their eyes and closed their ears lest they should see with their eyes and hear with their ears and be converted and He should save them. (See Matthew 13:15) Light had been given them, but they would not receive it. Darkness was upon them, and they would come and pick the little flaws, and draw the minds of the people away from the solemn truth that was for them. Now, how will it be with us? We don't want to kill ourselves here laboring for you, but will you labor for yourselves? We want to know whether we will have the rich blessing of the Lord resting upon us, and we realize that He sheds His rich light and glory upon us. This is my prayer.[12]

---
[12] Manuscript 2, 1889; MR 900.22.

Chapter 12

Behold Christ's Glory

[Morning Talk at Ottawa, Kansas May 14, 1889]

Brethren and sisters, just as surely as we begin to look earnestly to Jesus, and uncover our souls to Him, we shall go down deep into the valley of humiliation; and just as surely as we go down, we shall rise up again. The more humbly we live before God, the nearer we will come to Him, and the more distinct will be our view of Jesus Christ and His matchless light.

(2 Corinthians 3:18): "But we all, with open face beholding as in a glass the glory of the Lord, are changed into the same image from glory to glory." Now you see how important it is that we are beholding this. The enemy has come in, and his dark shadow has been thrown athwart our pathway so that we dwell on the dark side and talk of gloom until our way seems almost hopeless, and we stumble along without courage, hope, or love. But we do not want this to be so. We want this shadow to be swept away, and it will be if we look beyond the darkened shadow to the brightness beyond in Christ Jesus.

"Therefore seeing we have this ministry, as we have received mercy, we faint not." (2 Corinthians 4:1) It is the mercy of God that we are to enjoy every day and every hour. Talk of it: dwell upon it.

"But [we] have renounced the hidden things of dishonesty" (Verse 2) Here come in the works that go hand in hand with faith. We must not expect that the grace of Christ will work with us while we are practicing dishonesty.

"Not walking in craftiness, nor handling the word of God deceitfully; but by manifestation of the truth commending ourselves to every man's conscience in the sight of God." (Verse 2) All that we do is to be in harmony and corresponding with the holiness and purity of the truth.

"But if our gospel be hid, it is hid to them that are lost." (Verse 3) If they quibble and stumble over points of truth that are presented, why, they would stumble over the plainest statements.

"In whom the god of this world hath blinded the minds of them which believe not, lest the light of the glorious gospel of Christ, who is the image of God, should shine unto them. For we preach not ourselves, but Christ Jesus the Lord; and ourselves your servants for Jesus' sake." (Verse 4, 5) Is there not a whole volume here on which we can study?

"For God, who commanded the light to shine out of darkness, hath shined in our hearts, to give the light of the knowledge of the glory of God in the face of Jesus Christ." (Verse 6) How are we to get it? We are to be God's witnesses and reflect the character of Christ in our character. There is no use for a man to be low and sensual, with his mind on sensual things, and yet think he can reveal the knowledge of God that is Jesus Christ. He must have the grace of God in his own heart and practice it in his life.

"But we have this treasure in earthen vessels, that the excellency of the power may be of God, and not of us." (Verse 7) Have we received a bright thought? If so, we are not to think that it is because of any wonderful smartness or intelligence in ourselves. It is because God is the Author of it. If anyone tells you you have preached a good sermon, tell him the devil told you that before he did, and for him not to be an agent for the devil. There is pride in our hearts that must be emptied out, and then Jesus Christ will come in and take possession of our whole heart.

I love my Saviour this morning because He first loved me. If there is anything in my life, my words, my teachings, that is good, it is because Christ has put it there. It is not because of any goodness in me, and there is no glory to be directed to myself. The fruit of the Spirit is love, joy, peace, longsuffering, gentleness, goodness, faith; against these there is no law. We should experience this, and then we will not be under the bondage of the law of God by any means. You are free in Christ Jesus. We shall walk in liberty because our will is in harmony with the will of God and we love all His commandments.

"We have this treasure in earthen vessels," but we are hid in Christ, and Christ is in God; so, our lives are hid with Christ in God and we reveal Christ, and in doing so we reveal the Father. Let this be a season when if you have sins to confess, or if you have wronged your brethren and have not right feelings toward them, for Christ's sake get these things out of the way. We want to be getting ready for the future life. Our Lord is coming with power and great glory. We are not to be surfeited and drunken with the cares of this life, but we are to keep our minds uplifted; and if we do this we shall see of the salvation of the Lord, and our hearts will be all light in the Lord, and we shall talk of His love and tell of His power and reveal Him to all around us.

It is our privilege to go on from strength to strength and from glory to glory. Do not think that because we have a glimmer of the light of God, that we have it all. It will soon leak out of your hearts as water out of a leaky vessel if your eyes are not fixed on the mark of the high calling which is in Christ Jesus. Unless you work with earnestness, the devil will sow doubts in your mind.

When you start out, the enemy may put into your minds some cheap, common, sensual thought; but lift your souls to Jesus Christ and think of His purity, and they will not long remain. Talk of His glory, think of His life; and when affliction comes to you, let it prove you to be God's workmen, working out a far more exceeding and eternal weight of glory. Then talk of His glory, and let your soul be full of the love of Jesus, and your hearts be uplifted to God every morning and noon and evening and if we fight the good fight of faith we shall come off victorious.[13]

---

[13] Ms. 3, 1889; MR 900.15.

Chapter 13

Preparation for Christ's Coming

[Talk at the Ministers' Meeting Kansas camp meeting May 14, 1889]

We take the words of Brother [O. A.] Olsen in regard to the coming of the Lord, and we think how it has been presented to us in a striking manner that the end of all things is at hand; the Lord is at the door. What influence has it had to solemnize our minds and arouse in us an earnestness to separate from us everything that is offensive to God? Then to think that, after all, He is nearer now than when we first believed. The day of the Lord is right at hand, and it is not safe for us to delay [to prepare for] His coming. Do you think that any of us, when He comes, will be brought before the great Judge and will feel that we have devoted too much time to preparation? Will such thoughts come into our minds? Shall we think that we have been altogether too sympathetic, that we have devoted too much time in winning souls back to Christ, and binding up the brokenhearted? No indeed. Our thoughts will be these as we look back to those who stand before the Judge: "Why didn't I help them at such a time when I ought to?" or, "O, I am glad I did deny myself and help them to stand on the solid rock." These are the very thoughts that will come up to us in the judgment when everyone is judged according to the deeds done in the body.

And as many are weighed in the balance, they will be found wanting. Then they will proclaim their sins upon the housetop. They will not be afraid to have everybody know their sins, if they can only make restitution for them and save one soul. But let us thank God today that we are not yet before the judgment seat of God, but we have an Intercessor, one who has loved us so that He gave His own precious life for us individually, just as though there was not another soul in the universe. He died for us, and we are of infinite value to Jesus Christ. How can we measure the sacrifice He has made for us? Then we should feel how we have wounded and bruised the Son of God and put Him to an open shame when we deny Him. It is not that you come out in words and deny Him, but in your actions you deny Christ so that He is ashamed to call you brethren. We want every one of us to be consecrated to God.

Let the plowshare go deep, and uproot all this Phariseeism, and let this self-righteousness be torn all to pieces. The very best way to have this done is to fall on the Rock and be broken. Just as soon as you see there is nothing in you that is righteous, just as soon as you have a dread of sin, you will fall on the Rock, and then it is that Christ can take you and mold you and fashion you into a vessel of honor. But just as soon as you allow your thoughts and feelings to be turned against one another, this is unlike Christ, and just so sure it is that you are not vessels unto honor, but dishonor. You don't give God a chance; you are trying to fashion yourself after a mold of your own imagination, but you want to take that out of your mind, and keep Christ before you every day—when you rise up and when you sit down, when you go out and when you come in.

You want to exercise all that Christian politeness and respect because you are the purchase of the blood of Christ, and He has died upon Calvary's cross that we might live. Christ Himself has bridged the gulf for us. It is our duty to help those who are downcast. Recollect what their privileges are, and don't talk of the difficulties, but go right to them and try to bind up the brokenhearted. These are right in the church all around us. Never have an idea that you know more than your brethren, but just keep humble. It was this spirit of surmising that brought all the weakness into the Jewish nation.

We want to learn in the school of Christ meekness and lowliness of heart, and from whom are we to learn these lessons? Jesus says, "I am meek and lowly of heart." "Learn of Me." Now, if there is anything in us like self, then Christ cannot dwell there. We want to represent Christ to the world. We must have self hid with Christ in God, and when this is the case we will represent Christ to the world. Oh, there is something wonderful about it—He loves us as He loves His Son. (See John 17:23) Just think of it—loves us as He does His Son! This is wonderful, wonderful. In Him we have all heaven presented to us, and the more we see in Jesus the less we see that is good in self. You know, just as soon as the heavenly Messenger came from heaven and revealed Himself to Daniel he said, "My comeliness was turned in me into corruption." (Daniel 10:8) He had such a view of the glory of God that he fell as one dead. He could not talk; he could not see; but the angel took him and set him upon his knees, and yet he could not look at Him. Then what did he have to do? Veil His glory, and come to him just as Christ came to this world. He took upon Him humanity, then He could talk with Daniel. Brethren, the more we see in Jesus, the less we will see in self; and the more self-esteem we have, the more we are puffed up by the devil. May God help us to put away self and cling to Jesus; then we will spring up and bear fruit to the glory of God.[14]

---

[14] Ms. 4, 1889.

Chapter 14

Christ and the Law

[Sermon given at Rome, New York, June 19, 1889]

(Matthew 5:14-16 quoted)

We read in the following verse, Verse 17, "Think not that I am come to destroy the law, or the prophets: I am not come to destroy, but to fulfil." What made them think that? It was because, notwithstanding they had had Christ represented in the typical offerings and sacrifices, they could not get it out of their minds that it was the law, the law, the law that they must dwell upon as their entrance into heaven. And here Christ comes in with His lesson, not to detract from the law, but to reveal to them the old light in new settings. He comes to reveal that light in the framework of the gospel, that they might understand in regard to this light that it was essential for them to have.

Here He shows the exceeding breadth of the law of Jehovah—its extended character—and He presents it before them in a light they had not comprehended before. And the moment He does that, there arises a resistance against that light. Why should they accept it? It was not as they had taught it; it was in a different setting; and they could not harmonize this with their misconceived ideas.

Christ reads their thoughts, and their thoughts were that he did not make the law as prominent as they had done. He takes up their thoughts and says, "Think not that I am come to destroy the law, or the prophets: I am not come to destroy, but to fulfil.... Whosoever therefore shall break one of these least commandments, and shall teach men so, he shall be called the least in the kingdom of heaven: but whosoever shall do and teach them, the same shall be called great in the kingdom of heaven." (Verses 17, 19) And He makes it still more plain: "For I say unto you, That except your righteousness shall exceed the righteousness of the scribes and Pharisees, ye shall in no case enter into the kingdom of heaven." (Verse 20) Now, they had built over that law, and around it, exactions, and they had burdened it with their own laws and ideas emanating from human, finite beings, until there could no one observe that law, even the letter of it, as they interpreted it; it was impossible.

Now Christ goes on and tells what the principles of the law are, and shows them that it reaches into the inmost parts of the mind. Thus He brings out the purposes of God's law.

When Christ came into the world, He was the origin of truth. The lessons He had given to the prophets had been placed in false settings, and it was His work to place them in the true. He was the foundation and the originator of all truth, and His work was to strip off all traditions of men, for they taught the commandments of men instead of the commandments of God. Those who had been in the school of the prophets, and had been obtaining their education, were considered to know more than all the nations and all other people upon the face of the earth. He turns to them and says, "Ye do err, not knowing the scriptures, nor the power of God." (Matthew 22:29) They saw trees as men walking. And why was not the truth distinct in their minds? The reason was, they were not connected with the God of all truth.

One part of Christ's great work to the world was, He came to it as a representative of the Father. But the world did not know God, and it is very much the same at the present time, even among those who claim to be following the truth. I don't know but you have heard me say it in years past, "I long to introduce you to Jesus Christ, to behold Him as a Christ of love, mercy, sympathy, and tender compassion."

There was one who came to me and said, "Sister White, can you tell me how I am to know that Jesus forgives me my sins as I repent of them?" "Yes, I can. I point you to Calvary, to the dying Saviour upon the cross." There is the evidence that we present to the mind. It is the evidence that you see, that Christ forgives sins. The light reflected from the cross of Calvary speaks to us of the blood of Jesus Christ which was shed for the remission of sins, and it tells us that we may be cleansed and sanctified.

I remember one woman who said, O, if the Lord would only show her in a dream that He would have mercy upon her and save her! Well, He did teach her, and she was taught in a dream, and then the first impression was, "Is that dream any stronger than a 'Thus saith the Lord!?" I want every one of you to take that, because I have found out that whenever I have been pleading for some special light, some strong evidence, I have found I had to wait a long time before I got it. I have found out that I had to take what the Lord said, and believe it as spoken to me. I am one of the daughters of Adam, one for whom Christ died, and have a right to lay hold upon the merits of the blood of a crucified and risen Saviour, because I am a sinner.

And when the devil comes and points to your sins and hateful crimes, tell him,

"Yes, I am a sinner, but Christ is a Saviour, and He says, 'I am not come to call the righteous, but sinners to repentance.'" (Matthew 9:13) Thus you arm yourself with the whole armor of Christ's righteousness. How is it you have not on the armor of Christ's righteousness? What did He come to this world for? Why, if it had been a possible thing for us to have been brought back to keeping God's commandments, He never would have come to this world; but He came here because it was impossible for man to redeem himself and bring himself into a position where Adam stood before the fall. Then what was he to do? Christ came, our substitute and surety.

Before He came they were under a yoke; but Christ was above law, He was the originator of the law, so there was no yoke upon Him; and the angels were in obedience to Christ, who was not under the yoke. He could come as one equal with the Father, and He could open His breast to the whole woe, grief, sin, and misery, and by an offering of Himself He could bring life and immortality to light through the gospel. This is the only hope of life, and when Christ cried out, "It is finished," He carried out the devised plan. He had died in behalf of the race, as a freewill offering to God. He was not urged to do it, but He took it upon Himself that He might save the fallen race. He goes down into the grave and comes up out of the grave.

As Satan was triumphing in His death, it was not long before he found out he had overstepped the boundary. In seeking to cause the death and crucifixion of the Son of God, what did he do? He claimed in heaven, and he claims today among the Christian world, that in taking away the law of God they could establish one of their own that would be better. All the universe of heaven were looking to see what would come out of it.

Why did not God blot Satan out of existence? Why did He not blot sin out? Satan was permitted to develop his character, and unless he had had this opportunity, he would have laid the whole cause of his disaffection upon Christ and the Father. But he had an opportunity here in this world to develop his new principles, and he did it when he crucified the Lord of glory. He acted out his principles, and showed what they would lead to, and we see the same acted out in our world today—what these lawless principles will lead to.

The enemy has worked, and he is working still. He is come down in great power, and the Spirit of God is being withdrawn from the earth. God has withdrawn His hand. We have only to look at Johnstown [Pennsylvania]. He did not prevent the devil from wiping that whole city out of existence. And these very things will increase until the close of this earth's history, because he has come down in great power, and he works with all deceivableness of unrighteousness in them that perish. What is he doing? Going about like a roaring lion, seeking whom he may devour. And when he sees those who are resisting the light, and that God does not shelter them, he will exercise his cruel power upon them. This is what we may expect.

What is God going to do for His people—leave them with no new light? "Ye are," says He, "the light of the world." Then we are to get more light from the throne of God, and have an increase of light. Now, we do not tell you in the message that has been given to you here and in other places that it is a grand new light, but it is the old light brought up and placed in new settings. Jesus gave light, the most wonderful light, as He spoke from that cloudy pillar. And just prior to the time when the children of Israel left Egypt, one plague after another was brought upon the Egyptians, because Pharaoh refused to let the Israelites go to worship God. Finally, the God of heaven suffered the firstborn of both man and beast to be slain, and when Pharaoh looked upon their dying forms he began to understand who the great I AM was—that there was a power above, whom Pharaoh, the king of Egypt, could not compete with or overcome with all his experience and resistance. Therefore he said to the children of Israel, "Go."

But what was there to do the last night? They were to kill a lamb and take the blood and mark the lintels and the doorposts. What for? To evidence to the whole of Israel, as they shall see these things, that there was something that connected them with God. And as the angel would pass over the land to slay the firstborn, and would see the blood that marked the lintels and the doorposts, he was to pass over those who had the blood upon the doorposts.

Just prior to the coming of the Son of man, there is and has been for years a determination on the part of the enemy to cast his hellish shadow right between man and his Saviour. And why? So that he shall not distinguish that it is a whole Saviour, a complete sacrifice that has been made for him. Then he tells them that they are not to keep the law, for in keeping that law man would be united with the divine power, and Satan would be defeated. But in keeping that law man would be united with the divine power. Notwithstanding man was encompassed with the infirmities of humanity he might become a partaker of the divine nature, having escaped the corruption that is in the world through lust. Now here is the redemption.

He did not come to destroy the law, for He says, "One jot or one tittle shall in no wise pass from the law till all be fulfilled." Then they remain today. Yes, there is not a jot or tittle dropped out, and everyone is under law. This is the position that we stand in today; and if any oppose the law, they are the ones that God condemns, because we are not left in uncertainty.

I want to keep God's law and live. But that man of sin has taken it upon himself to change the fourth commandment, and shove in a spurious Sabbath, to show his greatness and power to exalt himself above all that is called God or that is worshiped.

Now the test is coming between the Sabbath that the man of sin has introduced and the Sabbath of the Lord God Jehovah, the seventh day.

There are to be trying times before us, and what does God mean? He means that we seek to understand what He wants to say to us. We have not understood it; we have been going on here, groaning and groaning. When I tried to do good, evil was present with me and sin is constantly at work to have the supremacy. If you could see what Christ is, one that can save to the uttermost all that come unto God by Him, then you would have that faith that works.

But must works come first? No, it is faith first. And how? The cross of Christ is lifted up between heaven and earth. Here comes the Father and the whole train of holy angels; and as they approach that cross, the Father bows to the cross and the sacrifice is accepted. Then comes sinful man, with his burden of sin, to the cross, and he there looks up to Christ on the cross of Calvary, and he rolls his sins at the foot of the cross. Here mercy and truth have met together and righteousness and peace have kissed each other. And Christ says, "I, if I be lifted up, will draw all men unto Me."

"Then," says one, "you cannot be accepted unless you repent." Well, who leads us to repentance? Who is drawing us? Here the law of God condemns the sinner. It points out the defects of his character. But you can stand before that law all your lifetime and say, "Cleanse me. Fit me for heaven," but can it do it? No; there is no power in law to save the transgressor of law in sin. Then what? Christ must appear in that law as our righteousness, and then Christ is lifted up. "And I, if I be lifted up from the earth, will draw all men unto me." (John 12:32)

Here we look at the cross of Calvary. What has made us look at it? Christ is drawing us. Angels of God are in this world, at work upon human minds, and the man is drawn to the One who uplifts him, and the One who uplifts him draws him to repentance. It is no work of his own; there is nothing that he can do that is of any value at all except to believe.

As he sees Christ hanging upon the cross of Calvary he sees that He loves sinners, those who were at enmity with God. He begins to marvel, and is abased.

What is the reason for this? Why, he sees that there is a transgressed law, and that man cannot keep it, but he sees Christ, and with hope and faith he grasps the arm of infinite power and repents at every step. Of what? That he has violated every principle of the law of Jehovah.

Paul says he taught from house to house repentance toward God and faith toward our Lord Jesus Christ. What did Christ come to our world for? To attract the mind and bring it to repentance. Here we have the love of the Father in giving His Son to die for fallen man, that he might keep the law of Jehovah.

Now Jesus stands in our world, His divinity clothed with humanity, and man must be clothed with Christ's righteousness. Then he can, through the righteousness of Christ, stand acquitted before God.

O, I am glad I have a Saviour! We must have the Holy Spirit to combine with man's human effort. We can do nothing without Christ. "Without Me, ye can do nothing." "Behold, I stand at the door, and knock: if any man hear My voice, and open the door, I will come in to him, and will sup with him, and he with Me." (Revelation 3:20) I am so glad that we can be partakers of the divine nature, and that through Jesus Christ we can be conquerors. This is the victory—even your faith, feelings, and good works? Is that it? No; "This is the victory ..., even your faith." (1 John 5:4)

What is faith? It "is the substance of things hoped for, the evidence of things not seen." Then what? "Faith, if it hath not works, is dead, being alone." (James 2:17) Therefore we lay hold upon the merits of the blood of a crucified and risen Saviour. Our lives are hid with Christ in God. There we have the whole of it. We can do nothing of ourselves, but the fire of God's love is burning on the altar of our hearts. We are not following cunningly devised fables, no indeed; but we have been revealing Christ our righteousness. If you boast in your own good works, you cannot boast in Christ.

Now, there has been coming in among us a self-sufficiency, and the message to the Laodicean church is applicable to us. I will read it: (Revelation 3:14-16 quoted)

What is the matter? They have left their first love. "So then because thou art lukewarm ... I will spue thee out of My mouth." What does He mean by that? Why, if the people have great light and knowledge and yet they are not striving to give that light and evidence to the world in their works, which are living principles that they shall present to the world, Christ is dishonored, and He becomes so disgusted with them that he will not take their names into His mouth to present them to the Father.

"I know thy works." "Because thou sayest, I am rich, and increased with goods, and have need of nothing; and knowest not that thou art wretched, and miserable, and poor, and blind, and naked." (Verse 17)

Now what is the difficulty? "Tried in the fire." Christ had such love for us that He could go through all that trying of the crucifixion, and come off conqueror. And the white raiment, what is that? Christ's righteousness. "Anoint thine eyes with eyesalve"—spiritual discernment, that you may discern between true righteousness and self righteousness. Now here is the work. The heavenly merchantman is passing up and down before you saying: "Buy of Me. Here are heavenly goods; buy of Me." "Will you do it? It is "Me" you are to buy of. There is no other source in heaven from which we may receive liberty and life but through Jesus Christ our righteousness.

Then He says, "Be zealous therefore, and repent." That message is to us. We want the brethren and sisters in this conference to take hold of this message, and see the light that has been brought to us in new settings.

God has opened to us our strength, and we need to know something about it and be prepared for the time of trouble such as never was since there was a nation. But here is our strength, Christ our righteousness. Let us ask Isaiah who is to be our strength. Well, he answers, and it comes echoing down along the lines to our time: "For unto us a child is born, and unto us a son is given; and the government shall be upon his shoulder: and his name shall be called Wonderful, Counsellor, the mighty God, The everlasting Father, The Prince of Peace." (Isaiah 9:6) Is not that enough for us? Cannot we cover ourselves all over with it? Do we need any of our own self esteem? No, we cannot have that. We must hide in Christ, and we can hide in the mighty strength of Israel's God. Thus we work to meet the powers of darkness. We fight not against flesh and blood, but against principalities and powers, and spiritual wickedness in high places. And it is only in Christ that we can meet them.

Brethren, do not let any of you be thrown off the track. "Well," you say, "What does Brother Smith's piece in the Review mean?" He doesn't know what he is talking about; he sees trees as men walking. Everything depends upon our being obedient to God's commandments. Therefore he takes those that have been placed in false settings and he binds them in a bundle as though we were discarding the claims of God's law, when it is no such thing. It is impossible for us to exalt the law of Jehovah unless we take hold of the righteousness of Jesus Christ.

My husband understood this matter of the law, and we have talked night after night until neither of us would sleep. And it is the very principles the people are striving for. They want to know that Christ accepts them as soon as they come to Him. I want to tell you, brethren, that light is sown for the righteous, and truth for the upright in heart.

Now, we want to be a people who carry with us joy and gladness and we never can do it unless we carry with us Jesus Christ. If we sin, we have an Advocate with the Father, even Jesus Christ the righteous. Then I do not need to be mourning all the days of my life, for Christ has risen. He is not in Joseph's new tomb, He is with the Father. And how is He there? As a Lamb slain, and He bears in His hands the marks of the crucifixion. "I bear them on the palms of my hands." O, if this does not fill us with hope and gratitude, what will?

I have had the question asked, "What do you think of this light that these men are presenting?" Why, I have been presenting it to you for the last 45 years—the matchless charms of Christ. This is what I have been trying to present before your minds. When Brother Waggoner brought out these ideas in Minneapolis, it was the first clear teaching on this subject from any human lips I had heard, excepting the conversations between myself and my husband. I have said to myself, It is because God has presented it to me in vision that I see it so clearly, and they cannot see it because they have never had it presented to them as I have. And when another presented it, every fiber of my heart said, Amen.

Brethren in New York, we want you to go forward. Advance from light to clearer light. Here are the mines of truth. Work them; dig for the truth as for hid treasures. As you go to the Scriptures and ask God to help you, He will illuminate your minds, and the Holy Spirit will bring all things to your remembrance and the light of heaven will shine upon you.

I ask you in the name of Jesus Christ of Nazareth to arise and shine, for thy light has come. We do not want the work bound about. As you see men and women who have some ability, encourage them. God doesn't want novices to do His work. He doesn't want His work crippled. He wants you to place yourself where you may have a knowledge of the truth as it is in Jesus.

He wants you to attend the school where Biblical lectures are being given. "Well," says one, "I will go to the school in Battle Creek." But they are about full there, and are going to start a school in Kansas. But here is South Lancaster; now why not, you who are so near, patronize South Lancaster? There will be those there who will be able to teach and stand at the head in giving Biblical lectures.

No man should go out to teach the truth unless he has had training and knows how to use the ability and capabilities God has given him. Now, you would not think of such a thing as going to a man who never worked at the carpenter trade and asking him to put you up a fine building; and so it is in God's work. God wants you to learn, and the angels will be right by [you] to impress your mind, and if you will go to the Scriptures as Daniel did, you will understand all God would have you understand. As you learn to practice, and learn to teach, [teach others] as God commanded Timothy to take the things He had given him and commit them to faithful men who would be able to teach others also. Now this is the very work to be done in New York. Let the mind be elevated, ennobled, sanctified, and then the minister will not be worked to death and you can take them and drill them in the truth, and their hearts be burning with it and they want to tell it to others.

Now, you have had light here, and what are you going to do about it? Are you going home and sit down, or are you going to work to build one another up in the most holy faith? God grant that you may work to the point. Oh, how I long to see the work as we may see it! How I long to see the tidal wave pouring over the people! And I know it can be, for God gave us all heaven in one gift, and every one of us can accept the light, every ray of it, and then we can be the light of the world. "A city that is set on a hill cannot be hid."

Now, brethren, go to work. Parents, send your children to these schools. Those near to South Lancaster can go there, and those near the college, go there. God is at work to drill laborers to go forth from there. Now let every one of us arm ourselves and work intelligently, just as the carpenter works intelligently at his trade. He cannot work intelligently unless he learns his trade; no more can you. We want to be growing in every sense of the word. O, I love the truth, and I mean to triumph with it. Not only the ministers but everyone can do something. Taste and see that the Lord is good. May God bless you as you go to your homes.[15]

---

[15] Ms 5, 1889; MR 900.12.

Chapter 15

Responding to New Light

[Remarks at the Bible School, Battle Creek, Michigan, Monday, February 3, 1890]

My brethren, I am laboring most earnestly day and night. My mind is traveling. Things are constantly being revived to my mind that have been revealed in times past, all the way along. I feel such a burden pressing and urging upon me that I cannot keep my tongue silent. Now, we have talked it, and we have urged it, and we have set it before you, and begged and pleaded and prayed and wrestled with all the strength of our being, until we have felt afterward—after the occasion was over—the whole being was so feeble that my breath might stop and my life end at any time. Still on another occasion I am urged in behalf of the people. Now, why can't you do some of this? Every time our people assemble, they come, and they hear, and they go away as they came. They may have a little light, but they do not act on it. They do not take their position on the Lord's side. You do not see that they have opened up the avenues of the heart where the Spirit of God, with its illuminating power, can come right into the heart and soul, so that they will respond.

If God is working upon me in this direction, why is there not a more decided response from our brethren, and they take hold of the work too? Is it so that the burden may press upon me constantly, and yet my brethren and sisters sit as though it must always be so, and as though they had no special work to do in this matter? Now, brethren, we want to know whether we will take hold of that which is our privilege to lay hold of in Jesus Christ.

I know there have been efforts—a contrary influence—to throw back the light, the light which God has been forcing in here upon us in regard to the righteousness of Christ; but if God has ever spoken by me, it is the truth, brethren. It is the truth that every soul of you will receive, or your soul will be left in darkness as barren as the hills of Gilboa—without dew or rain.

The question will come up, How is it? Is it by conditions that we receive salvation? Never by conditions do we come to Christ. And if we come to Christ, then what is the condition? The condition is that by living faith we lay hold wholly and entirely upon the merits of the blood of a crucified and risen Saviour. When we do that, then we work the works of righteousness. But when God is calling the sinner in our world, and inviting him, there is no condition there; he is drawn by the invitation of Christ and it is not, "Now you have got to respond in order to come to God." The sinner comes, and as he comes and views Christ elevated upon that cross of Calvary, which God impresses upon his mind, there is a love beyond anything that is imagined that he has taken hold of. And what then? As he beholds that love, why he says that he is a sinner. Well, then, what is sin? Why at once he has to come here to find out. There is no definition given in our world but that transgression is the transgression of the law; and therefore he finds out what sin is. And there is repentance toward God; and what then?—why, faith toward our Lord and Saviour Jesus Christ that can speak pardon to the transgressor.

Christ is drawing everyone that is not past the boundary. He is drawing him to Himself today. No matter how great that sinner is, He is drawing him. If the sinner can get his arm fixed upon the cross of Calvary, then there is no conviction of sin. What is he there for? Because the law has been transgressed, and he begins to see that he is a sinner; and Christ died because the law was transgressed. And then he begins to look to the righteousness of Christ as the only thing that can cleanse the sinner from his sins and from his transgressions.

Now, we want to have an intelligent knowledge of this thing. We want to take hold of the righteousness of Jesus Christ by living faith, and know that we have not any. We may work to the very best of our ability, but we cannot make a single virtue in ourselves; it is the righteousness of Jesus Christ alone that can do it. Then, as we are clothed with the righteousness of Christ, we have a power and a strength that is imparted unto us, and we will not want to sin; we cannot do it with the righteousness of Christ, and with ourselves in a position where we shall have Christ working with us and by us. We may make mistakes; we may make errors; but we shall hate these sins—the sins that caused the suffering of the Son of God in our behalf because we were transgressors of the law of God.

Now, I want to say, brethren, there is a door open, and no man can close it to you—no matter whether it is those in the highest position or the lowest position—they cannot close it. But you can. You can close the door of your heart that the light which God has sent you for the last year-and-a-half—or nearly that—shall not have its influence and its effect upon your life, nor be brought into your religious experience. This is what God sends His messengers for.

As John went forth to proclaim his message, God gave him a work to do. He had to do that work and arouse the attention of the people. He had to cry aloud, lift up his voice like a trumpet in the wilderness, just as spoken in Isaiah: "Cry aloud, spare not, lift up thy voice like a trumpet, and shew my people their transgression, and the house of Jacob their sins" (Isaiah 58:1). Well now, Christ had not come yet upon the stage of action as a minister. But after the ministry of Christ commenced, here was John to prepare the way for the ministry of Christ, that the minds of the people might be agitated, that their hard hearts, and principles, and customs, and practices might be all stirred up. He condemned their course, and condemned their practices, calling them a generation of vipers. The Christ comes in with a healing balm, with a message which, with the heart broken up, the seed can fall into prepared soil.

When John's disciples became jealous of Christ, they say, "This man, Christ, is baptizing, and all men go unto him." And they bring it in to stir up jealousy. John tells them, "There cometh one after me who is preferred before me, whose shoe's latchet I am not worthy to unloose" (See John 3:26; 1:27). Here was the very work to be done. Well, now, do you think that John had no human feelings? Of course he had! But those human feelings should not have a power over him on that occasion. No; when he sees Christ in the crowd, why he says, "Behold the lamb of God, which taketh away the sin of the world" (John 1:29). He directed the people right to Christ, and two of the disciples immediately followed Him.

God has workmen. They carry the work so far and they can carry it no further, because it is just as natural for the mold of man to be placed upon man as it is to breathe. Now, God calls upon another workman to come right in and advance that work. The one that was working becomes circumscribed. He cannot see that the very line of work that he is working in is not to be pursued to the very close of time. There has to be more light and power infused into the work than we have had. There are workmen to come and carry that work upward and forward. That breaks up the old mold that would be an injury to them, and which would have crippled their experience and advance. But this mold has got to be taken off. The mold of man, the peculiarities of man, are stamped upon it, and it comes to be deified by all those that receive of his labor. Now there comes in another element that takes the old mold off. This work is to be carried upward and forward, and the building is to go up. Thus God has worked with His workmen; He buried the workmen, but the work progresses still.

When I sat with the hand of my dying husband in my own, I knew that God was at work. While I sat there on the bed by his side, he in such feverness, it was there, like a clear chain of light presented before me: The workmen are buried, but the work shall go on. I have workmen that shall take hold of this work. Fear not; be not discouraged; it shall go forward.

It was there I understood that I was to take the work and a burden stronger than I had ever borne before. It was there that I promised the Lord that I would stand at my post of duty, and I have tried to do it. I do, as far as possible, the work that God has given me to do, with the understanding that God was to bring an element in this work that we have not had yet.

Our young men look at the older men that stand still as a stick and will not move to accept any new light that is brought in; they will laugh and ridicule what these men say and what they do as of no consequence. Who carries the burden of that laugh, and of that contempt, I ask you? Who carries it? It is the very ones that have interposed themselves between the light that God has given, that it shall not go to the people who should have it. I know what I am talking about. These things have not been revealed to me for the last forty years and I [remain] in ignorance in regard to them.

Now, brethren, I say, clear the King's highway, for your soul's sake. If you have interposed between the people and the light, get out of the way, or God will move you out of the way. I tell you that God calls for men to come up to the help of the Lord, to the help of the Lord against the mighty. They are not to pull back; they are not to put their weight against the chariot so as to pull it back; but they are to push with all the might and energy that God has given them.

Now it is just exactly as in the days of the Jews. When a message came in, why all the power of the leaders was put against it, that it should not have access to the people. Now, brethren, go to God for yourselves, and on your knees plead with God. We cannot bear that men should go away from the very center and heart of the work here with wrong impressions. I cannot bear that they should go away from here with a cloud on their minds. If God sends us light, let it come to us, and let no man close the door, or try to close it. Don't close it yourselves. Open the door of your heart and let the brilliant rays of light shine into your heart and into your mind. I pray you, let the Sun of Righteousness in.

Now, if it is my work, and if God wants me to stand and oppose this matter to the end, I can. But how long before you decide you will receive my testimony? How long before it shall have any weight with you? How long before you will accept the word that has been among us from its very commencement? How long will you reject or turn from the testimony to your own feelings, and your own ideas, and your own impulses? I have stood here and fought every inch of ground that we may have the very message that this people has had, that I might work together with God. I want to know how that God will let His people deny and hedge up the way, that the light He has sent to His people cannot reach them. How long is this thing to be tampered with? How long is the grace of God to come to this people in vain? I plead with you, for Christ's sake, clear the King's highway, and trifle not with the Spirit of God.

We have traveled all through to the different places of the meetings that I might stand side by side with the messengers of God that I knew were His messengers, that I knew had a message for His people. I gave my message with them right in harmony with the very message they were bearing.

What did we see? We saw a power attending the message. In every instance we worked—and some know how hard we worked. I think it was a whole week, going early and late, at Chicago, in order that we might get these ideas in the minds of the brethren. The devil has been working for a year to obliterate these ideas—the whole of them. And it takes hard work to change their old opinions. They think they have to trust in their own righteousness, and in their own works, and keep looking at themselves, and not appropriating the righteousness of Christ and bringing it into their life, and into their character. We worked there for one week. It was after one week had passed away before there was a break and the power of God, like a tidal wave, rolled over that congregation. I tell you, it was to set men free; it was to point them to the Lamb of God which taketh away the sins of the world.

And there at South Lancaster, the mighty movings of the Spirit of God were there. Some are here that were in that meeting. God revealed His glory, and every student in the College was brought to the door there in confession, and the movings of the Spirit of God were there. And thus [it was] from place to place. Everywhere we went we saw the movings of the Spirit of God.

Do you think, like the ten lepers, I shall keep silent, that I shall not raise my voice to sing the righteousness of God and praise Him and glorify Him? I try to present it to you, that you may see the evidence that I saw, but it seems that the words go as into empty air. How long is it to be thus? How long will the people at the heart of the work hold themselves against God? How long will men here sustain them in doing this work? Get out of the way, brethren. Take your hand off the ark of God, and let the Spirit of God come in and work in mighty power. I feel to stand at my post of duty. I may fall here as my husband fell, but I need to do a work for God. I need to do a work for eternity.

What is the testimony that has been given here? Who are the men to come in and give you anything, infusing new light, and bringing you up to a higher standard? If you can show them to me, if you can show me that the work is advancing, we say amen; but we cannot see it. We want to see that God puts His impress upon the work. We want to see men that bear heavenly credentials carry this work in the very last days to its completion. God will give every man here a chance if he will accept it. ...

Now, brethren, I entreat of you, for Christ's sake, let us be reasonable. Let the Spirit of God have influence upon your hearts. I feel an intense interest for every soul here. Why? Because I look to Calvary, and I see the value of the price that has been paid for the soul; and therefore I do not want that soul to close the door of his heart to God. I entreat of you, brethren and sisters, that you should come near to God, that you should take hold of His power, and that you should not deprive yourselves of the very blessing that God wants you to have.[16]

---

[16] Manuscript 9, 1890; MR 900.9.

Chapter 16

Who Will Accept the Light from Heaven?

[Remarks of Mrs. E. G. White, February 6, 1890]

Jesus has some very precious words I want to read to you: "Neither pray I for these alone (that is, the disciples immediately around him), but for them also which shall believe on me through their word." (John 17:20) That is us. That means us brethren. "That they all may be one; as thou, Father, art in me, and I in thee, that they also may be one in us: that the world may believe that thou hast sent me." (Verse 21) The unity and the harmony.

Now, I have thought of a good many that ought to be here that are not here. Where are Leon Smith, and Brother Ballenger, and Brother Smith? Can't they spend an hour? Will they draw off for fear that they shall be won? Why not gather these men in here? And if they do not know what they are opposing at all, they will not understand. No, brethren, where is your burden? Is it that you should get those that do not understand these things, and are all the time firing in the dark against them? We know they will not come to hear, and where the Lord can impress their hearts and their minds. Can't you see, that is not the way for man to work?

Now, brethren, let us look at these matters in the right light. If we have precious things, we want they should have it, we want they should understand where the Spirit of God is; but if they keep on the outskirts of the camp all the time, they do not know the impressions that the Lord is making upon His people. We want them to come right in with us, that we may [have] a unity in faith and in purpose, and we may understand where the Spirit of God is working. And there are a great many others that ought to be here.

Now, here is the word: "That the world may believe that thou hast sent me, And the glory which thou gavest me I have given them." (Verse 21) That is what we are waiting for here; we want some of that glory; and it is our privilege to have it. There is darkness enough in the world, and we want the light of the glory of God to lighten our pathway and to lighten the pathway of others. We want some of that glory, that you may go forth to your labors with that glory shining upon our countenances, expressed in your words and in your testimonies, that it will make an impression on minds wherever you go.

"And the glory which thou gavest me I have given them; that they may be one, even as we are one." Who is it that is burdened that they may get into unity? Who are they? Where are they? God help us that we may understand what spirit actuates and moves us. "I in them, and thou in me, that they may be made perfect in one." (Verse 23) Now their profit is not in seeing just how far they can keep off, and keep another mind, and their own ideas, and cherish their own ideas, and water their own ideas. No, it is that they may be made perfect in one; and they want to be made in one, and they are trying to be one, and they are trying to get where they may be in unity.

"That the world may know that thou hast sent me." Those are the credentials they bear to the world. "And hast loved"—now, mark this. O, it is such a power with me. It has such a power for my heart; it melts and dissolves my very being as I read this. "And hast loved them, as thou hast loved me." Why, brethren, can we comprehend this? Can we take hold of it? Can we measure it?

"Hast loved them, as thou hast loved me." Why, that ought to bring every soul of us in gladness and joy and thankfulness and gratitude the whole time to God, that the preparation has been made that this shall be done; that God loves us as His Son. Why? Because we are united in Christ as He is united with the Father.

There is a oneness with those that are partakers of the Spirit of Christ. You may bring the horse to the water, but you never can make him drink; he has got to drink for himself. Just so it is with us; we may have a house around us, and the words of life may be presented in all their beauty and in all their clearness, and it is like the bright shining of the candle; but unless they will kindle their tapers from it, unless they are willing to get some light, they won't have any, no, indeed. Now, that is the most precious to me.

And He says, "Father, I will that they also [that thou lovest], whom thou hast given me, be with me where I am." Why, in His kingdom they will be right around Him, right about Him. Oh, what a thought! It makes me willing—even if I die at my post—it makes me willing to make an entire sacrifice for the truth's sake. Oh, if I can be with Him where He is! He is my love, my crown of rejoicing; He is my hope and comfort.

Now what? "That they may behold my glory." We have felt Him in the humiliation; we have felt Him in the sacrifice; we have felt Him in the trials; we have felt Him in the test; now that we may behold Him; that we may see Him as He is; that we may behold His glory; and if we behold Him we will be a partaker with Him of His glory.

"And the glory which thou gavest me I have given them.... For thou lovedst me before the foundation of the world. O righteous Father, the world hath not known thee" (Verses 24, 25) Oh, how little we know "Thee," and we profess to be His followers. He says, "The world hath not known thee." God forbid that it should be of those that carry the truth to those who are in darkness that Christ will say, "They do not know Thee." How few know my Saviour!

"But I have known thee, and these have known that thou hast sent me. And I have declared unto them thy name, and will declare it: that the love wherewith thou hast loved me may be in them, and I in them." (Verses 25, 26) That is His word. We have been reading it for more than the last year more distinctly. "I have declared unto them thy name"—Thy name, its goodness, its mercy, its love, its compassion, that you may gather up your forces and think, and that you may plant yourselves upon the rock Christ Jesus and believe Him. "I have declared unto them thy name, and will declare it." That is what He came here for.

"That the love wherewith thou hast loved me may be in them, and I in them." I am so glad, brethren, I am so glad that we have the privilege. But our minds have become separated from God; and the enemy meant it should be so. He cast his hellish shadow right between us and our hope, and our strength, and our comfort, that we should not see Him; that he might eclipse Jesus, that we should [not] discern Him and what He was to us, and what He would do for us, and what He would be to us—that he should cast this dark and gloomy shadow between us and our Saviour.

Now, we have been getting just a glimmering of faith. We have but a little of it. Yet it is so very hard for the mind that has been looking on the dark shadows, and that has been hanging memory's hall all through with disconsolate things and pictures that are draped in mourning, that it seems as though we cannot look upon anything else. But may God help to gather up the jewels of Christ. God help us that we may hang memory's hall all through with the rich promises of God, that when Satan shall come to cast his hellish shadow between us and the source of our strength we may just be armed; we have got the memorials all surrounding us—barricaded with the promises—and we can say, "Although the fig tree shall not blossom, neither shall fruit be in the vines; the labour of the olive shall fail, and the fields shall yield no meat; the flock shall be cut off from the fold, and there shall be no herd in the stalls: yet I will rejoice in the Lord, I will joy in the God of my salvation." (Habakkuk 3:17, 18)

And when sometimes it seems that the Word is made so hard because unbelief is planted in the hearts where faith ought to be flourishing, I repeat that text over and over and over again, and I bring myself in position where the light and the brightness of the Sun of righteousness I can perceive. I will not look at the darkness.

Brethren and sisters, I beg of you for Christ's sake, to lift Him, up—the Man of Calvary. Lift Him up, the sinner's only hope. Learn of Him, every one of you. Oh, may chapters be opened in your experience that you never have opened before in regard to the blessedness and the trust and confidence that you may have in God.

Just see what our Saviour says: "When the Son of man cometh, shall he find faith on the earth?" (Luke 18:8) Why? Why, because the devil has put his dark mantle to enshroud the people, when we want light, light, brethren, light, precious light from the throne of God. Well, then, you want to be sure that you learn how to tell it when you go from here; you want to be so rooted and grounded in it that when you go to those that are fastened in unbelief that they shall not throw their darkness over your mind; that you shall become so settled as to what is truth that you will not be shaken away from it; but that God can reveal to you His precious, precious light.

Now, Paul knew that he was not going to stay very long with Timothy, and he kept giving him lessons all the time; and he says, "My son, be strong in the grace that is in Christ Jesus." (2 Timothy 2:1) That is what every one of us wants—not any of your own opinions, or smartness, or intellect, or any of these things; but be strong in the grace that is in Christ Jesus.

"And the things that thou hast heard of me among many witnesses, the same commit thou to faithful men, who shall be able to teach also. Thou therefore endure hardness, as a good soldier of Jesus Christ." (Verses 2, 3) There is the very word before us. And the very men that ought to be here to feel their interest of having the truth for their positions of trust here in Battle Creek, on this missionary soil—the very men that ought to be fitting for these positions, they are not here at all; they do not come near.

Now, brethren, that is not as it ought to be. I want you to meditate over these matters. I want you to seek God in regard to it. I want you to tell the Lord to stir up these souls, that they may begin to feel that they need something more than they [have] got. Brethren, we want light, precious light from the throne of God; and in the place of quibbling, and in the place of fastening upon hooks that you can hang your doubts upon, for Christ's sake go to your knees in prayer; for Christ's sake see the error and mistake of the Jews; because Christ has said, "Light has come, and ye choose darkness rather than light." (See John 3:19) Now, this can be done right where light is shining. You meet men who say, Beware, beware; we must go careful; we must be very careful to press out the darkness, and let the light come in.

Brethren, we want to come right up as a man and obtain a living experience here in this meeting. You want light enough that you can carry it with you into eternity. That is what you want. We have not half faith enough. We are only just beginning to learn as little children. The child first takes a step, and falls; and then takes another step, and finally learns how to walk. Now, we want to learn how to exercise faith.

When the centurion came to Christ, just look at his faith. Why, he did not claim all the knowledge of the Jews; but here this centurion came, and he says, O Lord, You need not go away down there to heal my servant; You just say it and it will be done. What kind of power did he think was in Christ? Just what was invested in him. Now, said he, You may just say the word. I say to my servant, go, and he goeth, and I say to him, do this, and he doeth. Well now, all You have to say is to command, and it will be done.

What was his insight? That there were angels all around Christ; the word of Christ would go right to that sick chamber and heal that soul. The Jews saw how Christ said to him, "I have not found so great faith, no, not in Israel." Now there are those outside of us that are standing in greater favor to God than we are; and why? Because they live up to every jot of light that they have. And we have light pouring in on us, and for months we have been pleading that the people would come up and accept the light; and they do not know whether to do it or not. They do not seem to see that they can come and drink, that they can open their hearts and let the Saviour in.

My soul is agonized at times over these things. But I cannot do anything, I cannot speak to the heart; but God alone can speak to the heart. I entreat of you, as an ambassador of Jesus Christ, to bruise Satan under your feet. I beseech of you to begin to labor for yourself, labor for souls that are in darkness and unbelief. I beseech of you to spend your efforts in order to bring them where they can come where the living waters flow—where the light of heaven may come upon them, that they can stand amid the people as a light, and not as a shadow of darkness.

Well, yesterday morning I awoke about two o'clock, and I could not rest; it seemed as though there was an agony of soul upon me, and I could not say anything. I knelt right down before the Lord and I said, You know all about it; You know what the burden is. And I must have something more than this. I cannot carry this load. I feel such a responsibility when I know that men are not walking in the light, when I know that they are going contrary from what God has told me.

And it seemed as though there was a light-wave came right down upon me and the peace of God came upon me; and the words, I will be with you; I will give thee My strength, came to me. And since yesterday morning I have felt that I could die for Jesus Christ. And I am not going to worry or put myself under this load; I am going to leave it right in the hands of God. Brethren, do we carry our loads there and leave them? Let us do it. Let us roll it right on the Burden-bearer; and when we have a part to act we will act it. And when you go from this place, Oh be so full of the message that it is like fire shut up in your bones, that you cannot hold your peace. It is true men will say. "You are too excited; you are making too much of this matter, and you do not think enough of the law; now, you must think more of the law; don't be all the time reaching for this righteousness of Christ, but build up the law."

Let the law take care of itself. We have been at work on the law until we get as dry as the hills of Gilboa, without dew or rain. Let us trust in the merits of Jesus Christ of Nazareth. May God help us that our eyes may be anointed with eyesalve, that we may see. God helping us, we will draw nigh to Him, and He says he will draw nigh to us. Do we believe? Will we come in God's appointed way? May the Lord help us and enlighten us, that we may go forth from this place as they went forth to proclaim the truth after the day of Pentecost; and there were souls converted; they could not resist the testimony.[17]

---

[17] MR 900.17.

Chapter 17

The Spirit of Discernment

[Sermon by Mrs. E. G. White, March 9, 1890]

(Re Minneapolis Meeting)

I want to read a few words from the first chapter of Acts—[the] eighth verse: "But ye shall receive power, after that the Holy Ghost is come upon you: and ye shall be witnesses unto me both in Jerusalem, and in all Judea, and in Samaria, and unto the uttermost part of the earth." Now we read in the second chapter (Verses 1-4), "And when the day of Pentecost was fully come, they were all with one accord in one place. And suddenly there came a sound from heaven as of a rushing mighty wind, and it filled all the house where they were sitting. And there appeared unto them cloven tongues like as of fire, and it sat upon each of them. And they were all filled with the Holy Ghost, and began to speak with other tongues, as the Spirit gave them utterance."

Now, brethren, the blessing that is here spoken of we may receive when we come to God with our whole heart, when we empty it of every kind of prejudice and all this doubting and unbelief; then we can expect the Spirit of God. But it is the case as I presented before you one morning in regard to the presentation of Christ in the temple. The priest took Him in his arms, but he could see nothing there. God did not speak to him and say, "This is the consolation of Israel." But just as soon as Simeon came in, the Spirit of God led him, and because he was under His influence, the Holy Ghost being upon him, he sees there that little Infant in His mother's arms and every indication of the little family being in poverty, but the moment he beholds that, God says to him, "This is the consolation of Israel."

Now we have two distinct characters. The priest that was there officiating did not know Him; but here was one who recognized Him because he was where he could discern spiritual things. He was living in close relation with God. He was living in connection with the future eternal interest, and therefore he recognized the Spirit of God.

And how is it with us individually? We know that the Spirit of God has been with us. We know that it has been with us time and again in the meetings. We have not a doubt but that the Lord was with Elder Waggoner as he spoke yesterday. We have not a doubt of that. I have not a doubt that the power of God in rich measure was hanging over us, and everything was light in the Lord to me yesterday afternoon in the minister's meeting. Now, if there had been a throwing open the door of the heart and letting Jesus in, we would have had a precious season there yesterday. I have not a doubt of it.

It makes every difference to us in what kind of spirit we come to the investigation of the Scriptures. If we come with a teachable spirit, ready to learn, with our hearts emptied of our prejudices, not seeking to bring the Scriptures to our ideas but to bring our ideas to the Scriptures, then we shall know of the doctrine. We shall understand it. But let me tell you, brethren, if you have discernment you can understand where God is working. You do not need wonderful miracles to testify of this, because you see the miracles did not do any good to the Jews. They had it right in their sight but it did not do any good to them.

The woman of Samaria who came and listened to Christ—she accepted Him without miracles at all, because she believed His word. She was glad for the light and went and published it to her neighbors. Here were the very ones who were hated of the Jews. The Samaritans were receiving the light. When Christ came to the Jews with all the power of His majesty, all His grace manifested in mighty healings and in the mighty out-pouring of His Spirit, they would not recognize that. Well, why? Because the very same prejudices that had been in their hearts reigned there, and the most mighty miracles that He could do would have no effect on their hearts at all.

If we place ourselves in a position that we will not recognize the light God sends or His messages to us, then we are in danger of sinning against the Holy Ghost. Then for us to turn and see if we can find some little thing that is done that we can hang some of our doubts upon and begin to question! The question is, has God sent the truth? Has God raised up these men to proclaim the truth? I say, yes, God has sent men to bring us the truth that we should not have had unless God had sent somebody to bring it to us. God has let me have a light of what His Spirit is, and therefore I accept it, and I no more dare to lift my hand against these persons, because it would be against Jesus Christ, who is to be recognized in His messengers.

Now, I want you to be careful, every one of you, what position you take, whether you enshroud yourselves in the clouds of unbelief because you see imperfections; you see a word or a little item, perhaps, that may take place, and judge them from that. You are to see what God is doing with them. You are to see whether God is working with them, and then you are to acknowledge the Spirit of God that is revealed in them. And if you choose to resist it you will be acting just as the Jews acted. You have all the light and all the evidences that they had. They rejected the light notwithstanding the mighty miracles of God were there. Their hearts were so filled with prejudice that they said at last, Oh, He does miracles by the power of Beelzebub, the prince of devils; that is how He does His miracles.

Now, brethren, God wants us to take our position with the man that carries the lantern; we want to take our position where the light is, and where God has given the trumpet a certain sound. We want to give the trumpet a certain sound. We have been in perplexity, and we have been in doubt, and the churches are ready to die. But now here we read: "And after these things I saw another angel come down from heaven, having great power; and the earth was lightened with his glory. And he cried mightily with a strong voice, saying, Babylon the great is fallen, is fallen, and is become the habitation of devils, and the hold of every foul spirit, and a cage of every unclean and hateful bird."

Well now, how are we going to know anything about that message if we are not in a position to recognize anything of the light of heaven when it comes to us? And we will just as soon pick up the darkest deception when it comes to us from somebody that agrees with us, when we have not a particle of evidence that the Spirit of God has sent them. Christ said, "I come in the name of my Father, but ye will not receive me." (See John 5:43) Now, that is just the work that has been going on here ever since the meeting at Minneapolis. Because God sends a message in his name that does not agree with your ideas, therefore [you conclude] it cannot be a message from God. How dare you run the risk of trying in the least to shut [Remainder Missing]

Chapter 18

Cherishing Faith, Not Doubt

[Sermon by Mrs. E. G. White, March, 16, 1890, Battle Creek, Michigan]

I want to say a few words in reference to faith. I want to say, brethren and sisters, it is not natural for us to believe, but it is very natural for us to foster unbelief. This is the besetting sin, and has been the besetting sin of God's people. It has not been natural for me to believe for myself, and I have had very severe lessons on this point until I know that it is not safe for me to cherish for one moment any doubt. I never doubted the truth, but to cherish doubt in regard to myself and my work.

Now, I have great sorrow of heart—I have had nearly ever since the Minneapolis meeting—and I will tell you why. Because God has been speaking to me as He has done for the last forty-five years, and I have presented these matters, and the brethren have known and have seen the fruits, and yet unbelief has come right in. But why? They will take the testimony of somebody else, and they will all be credulous in regard to that. Now, when it comes to the manifest movement of the Spirit of God, if the Spirit was in their hearts they would recognize it in a moment. But the trouble is, the Spirit is not in them. And they never will search these things to see if they are so.

The reason why I felt so at Minneapolis was that I have seen that everyone who has taken a position similar to the one they took in Minneapolis would go into the darkest unbelief. Have we not seen it acted over and over again? Then when we see just how Christ was tried, when He came upon earth; when we see the hardness of the hearts; when we see what the enemy can do with human nature, putting unbelief into the heart, I should think it would be such a terror to our souls that we would not dare to open the heart to the miseries of unbelief and dwell in that atmosphere, such as there has been since we were in Minneapolis.

Well, we wonder why Christ prayed with such an agony. It was not for His own sake, but it was because of the hardness of hearts, that notwithstanding He was the Way, the Truth, and the Life, yet people were so hardened that they could not see it and accept it. And as you took their steps, here was my trouble. As they took their steps in the path of unbelief that day, others are taking the same steps this day, and my grief is the same as Christ's was. They are placing themselves where there is no reserve power that God has to reach them with. Every arrow in His quiver is exhausted.

Now, I feel this in every meeting where I have been. I have felt that there is a pressure of unbelief. It is just as evident as it ever has been. I can go among the unbelieving (just as Christ spoke to the Samaritan woman, and the Samaritans came out and heard); I can go among those that have never heard of the truth, and their hearts are more susceptible than those that have been in the truth and had the evidences of the work of God. But they excuse it all. "Why, we did not know that some things were so and so." When we get the Spirit of God in our hearts, He will speak to us. There is the trouble. When they see that God is working in a certain line, they commence with all the power of brain, and all the power of thought, and all the power of talk, as it has been the case here, to stay the work of God. Let me tell you, the testimony will be this: "Woe unto thee, Chorazin! Woe unto thee, Bethsaida! For if the mighty works, which were done in you, had been done in Tyre and Sidon, they would have repented long ago in sackcloth and ashes." (Matthew 11:21)

Now, I know what I am talking about, and as I do not expect to have many opportunities to speak to you, I will say again: "Fall on the Rock." I have no hope for you unless you do. I am glad—yes, I am so thankful—that some are beginning to see that there is light for us. If we want to stay in the cellar, we can do it; but the only way for anyone of us is to fight the good fight of faith. It is not anything that is going to come naturally; but we have got to fight the good fight of faith instead of absorbing all the filth of unbelief. If it is a suggestion of unbelief, credence is given to that at once.

You will never have greater light and evidence than you have had here; if you wait till the judgment, what you have had here will condemn you. But God has been speaking and His power has been in our midst, and if you have not evidences enough to show you where and how God is working, you never will have it. You will have to gather up the rays of light that you have had, and not question so.

"But there are some things that are not explained." Well, what if everything is not explained? Where is the weight of evidence? God will balance the mind if it is susceptible to the influence of the Spirit of God; if it is not, then it will decide on the other side. They will come just exactly where Judas came; they will sell their Lord for thirty pieces of silver or something else. They will sacrifice everything to unbelief.

I will tell you why it makes my heart so sad. It is because every such mind that is susceptible to unbelief and the say-so of this one and that one, and that works against the light and the evidences that have been presented since the Minneapolis meeting—I tell you, brethren, I am terribly afraid that they will fall at last. I am terribly afraid that they will never overcome. But the blood of the Lamb and the testimony of the Lamb must be on the right side of the question. When God is working—and they have got no light to know that he is working, and they just place themselves right under the enemy's power and work right in that line—then they make excuses and say, they did not know. "Oh," said Christ, "if they had known that it was the Prince of light, they would not have crucified Him." Well, why did they not know? Well, if they had only known that these objections that we have been fighting were no objections, then they would not have done it. Well, is that any excuse? Why did they not know? They had the evidences of the Spirit, and it was only the false reasoning, perversion of words and positions, and the misunderstanding, that has led them to this position of danger.

Now, I tell you, God will not be trifled with. God is a jealous God, and when He manifests His power as He has manifested it, it is very nigh unto the sin of the Holy Ghost to disbelieve it. The revealings of God's power have not had any effect to move and to stir persons from their position of doubting and unbelief. God help us that we may remove ourselves out of the snares of the devil! If ever a people needed to be removed, it is those that took their position in Minneapolis at that time on the wrong side.

It is a true saying that we cannot do anything against the truth, but for it. The precious truth of God will triumph; it has the triumph in it, and it is not going to fall to the ground, but somebody will fall, just as in the days of Christ. They have their boundaries and lines, and God has got to work in their line. God disappoints people a good deal. He works right contrary to what they expect. The Jews expected, of course, they were going to be blessed with a Messiah. You see, there was no place for Christ. He had to make new bottles in order to put His new wine of the kingdom in. Just so He will here. The crown is there in the hands of Christ, but many will lose it, and why? Because they have not run the race.

Now, I have seen how the enemy works. He doesn't want to let go of the people here. But, oh, let no soul go out from here with darkness, for he will be a body of darkness wherever he goes. He scatters the seeds of darkness everywhere. He carries all these seeds and he begins to sow them, and it unsettles the confidence of the people in the very truths that God wants to come to His people. I have told our brethren here again and again that God has shown me that He raised up men here to carry the truth to His people, and that this is the truth. Well, what effect did it have on them? They were just the same; so that it should not be made of any account. What is the matter? Brethren, I say again, Fall on the Rock and be broken! Don't try to begin to make excuses. Well, here Christ says when they should bring their offerings and make confession of their sins, if afterward they found that other things came to their remembrance, notwithstanding but one, they should come and make an offering for that.

Now, brethren, we want to have the simplicity of Christ. I know that He has a blessing for us. He had it at Minneapolis, and He had it for us at the time of the General Conference here. But there was no reception. Some received the light for the people, and rejoiced in it. Then there were others that stood right back, and their position has given confidence to others to talk unbelief, and cherish it. Now, brethren, if you expect that every difficulty is going to be laid out in clear lines before you, and you wait until it is, then you will have to wait until the judgment, and you will be weighed in the balances and found wanting.

Now, brethren, can there not be some means insured by which we can have a season of prayer? My strength is about exhausted. If it is possible, I want to get away before the last atom of strength shall be gone here. Brethren, why not pray to God? Why not get in such a position that you can lay right hold of the hands of God? Why wait for God to humble us? Now God has been waiting for those men that have stood in the way, to humble themselves; but the word has come to me, "If they do not humble themselves, I will humble them." Now, God will work. He will have the work prepared for His Spirit. There is to be a preparation for the last great day, and we want to come into a position where we can work unitedly with intense earnestness and courage for God.

I want that some of these shall assemble again, and then I want those that have been standing here and questioning, and been just about ready to give up the Testimonies—we want to know why; and if anything can be taken out of the way, God help us to do it! We want to know why the enemy is having such power upon human minds as he has here. It is something beyond anything I ever saw in all my experience since I first started in the work. The people of God who have had light and evidences have stood where God would not let His blessing fall upon them.

In the chapel hall the power of God was all ready to fall upon us. I felt for a little time as though I could look right into glory; but the spirit that was there drove it away. We want to understand how we are working. I speak these plain things because I know that there is nothing else that will do. We have tried to encourage in regard to faith.

One brother thinks that Sister White doesn't understand her own testimonies.

Heard that in Minneapolis. Why? Because the brethren did not agree with them. Well, there are some things that I understand. I understand enough to acknowledge the Spirit of God and to follow the voice of the Shepherd. I understand that much.[18]

---
[18] MR 900.13.

Chapter 19

The Importance of Excerising Faith

[A talk presented at Harbor Heights, Michigan, July 22, 1891]

(Matthew 7:1-7) [Verse 7 says, "Ask, and it shall be given you.] Are there any "ifs" in this matter? There is no "if" except "if ye ask." There is no condition of the mind that excludes from asking, if only you desire those things for which you ask. [There are] no conditions spiritually. So, if we desire the things of God we must comply with the condition of seeking them. (Verses 8-11) "Good things," according to Luke, is [the gift of the] Holy Spirit, and that is what we want, to thirst after godliness. (Verse 12)

This morning we want to dwell especially upon the importance of our exercising that simple faith which takes God at His word. We feel sorry that there is a necessity of presenting this matter again. I do not know as we are sorry that it is presented, but [that] notwithstanding that it is presented that minds fail to grasp it. But our minds must be broad enough to comprehend the promises made to us.

I have taken one of the very promises so simple that a child can understand it (Verse 11), and we are told what kind of asking this is. If we ask, there is a possibility of our having the things promised; is that the way it is put? Is there any hesitancy in this matter? We would think so from the actions of those who ask, but there is no need of it; there is no excuse for one doubt. We receive the things we ask, not because we are good; if you expect to wait until you are good enough to receive the blessing, you will never receive it. If you are going to wait until you are good enough to receive the promise, you will wait until after Christ comes, and it will be too late. You may come just as you are, because He is your Saviour; He died for you; in Him dwelt all the fullness of the Godhead bodily; and because He has the whole heaven of gift, of light, of power, of blessings, that He may bestow on every one who will seek them and open the door for Jesus to come in. Do you want it enough to open the door? If you will open the door to receive these blessings, there will be an emptying out of the love of the world, of the pride of life, and the vacuum must be supplied by the Holy Spirit just as soon as there will be an emptying of the heart of its idols.

We want to be very particular to stand on the very ground on which the Lord wants us to stand—that is, to recognize that all the blessings that we receive come through the mercy and compassion and goodness of our God, while we are undeserving. It is not because we regard ourselves good in many particulars, but it is because "God so loved the world, that He gave His only begotten Son, that whosoever believeth in Him should not perish, but have everlasting life." It is not one now and then in one hundred or one thousand, in five or ten thousand [who] may have life. No. Whosoever believeth on Him shall not perish but have everlasting life.

Now, have we that inward faith? It rests with us. There are two classes to the end of time—a party to be separated on the left hand He calls "goats," and there is a party to be on the right hand He calls "sheep." Every soul may be saved if he believes in Christ as his personal Saviour. [But] not all will be saved. Not because Jesus does not want them to be saved, for He is drawing every soul. Whatever may be their position, whatever may be their education, their nationality, or their training, He is drawing every soul to Himself. Why? Because in Him is life and light and truth, and all of these are essential to us for our happiness daily in this present life; and all these things are going to help us bear with greater ease the burdens and trials and perplexities of life, and Christ says in His invitation, "Come unto Me, all ye that are weary and heavy laden, and I will give you rest."

Now, I receive letters constantly, so many that I could do nothing else than answer them, begging me to pray the Lord that He may have mercy upon them. Now, I am not their Mediator, and do not ever expect to be, and I am not one who shall open my heart to those individuals as though I was capable of blessing them. I am riding in the same boat with yourself, trusting for salvation in the merits of a crucified and risen Saviour. I want salvation, I want eternal life, and I must know the conditions of my obtaining life eternal. You must know it.

How is it so natural for us to pour out all our soul troubles and perplexities upon finite beings as ourselves? I leave you to answer the question. Why do we do this? [The practice might be excusable] if we had not the promise, "Ask and receive," and "Come unto me, all ye that labor and are heavy laden, and I will give you rest. Take My yoke upon you, and learn of Me; for I am meek and lowly in heart: and ye shall find rest unto your souls. For My yoke is easy, and My burden is light." It is not "My yoke" that makes your work so hard, that makes your journey so difficult.

What is "My yoke"? It is perfect submission to God. Our wills must be submerged in the will of God. In coming to Jesus it is to feel that there is no help for us except in Jesus; (therefore when the Father) gave His Son for the life of the world He is of no avail to anyone who does not receive Him by faith as their personal Saviour. When the worried, perplexed souls come to human, finite mortals for relief, conduct them to Jesus, pray with them and for them in faith, and educate them by precept and example to bring every trial, great and small, to Jesus. We can help these poor souls who bring their troubles to us, only by leading them to Him, to take their cares and burdens to Jesus, and leave them there. I want to be able to stand in that position where I can be a help, and all that I can do is to recommend them to Jesus, pointing them to Calvary.

John pointed the people to the Lamb of God who taketh away the sins of the world. He said, "Behold the Lamb of God, which taketh away the sin of the world." There is a great deal in that "taketh away." The question is, Shall we keep on sinning as though it were an impossibility for us to overcome? How are we to overcome? As Christ overcame. He prayed to His heavenly Father; we can do the same, and that is the only way. Then we are to overcome something, for it is stated that those who shall see Him in His beauty shall be "without spot, or wrinkle, or any such thing." Now, if there is a spot or wrinkle in your character, is it not now the very time for you to begin to understand what that defilement is, that you may trust in the blood of Christ to wash it away?

"How shall I," says the trembling one, "put it away?" You are to say, "I will try." But you are to put it away by believing that Christ is your Saviour today, and that He cleanseth you from all unrighteousness. You have the lesson in the word that was spoken. When tempted to speak wrong, and do wrong, resist Satan and say, "I will not surrender my will to your control." I will cooperate with divine power, and through grace be conqueror."

Satan says to Christ [in the wilderness], "It is certain that the angels shall have charge over You and bear You up in their hands lest at any time You shall dash your foot against a stone." But what did he leave out of that quotation? He was to be kept in the way; in all Thy ways. That was not His way at all. God's way is Christ's way. There is a plan of salvation laid for the race that Christ should not work a miracle on His own account to relieve Himself of any of the necessities of humanity and He was kept in all His ways. The enemy did not quote that at all, but [he did quote that] the angel shall keep Thee lest at any time Thou shalt dash Thy foot against a stone; he was to bear him up.

Now, the enemy will have all these attractions for us, and the question is which has the most weight with us. Is it to put ourselves in the channel of the bright rays of the Sun of Righteousness? Is it to go into a meeting and consider that there is the place to be a Christian and that out of the meeting we are to lay it off as a man lays off his overcoat? Are we thus to lay off our religion? Watch unto prayer, says Christ; "watch ye and pray, lest ye enter into temptation."

The temptations will surround us just as long as we live. Satan will try us in one way, and if he doesn't overcome us he will try us in another way. And thus his efforts will never cease. But we are always to remember that we are members of the royal family, subjects of the heavenly King, and we are born anew with a new character unto God. The old cheap character, the frivolous character, the character which leads to the world, to pride, to vanity, and to folly, we have parted with that. We have left that, but not in our own strength. We have asked wisdom of God, and He says He giveth to all men—how? In such a stinted measure? No, liberally; and what? Upbraideth not.

And what does He say? You ask in faith, and do not waver about it. There is the trouble. We go from our petitions and do not know whether we are blessed or not. We say, "I wish that I did know." What does that mean? "You said it, Lord, but I don't believe it." You must ask without wavering, "for he that wavereth is like a wave of the sea driven with the wind and tossed." He is tossed right between the waves. One wave after another comes, and our faith goes out like water out of a leaky vessel. It is to believe and to watch unto prayer.[19]

---

[19] Ms 83, 1891; MR 900.53.

Chapter 20

The Danger of an I Spirit

[Counsel of Experienced Workers Needed in Australia, New Zealand, and Everywhere. A talk presented at Harbor Heights, Mich., Aug. 20, 1891]

There is much talk in regard to our journey to Australia, but I cannot see my [way] clearly to go. Brethren say that Sister White will have no such burdens to bear, as she has here in America, that she can write her books so much more readily without carrying so many responsibilities, but I know it is no use to tell them that all their flattering anticipations on my behalf do not lessen my ideas that going to Australia means work, responsibility to bear a message to the people who are not what the Lord would have them to be. If it were not thus, I would feel authorized to remain in America. As it is, I dare not mention the state of things in the office [of publication in Australia] presented to me, for I am then sure they would firmly conclude I must go.

There is work to be done there, and although those who have been there all testify that they will gladly receive any message that the Lord will give me to bear to them, I am not so sanguine in regard to this as my brethren in Australia. They know nothing of me and my work personally, only through my writings. Reproof is not pleasant to the natural heart, and the reproof coming to the people, as I know it will come to them, will meet with opposition. Already envy and evil surmisings and jealousies are at work, lest someone shall have a higher place in the work than themselves. There is want of spiritual knowledge, spiritual eyesight to discern the work that needs to be done as the Lord shall open the way.

The same enemy that has wrought upon human hearts in America, leading human minds to feel wise in their own conceits, is working upon the human minds in that far-off country. The work is now almost [at] a standstill. A messenger must be sent to Australia, but God forbid it should be I. I long for rest, for quietude, and to get out the Life of Christ. There is a cloud over the workers in Australia. The work must be reconstructed from its foundation of the office building, and there is not being done that which must be done in warning the world. The work of the Lord is aggressive. There should be a large number of souls converted to the truth in Australia.

As I stood before you Monday and spoke to you, the power of the Lord came upon me. The light previously given me flashed upon my mind. I had to speak. I knew that there must be a different mold put upon the work. I have been shown of the Lord that there must be a setting [of] things in order. There is not harmony between the workers sent as missionaries from America. There are envious feelings [as to] which shall be the greater. The Lord is ready to work for His people if they will come where He can safely bless them, seeking to answer the prayer of Christ that His disciples may be one as He is one with the Father.

Workers have been sent from America. The Lord will send by whom He will, and you will meet with great loss unless you take heed how you hear. There has been a spirit unlike Christ. There has been a jealousy among you, lest the American brethren shall have too much influence in your midst and too much to say in regard to the plans to be devised to be followed; and there is the enemy at work to sow tares while men slept, for they were not watching and praying and guarding the garden of the soul, because you do not take heed how you hear. To take heed how you hear is to sit at the feet of Jesus and learn of Him.

Those who are teachers should feel the necessity of being taught, learning of Jesus Christ through His sent messengers, that they may communicate to you, that you may communicate freely to others as you have received. Ministers and people should show the same earnestness to learn the truth anew, and receive it afresh, as to learn it the first time. It will bear repetition and will need to be oft repeated, to be appropriated, being heard from other lips.

The gems of truth become dimmed in our possession unless we are increasing in love for the truth, and practicing that faith which works by love and purifieth the soul. The gems of truth grow lusterless to the receiver unless put to a practical use. Hearts must be softened and subdued by the Spirit of God, receiving the truth in the soil of an humble, contrite heart. Isaiah 57:15-19. They will be active, and willing to be refined, longing to be purified and ennobled by the truth. And thus they show its power upon human minds by what it accomplishes for the receiver. If the teachers of the truth think their own ways are perfect and, begin to criticize the messenger the Lord sends, be sure you will reap that which you have sown. You will reap the fruit born of your criticism.

We are too busy with intensity of desire to glorify His name through the human agents, because self is magnified, and should He work for the one who is not possessing humility, should He give him success, then he would take it for granted he is all right, and not see that he needs daily the converting power of God that he may be a vessel unto honor.

I have been shown that the work in the publishing interest would have been far in advance of what it is today were it not for the spirit of self-sufficiency, selfishness, and self-importance, and expressed sometimes in words but more in actions, "We know all about this matter, and we need not to be told, to be advised, or counseled," when this very spirit which was manifested revealed they needed to be educated, and needed to seek counsel of their brethren in many things. Why? Because they had larger experience.

Now the Lord has taken notice of this spirit which has been cherished, and He has not been pleased. Angels are sent down from heaven to give you knowledge only through the cooperation with human agencies.

Now, the Lord has presented to me that in New Zealand and Australia there are many things that have been done that have displeased the Lord. There has been a determined spirit which has been inclined to consider that those who had come to the truth in Australia and New Zealand had sufficient wisdom to manage matters in the office of publication and in the churches without counseling with those men whom the Lord had sent from America for this very purpose, that the wisdom of their years of experience should be of advantage to them in Australia, that men who have ability may receive knowledge of experience as well as from those whom the Lord has sent to do His own work in the most perfect way, and that the mistaken finite man shall not mar and retard His work.

The Lord is not pleased with the spirit that has been manifested by Brother Scott. He has naturally a selfish nature. He is self-centered and his influence has not been correct and amicable in the office. He had a jealous spirit, fearing others should get credit which he desired. He encircled things in his arms, [and] followed his own judgment in their management. His actions were [saying], This is my line of work; please do not step on my territory. It was unfortunate that he came to Australia, for men should have been placed here who were wholly surrendered to God, that had not a taint of selfishness. He also estimated his own capabilities too highly, and losses were sustained. If he had only been willing to ask counsel, he would have avoided many blunders.

Other things that some of our brethren brought from America revealed a want of judgment, a want of discernment and solid experience. They did not advance the cause of God, as it should have been, but rather increased expenses without bringing in an equivalent. They walked in this new missionary field in the sparks of their own kindling, The aftersight of these things made the brethren suspicious of all that comes from America.

Some have thought that if the Lord honored them to have a connection with the work that it was their privilege to carry it forward in their own way and according to their own plans. The Lord knew what the sure result would be in doing this. They might have all the zeal and earnestness, but that ambition must be sanctified. These men must have that knowledge that comes from men who have been led and instructed of God—they are [men who] have had long training and learned their trade under the special divine Teacher—else they will make many blunders.

It is in mercy that the Lord has sent at great expense to the conference from time to time men and women from America, some to make a short stay, others to abide with them longer to impart to them the lessons which they have themselves had to learn in a long experience in connection with the work of God. And as the work is not theirs but the Lord's, they will get out of their place in attempting to monopolize it and think they can run it without counseling with God's delegated workmen of larger experience.

The Lord's work must be done not according to men's finite judgment, but according to [God's] mind, according to the light He has been pleased to give from time to time to the workers. And in any new place or countries where the truth has found a foothold, men of experience have thought they could manage the whole matter if the American brethren would only keep out of their way. This was the mind of finite men but far from being the mind of God, for He has placed in connection with His missions in all parts of the world men who had experience as managers.

The Lord will not at present leave the work solely in the hands of those in Australia who are brought into the truth, to run His own work after their limited experience. The thought of their heart and inclination to do this is positive evidence in the sight of the Lord and in the sight of His workers that they are not competent to do this without the counsel and guidance of that wisdom, that knowledge, that has been obtained [by] experience, by mistakes that have been made in certain lines which have brought losses and great discouragement to themselves and to the workers.

The Lord God of heaven sees not as finite men. He knows the result of every movement. And God designs [that] His own work in the advance movements shall not be trusted to any who have not had orders from Him under similar circumstances. He has sent delegates to you from America [to] help you with their counsel. Remember, God has seen your need, and because He loves you He has sent you help.

There is need of seeking the Lord daily. There are precious entrusted capabilities in a business line whose hearts are interested in the work in the publishing house. The Lord is testing and proving those men whether they will confine themselves to merely business transactions without consecrating themselves to the work, having discernment that it is God's work, that His mold and superscription must be upon it. If they are willing to give themselves unreservedly to God, the result will be they will be qualified by the Holy Spirit to be faithful stewards of the Lord to stand firm as a rock to principle. They will be men whom God will endow with [wisdom] to devise and plan and execute.[20]

---

[20] Ms 29, 1891; MR 900.52.

Chapter 21

Remarks by Ellen White at the Michigan Conference Campmeeting

September 3, 1891

Everything connected with God's work is to teach; everything during campmeeting is to do good. It is to present this people before the world as standing refined, with nicety of purpose, with wise plans, and for everything to be presented before them in such a way that it has a telling influence upon unbelievers. This people is a model people, and that is the way it ought to be. The truth is a sacred truth. Everything that is connected with the truth is to stand upon the highest elevation. Here are some things presented to me regarding our campmeetings, written about one year ago while I was at Petoskey, Michigan.

We are never to graduate in this Word until Jesus shall change us to the future life, and then we shall learn through all eternity. You are ever to be a learner if you are to be a teacher, presenting things new and old. We shall be continually discovering rich veins of precious ore in this Word. It is a priceless treasure for God's people. There is not a moment of time that we are to spend in indolence, but we are to be all the time having our hearts open for the Spirit of God to rest upon us.

You need at campmeetings to labor to teach in different lines, as Christ did. Few sermons were preached by Christ. He was the great Teacher, and crowds gathered wherever He went, to listen to His instruction, and He taught as one having authority, and knew that He was teaching the truth. He spake as never man spake.

Ministers must be educated to work after the divine model. Many of you love to teach, but you have not taken up the work of teaching in the simplicity of the gospel of Christ. The people will listen to sermon after sermon, which are often double the length they should be, and they can retain but few points of the discourse because their minds have been all the time on temporal, earthly things. Therefore they hear with such earthly thoughts that the truth of God does not make any impression. It does not reach to the very depths of the soul, and the plowshare of truth does not go deep enough. Then they go from the meeting and fall back where they were before. The sermons being often double the length they ought to be, the words lose their force upon the minds of the hearers. Other things come in to choke the seeds of truth. The truth of God must be made impressive point by point. It is for their eternal interest to know. So deeply must the seed of truth be planted that it will become firm, and bear fruit to the glory of God. ... [Ellipses on pages 2 and 3 indicate where Mrs. White read extracts relating to the work in Michigan, which extracts were not reported.]

Now, when the truth is being presented, there are applications that need to be made, and appeals to press it right home for a decision, for an important decision. Who is there when this truth is being presented? Somebody besides you. The devil and his angels are there to catch away the seeds of truth. Are these all? Angels of God and Jesus Christ are on the ground. Then what? When you seek to impress the truth upon the heart, you will be a co-laborer with Jesus Christ. ...

I want to tell you that God does not want us to go with a sad, morose countenance, gloomy and despondent. He does not want us to do any such thing. He wants us to look at the bright beams of the Sun of righteousness, and catch these bright beams that they may shine in all the chambers of the mind, that they may shine in the soul-temple, and therefore you can bring forth from the treasure-house of the heart the precious things of God, for out of it are the issues of life. ...

Now, brethren, I have read this much, but it is a small part of what I have in reference to Michigan. I sat here last Monday while in your conference the resolution was discussed. [The resolution recommended that the tithe of the Battle Creek church, which previously had been appropriated to the General Conference use, again all be given to the Michigan Conference.] I was too weak to open my lips at that time. I did not dare to do it. My heart was so weak and throbbing so painfully that I felt that it might be at the cost of my life if I attempted to speak, because I knew that if I spoke I would feel deeply over these points. As I went home and was adjusting some of my papers for Australia, I came across some messages which had been written, and I copied some of them.

I see that the principle, not the money value, that was presented at that time before I left was not in accordance with the light that God had given me. It will not help your case any. It will only place you where you will not do the very things that God means shall be done. I did not understand that when the matter was presented here, that it was the tithes from the Battle Creek church, but that it included the whole of Michigan; but after I went home it presented itself clearly to my mind.

Now, if that resolution is passed, that you shall in Michigan keep all your tithes, it is the heaviest weight that you have ever brought upon Michigan, and you will realize it the coming year. If you want that weight to be lifted from your souls, you had better rescind the action taken on that resolution, and let it stand where it was. I know there is a deficiency in all Michigan. It has been presented to me again and again. They are folding their arms and saying, There is an abundance of tithes. Here is the Battle Creek church which gives so much; they do not need my tithes; but I guess I will place my tithes here where they will serve self. There is not one-twentieth part being done that might be done.

This matter was presented before me in 1888, and I was bearing a message to the Michigan Conference something of the very import I am bearing to you now; but I never act upon these things immediately unless the Spirit of God urges me, and now I feel urged by the Spirit of God to say that there is not a more liberal-hearted people in the world than in Michigan. They do not want anybody to help them out, but are selfish, covetous, and withholding from the cause and work of God.

When I understood how the matter was, I had not a single question about the matter in my mind. I tell you, brethren, that in the place of withholding, you ought to give more liberally, for fields are opening everywhere. Souls are coming into the truth, and many of them never heard a discourse. I wish you could hear the pitiful appeals they are making to me. They say, I want your books. I want Patriarchs and Prophets; I have no money to buy. I want Vol. IV; I have no money to buy it. I want the Testimonies, but have nothing with which to purchase them. These appeals keep coming in continually. Can I forbear helping them? I have sent armfuls of books away without receiving a cent for them, because I know that they should have these things, and the truth of God is entering everywhere.

There are missions that must be supported. I remember when I was in Switzerland, how oppressed they were for want of means. Ask a man how much he is receiving for his labor, and he says $150 a year. He had five in his family and labored for that amount. Now, that man was pressed for the necessaries of life. You would think you were starving if you were living on that much. You do not know how it is. I know how it is. It will do you good to tell you. One-half of the world do not know how the other half is living. While you have the comforts of life, you ought to do God's will in helping others.

When over in Oregon, Elder Loughborough made an appeal to the conference in Upper Columbia that they should donate to that conference. The conference needed it very much. The power of the Spirit of God circulated through that meeting. It was all light in the Lord, and they were so lifted up that they said they would do it. After that meeting passed, I do not know how it came in, whether somebody proposed it to them or not, but they said, We need all this money in our conference. I do not know who put it into their minds, but it worked just like leaven. All they needed was to make them think that they were really martyrs, and that more was required than they could give. These men were in a position of backsliding from God.

I went into Oregon when my husband was stricken with paralysis, and bore my testimony, and the power of God rested upon me. Next year I went into Upper Columbia. There were all these men of wealth. Those who had the most were complaining the most. Here they were with all their complaints, when I stepped into the desk and asked what they were complaining about. I knew what they were complaining about, and said to Brother Miller, "You invested so much money in the cause. What did you do after you pledged this much? You went and talked your disaffection, and God cut your crops down according to your withholding. According to this He has cut down your crops. We want to elevate this conference," said I, and turned around to Brother Van Horn, and told him to put my name down in place of Brother Miller's. "I will stand where he stands. I will be responsible for him." I called for another in the same way, and when I called for a third, they got ashamed and began to feel that they would not allow Sister White to pay their money.

"Now," said I, "Elder Van Horn told me how much money was paid by the General Conference to put the truth into Oregon. Now tell me how much money Oregon has paid to the General Conference?" It fell short something near $1,000 of what the General Conference had purely invested for them to bring the truth to them. That was a showing they had not looked at. They were ashamed of this. The light of heaven has not shone upon some of them since that time.

It means something to trifle with God. Suppose God should stop letting His blessings come to us. True, Michigan may not have been able this year to pay some of her indebtedness to her ministers. What if they did carry it a year and did more to bring up the resources in general? This is the work to be done, and I tell you that if you expect the blessing of God to rest upon you, you must put into the treasury that which will support the interests of the cause in different places. Those who have been investing their means in order to bring the truth into the different places in Michigan will stand in the light of heaven as doing the very work they ought.

You do not want this matter to stand just where it is. It will be the saddest experience in the life of those who have traveled over many places in Michigan; but do not let God's displeasure rest upon you. I do not believe that you mean it shall be so. I want to see this matter placed just where it was before. There is enough in Michigan to sustain every aggressive movement that shall be made in Michigan; but there are some who feel that if the cause can get along without it, they will invest it in their own special interests. God forbid that they should do this. Let us clear the King's highway. Let us make intelligent efforts to do everything in the sight of heaven we ought to do to bring His approbation and love upon us. I have more to bring before you, but I will say no more now.

[Later.] I could not understand that resolution when Elder Corliss read it, but I returned home, and the Spirit of the Lord impressing me, I know in myself that that was a mistake. Then reading this which I have presented to you, I copied it from that which I had written. It is not because the means of the Battle Creek church go to the General Conference that you are in this condition. It lies right within yourselves. If you are for God, He will be for you, and if you set the work in order in the churches as it ought to be, and bring them up in finances as they ought to be, you would have a surplus in the treasury next year, and the amount that goes from the Battle Creek church to the General Conference will go for the universal wants of the cause in different places where the work must be built up.

The Word of God has signified that people must be raised up to stand in the end. This matter, and much more I shall read you before I leave the ground, shows that there is an inward working right among yourselves and the churches that must take place, and then the finances will be brought up, if there is no robbery toward God. There is robbery toward God now. Now bring this up; let the conscience be touched; let God work upon your minds; and you will see salvation in your midst.

There are ministers who have not fed the flock of God. While their salaries have been paid, they are not men who are converted to God. There must be a weeding out of ministers; for they are not converted. We want to have the talent right in among us that has worked up to be used in our conference. But if there is no spirituality to discern where that talent is, or to train and discipline it for the work, what then? Why if there is talent in other fields, do not say, "We are going to furnish our own talent here in Michigan, and we do not want anybody to work in Michigan unless they are Michigan men." Who told you to prescribe for God? Who told you to say what men should be over you? This is contrary to all the light that God has given me. You have no right to pick and choose according to your plans. No, indeed. Ask God to send out the very men who will help you most; to send you the very men that are qualified to take and elevate and carry the churches in your place to a higher standard. That is what you are to do. When you do this, God will work with you. When we do this, He will lift what we are trying to lift.

If you are going to lay your mark how God is to work, He will work in an entirely different way from your mark. Every man must be in that position so that when he wants God the worst, he can get Him. We want God to teach us and lead us, and we should yield ourselves to him as little children, to learn in His school. These strong minds, these iron wills, how they must break before Jesus Christ can pour His Spirit into their hearts!

What we want is to be empty of self. We want Jesus Christ to work in us and by us and through us, and then we shall see the salvation of God. You say, "I am going to take just the men that are in Michigan." Is that the way God works? Not at all. You say, "Lord, Thou knowest just the men that will help us the most; give them to us, and we will accept them and uphold them." That is the way to do, and God will help you in doing it.[21]

---
[21] Ms. 11, 1891; MR 900.27.

Chapter 22

Work and Baptism of the Holy Spirit Needed

[Sermon by Mrs. E. G. White at the California Camp Meeting, Healdsburg, California, Sabbath, September 26, 1891]

(Acts 1:3, 12, quoted) And we read in another place, "They returned to Jerusalem with great joy." (Luke 24:52) Now, what made that joy? Was it because their Lord was leaving them? No, it was not that. It was because of the promise that He would come again, and that the Holy Spirit should come upon them.

You see, He bids them tarry in Jerusalem until a certain time; and when was it? Until the Holy Ghost should come upon them. We have altogether too little to say in our churches, in our camp meetings, in our assemblies, in our homes, about the descent of the Holy Ghost upon the people of God. The explanation is given here in the 14th chapter of John [as to] what is the Holy Ghost. "But the Comforter, which is the Holy Ghost, whom the Father will send in my name, he shall teach you all things, and bring all things to your remembrance, whatsoever I have said unto you." (Verse 26)

Why could they not receive it and accept it while Jesus Christ was with them on the earth? It is because of the false ideas which are constantly put forth by those who are in error, by those who are in darkness concerning the truth. The Pharisees, the Jews, the scribes and the rulers, were teaching for doctrine the commandments of men—mark, not "the commandments of God," but "the commandments of men."

These ["commandments"] had become so magnified, and they had listened to the misinterpretation of Scripture from their rulers and teachers so much, that they became confused and it seemed impossible to separate the truth from the error, the mysticisms of Satan's devising; the real from the false, the genuine from the spurious; and it was by constant repetition of the truth and what the truth means that they could get hold of correct ideas of what the Saviour meant. And the Saviour was full, oh, full of light and knowledge, and how He longed to communicate this fullness to His disciples; but He said, "I have yet many things to say unto you, but ye cannot bear them now." (John 16:12)

I want to tell you, dear friends, just now prior to the second appearing of Christ, you mingle with the earth, you mingle with the world; your business, your cares, your perplexities crowd upon you; the earthly becomes supreme, the heavenly subordinated to the earthly. Thus it was with the disciples. In order for them to understand the words of God and the Scriptures, there must be an application of the truth, a special divine enlightenment which they had not hitherto had; and He tells them that when the Holy Ghost shall come, the Comforter, He should bring all things that Christ had said unto them to their remembrance, and there would be an opening of their understanding.

When Christ met with the men as they were traveling to Emmaus, they saw in Christ only a man toiling, traveling like themselves; but He was the resurrected Son of God. And He asked why they were so sad, why they were conversing in such sadness. Why, they asked of this Stranger, are you only a stranger in Jerusalem, and do you not know what has taken place? That Christ, a mighty Man, a prophet that was mighty in power—why, wicked hands have taken and crucified Him. And then Christ opened to them the Scriptures, commencing at Moses and the prophets. He went right down and traced His very history, the Christ of God, and showed them that everything that had transpired was written there in the Scriptures, and laid [the prophecies] open to their understanding; but they could not take it in.

And when the disciples came to their place of abode, and they urged Christ to come in and abide with them because the day was far spent, in breaking of bread He revealed Himself unto them. They could, by the very manner in which He handled the bread, see the very marks—Christ's ways—and then, lo, the cruel marks of His crucifixion; and then He vanished out of their sight. Now they turned to one another and said: "Did not our heart burn within us, while he talked with us by the way, and while he opened to us the scriptures?" (Luke 24:32) What was it that made the heart burn within them? It was the illuminating power that was in the Scriptures that quickened their faith.

When we search the Scriptures with humble heart, when we take right hold of the truth as it is in its simplicity lying open in the Bible, when we believe it to be verity and truth, the heart will warm, it will kindle with the love of God, and from our hearts we can say ["Did not our heart] burn within us?" We realize that again and again. When in the institutions where they have been studying the Scriptures, how the tears would flow, and what gladness would be in the heart! There was not a particle of enthusiasm, only just that which was received by the precious jewels of truth that were unfolded to the hearers. This is what we want. We want the Bible for our standard.

Why is it that it is not a greater comfort to us? Well, I will tell you why. Christ has said that "ye cannot serve God and mammon." (Matthew 6:24) The one is against the other. However long you have been a professor of religion, even if it has been 20 or 40 years, if you have not learned to seek first the kingdom of God and His righteousness, you do not know God, neither are you acquainted with Jesus Christ if you allow the spirit of the world to come in and absorb the mind and take the whole attention.

Who gave you that mind? It was God. What right have you to commit day by day, hour by hour, week by week, month by month, and year by year, a system of robbery against God. What right have you to take the gift of reason, the gift of intelligence, and put that intelligence and reason largely to your own benefit in worldly profit? We are to yield ourselves up, all that there is of us.

Men in positions of trust, positions in our institutions, you become self-centered; you bring commercial business in. Men of responsibility that stand in positions of trust have contracted too big and heavy burdens to stop to pray. You are to consider the words of Christ, "Without me ye can do nothing." (John 15:5) Leave Christ out of your service and you cannot distinguish between the common and sacred fire. Oh, they are too crowded with the cares of life for them to pray. What is their positions before God? You can go on and load yourself with burdens and with cares and perplexities, and live [a secular life]. "Without me ye can do nothing." Now, what is the use to leave Jesus out of the question and go on with your bungling work, botchwork, and with your affections centered upon the things of this world, and absorbed and controlled by the business part—the temporal things of this life and that which is of no value to us—and that which is of eternal moment to us is put away as a thing to be taken up transiently, when most convenient? If you go to meeting, you cannot keep awake because you have robbed God of the nerve brain power in pressure of worldly cares and of the physical and of the spiritual. You have not been drinking of the life streams which made glad the city of our God. You have not been drinking of the snow of Lebanon, but you have been drinking at the malarious streams in the valley; and what you want [lack] is religion. It is what you will have to have or you will never enter the kingdom of God.

When the question was asked if there were many that should be saved, Christ said, "Strait is the gate, and narrow is the way, ... and few there be which go in thereat." (Matthew 7:14) Why? Because "wide is the gate, and broad is the way, that leadeth to destruction, and many there be which go in thereat." (Verse 13) They do not need to hunt to find it; they do not need to seek; they do not need to strive. They can drift with the current of the world. They have the maxims; they have their standard; they have the spirit of the world. The line of demarcation between saint and sinner is obliterated.

Now, if God has ever spoken by me, unless there is a reformation in our institutions, unless there is a reformation all through our churches, unless your eyes are opened by the baptism of the Holy Ghost, you will be lost just as surely as was Judas. You would sell your Lord just as readily as Judas sold Him for 30 pieces of silver, because Satan comes in with his temptations. His temptation is a bribe: All this will I give thee if thou wilt worship me. And many who suppose themselves loyal will sell their precious souls to Satan; and the things that are of interest, and that will live through eternal ages, are made a matter of minor consideration. You call the world an atom and you call an atom the world. You get that atom right before you, seeking for supremacy in these things, and talk of principles being maintained while worldly customs and worldly, unprincipled dealing is entered into and called principle to be maintained. Ungodly ambition is taking possession of the man not having an eye single to the glory of God but first for the glory of self. You get yourself and this atom right between you and your God, and you do not bring eternity into your reckoning.

Brethren and sisters, we had better come to our senses now, without delay. We had better cry for the vitalizing power of God to come upon us, and cure us of our spiritual paralysis. And, unless there is a thorough arousing, and you begin to cry unto God and change your course of action, you will be rated either with the unbeliever or you will be in that position that you have a name to live while you are dead; and your influence in the world is a living curse. Just because of your profession you lead people in the road to death and hell, and the account that God is to settle with you in the judgment you will not want the court to meet, for it decides your case forever.

We are here for a purpose. Here are souls to save. There is a voice to be raised among the people of God. "Cry aloud, spare not." Why, what is it? What is the matter? "Show my people,"—Oh, it is God's professed people, is it?—"their transgression, and the house of Jacob their sins." (Isaiah 58:1)

What we all need is a conscience, and with many it is dead. What souls need is to die to self and be born again. Conscience needs a resurrection. What is wanted is to know what religion is; to know what it is to have a living connection with the God of heaven; to know God and Jesus Christ, whom He hath sent, for we read, "And this is life eternal, that they might know thee the only true God, and Jesus Christ, whom thou hast sent." (John 17:3) Then there is a knowledge. Why, I ask you, do you devote so little time to prayer, so little time to your Bibles, searching the Word that you may be sure you are following the directions therein given that you may secure eternal life? Why do you feel so little burden to consecrate yourselves and your household to God? Why do you make it a mere form of worship? Many of you would be terribly surprised if Christ should answer your prayers. You do not expect it. You are not making calculations for it. You have a form, and the prayers of many of you do not rise any higher than your head. What do we want? Repentance of your sins. Confess your sins before God and be converted, that your sins may be blotted out when the time of refreshing shall come and He shall send Jesus (See Acts 3:19, 20)

Now then, on this occasion we have been teaching here and talking about the love of God, how freely He is to forgive your sins. It is all so. It was a whole Saviour that hung on Calvary's cross, and that is just where your condemnation comes in. It is because of the immensity and fullness of the sacrifice, and retaining your spiritual poverty and your spiritual death, that you do not lay hold of the hope set before you in the gospel and benefit yourself with the great and infinite sacrifice which has been made in your behalf. What can you answer to God in the day of final accounts? What can you say, that you have not received the missionary spirit to work for the conversion of souls?

Place some of you in a position of responsibility where any souls will be under you, and you will oft manifest the tyrant. You will order around God's property as though they were your own, not human beings; order them around in a manner that would hurt the dignity of even dumb creatures. Is that the spirit that is going into heaven? Is that the spirit that is to dwell with Him who dwells in light unapproachable? I tell you, Nay. These persons who exalt themselves to rule are to be converted through and through, experiencing the new birth Christ instructed Nicodemus he must have or he would never see the kingdom of God.

Religion is a personal matter. We are not saved by companies; we are not saved by having our names on the church books; we are not saved by numbers. The matter is, How is it with my soul? Have I made the surrender to God? Luke 10. Read the test made to Christ, "What shall I do to inherit eternal life?" Christ responds to the lawyer, "What is written in the law? How readest thou?" (Read the whole on this point.) Am I converted to God? Has His transforming power made me a new man? Am I kind? Have I the attributes of Christ, or the attributes of Satan? Am I polite to God whose property in souls I am responsible for? Am I kind? Am I patient? Am I tender? Do I have the love of Christ for the souls for whom He has died?

What we want is purity; what we want is love. None of your love-sick sentimentalism, but we want faith that works by love and purifies the soul. Have we it today—that love that Jesus had for us that He laid on the altar of sacrifice, that as a man He can make a sacrifice for the perishing souls of those in the world for whom Christ had died? He gave Himself a full and complete and perfect offering. He left the glory that He had with His Father before the world was; He came into our world to be a man of sorrows and acquainted with grief; wounded for our transgressions, bruised for our iniquities; the chastisement of our peace was upon Him; with His stripes we are healed.

What have we done as laborers together with God? Have we denied self? Have we lifted the cross? Have we manifested the intense interest for the work to be done in connection with the Lord Jesus Christ to save the souls ready to perish? It is our work to manifest the intense earnest desire to save souls proportionate with the greatest work God has committed to mortals. Then why so indifferent? Why so faithless? Why so worldly-minded? How can we meet the Lord in peace with our present showing?

Is there anyone that has any cause for boasting? Is there anyone that feels that he is very apt, and has great talents? Who gave them to him? They came to him from Jesus Christ. Then what are you doing with them? Are you employing these talents to represent to the world godliness and self-denial and self-sacrifice? If you do this, then it is you are imitating our Saviour Jesus Christ. What we want is religion, Christlikeness in character; what we want is the descent of the Holy Ghost. Talk it in your meetings; talk it in your families; pray to God for it. But let me tell you, it does not come upon a man that has made his soul the highway for worldly thoughts, for impure thoughts, for sensual thoughts, for corrupting thoughts; nor for the performance of wicked actions.

We point the sinner to One who can take away the sin of the world. He does not cover the world with His righteousness, but He takes it away, until sinners repent and wash their robes of character and make them white in the blood of the Lamb. And the heart that is divested of self is ready for something else. That is the inflowing of the Holy Ghost. Then you can no more repress it; it will come out. You will begin to work for the depressed and the suffering. You will forget self. Self will not be exalted, but you will forget self, and you will be hid with Christ in God. When self is hid with Christ in God, then the Spirit of Christ will flow forth in conversation. "Be ye holy," says the apostle, "in all manner of conversation." (1 Peter 1:15)

When Jesus Christ can present you before the Father spotless, the gates will be opened to you and you can go in; but if your soul is stained, and if your soul is spotted, the record is there and you must meet it in the judgment.

What we want is the deep movings of the Spirit of God. What we want is to be sanctified of God here, body and spirit. "Thou shalt love the Lord thy God with all thy heart"—not two-thirds of it, not a quarter of it—"with all thy heart, and with all thy strength, and with all thy mind; and thy neighbor as thyself."

Now, Jesus Christ did not come to man in His own divine character, but He clothed His divinity with humanity. He came to our world in His human nature, and in compassion, that you might behold Him. You could not behold Him if He had the light even of an angel. But He takes our nature; He comes right to us in the world to work for us, to teach all souls what we must do to be saved. And now every one of us can receive Him, believe on Him, if we will. But we are represented as the ten virgins, five of whom were wise and five foolish. They profess to be Christians. They profess to be religionists. But half of them have no oil of grace in their lamps, their hearts.

I beg of you to institute the inquiry, How many of you have the Holy Spirit of God, represented as oil in the vessel with the lamp. Here is the light; you have the truth, the precious gems of truth offered to you—the glorious unfolding of the truth from the Word of God. The coming of the Lord is presented before you, "Prepare to meet thy God." This subject is not dwelt upon half as much as it should be; preparation is essential. God has not given us any time to stop.

Some will say, It is no use now for us to raise money to send missionaries into foreign countries, because the time is so short it would not accomplish anything. Yes it will. You had better use your money in that way [rather] than have it left for the great day of conflagration to consume it.

There are thousands that do not feel the least responsibility to pay any tithes to God. They refuse to give to the Lord His own lent talents to them that they may trade upon them and double them. He knows you by name. He has all your names on His record. He knows the sum to a penny, and how much you have robbed Him of, His own lent money. He has given you the amount for your own sustenance and put His hand on a small portion; but you cannot see that God should receive any returns from you, that He has any right to it, so you use it all selfishly and rob God's treasury. God forbid that you should think that way, and continue this robbery. There is no reason why you cannot see the plain truth on this important subject, only because you have the selfishness of your own wicked heart right before you that you don't want to see, and that you don't mean to see.

But there is a time coming when every case shall be judged according to their works. Every action of robbery, of appropriating the Lord's tithe money, will be considered, unless you repent of your robbery toward God, that we may come to Him with His own and, as David said, "Of thine own, oh Lord, we freely give thee." (See 1 Chronicles 29:14) It is God that has given us everything. As we sit at our table He has given us this provision; through Jesus Christ it comes. The rain, the sunshine, the dew, and everything that is a blessing to us, He has given us, and yet many are so hard-hearted, so full of selfishness, that they cannot see the claims that God has upon them. Not all, thank God! There are many of us glad to give back to the Lord His own, and give it freely. We give it as freely as did David. Of Thine own, we freely give Thee.

Then, if there have been any that have been robbing God here, you may say, "I don't see it in the Bible." Yes you do. You are lying to God; you do see it. Your cases have been presented, specified in Malachi. You see it and you cannot help it, because if you have reasoning powers you can see it. But you do not want to see, and you encourage blindness of mind lest your selfishness should die, and Christ should come in and take possession of you. I am thinking of the judgment. I do not want to stand in debt to God, robbing God of the tithe and the offerings, and have Him say to me, as my name is called, "Ye are cursed with a curse." I do not want to hear that from the Master. I want to hear Him say, "Well done, thou good and faithful servant." Now, we are wondering why it is that we do not have more of the grace and power of God. You begin to institute Bible classes in your churches, at your homes, and humble yourselves before God, and earnestly pray and weep before Him, and give yourselves to Him without reservation; you would find that there is nothing in the way.

He says, "I stand at the door, and knock." What is the matter? Oh, you did not hear Him? Many don't hear when the Lord says, "This is My portion; give Me My portion. You may have the rest, but give Me My portion in tithes and offerings." So He knocks; He knocks, but you do not hear Him. What is the matter? Because the din of the world is sounding in your ears and you do not hear. You cannot stop long enough to seek God earnestly and listen to hear what the Spirit hath to say unto you. May God help us individually that we may divest ourselves of everything which separates the soul from God, and [may] there be such a reformation here in California that you have not dreamed of. You will see the salvation of God which will go through your minds, and the many souls that will be converted unto Him. That is everything to us.

When they tell me of losses of temporal goods, I feel like this: It is not a soul.

But the loss of a soul is of higher estimate than the whole world. "What shall it profit a man, if he shall gain the whole world, and lose his own soul? Or what will a man give in exchange for his soul?" (Mark 8:36, 37) Please consider how you will settle this question with your Maker, just now, without delay.

Now let us bring eternity into our reckoning. Let us live for God every day. We do not know at what time our period of life closes and He will come to us saying, "Give an account of thy stewardship." We each have a work to do. I will tell you when He will come to our world: After the gospel of His kingdom has been brought to all parts of the earth; and you had better be in a hurry. God help us to be faithful in the discharge of our duty to preach the gospel to all people, tongues, and nations; that we may arouse to our God-given responsibilities; that we may divest ourselves of every particle of selfishness; that there may be no money expended in flowers or feathers, or in decoration of the body; you cannot afford it. It may be at the cost of a soul. The time that you occupy in self-serving you want to be seeking to open your Bible to awaken the souls that are perishing around you out of the truth, that are ready to die.

Christ died that every soul might become a missionary. You need not look upon the ministers; you need not say they carry the burdens. They do carry the burdens, and the reason so many have fallen into the grave is because they carried the burdens that some of you refused to lift. They carry the burdens that you will not take upon your soul. If you would before God keep your own soul clean, if before God you would cleanse yourself from all filthiness of the flesh and of the spirit, perfecting holiness in the fear of God, your ministers would be where they could go forth, and your prayers could follow them like sharp sickles into the harvest field. But the temptations of the world have crazed you; the world has benumbed you; the world has paralyzed you; and we want now to get above the world and behold Christ, our only hope, that our eye shall be fixed upon Him who is the One altogether lovely and the Chief among ten thousand.

We want to know, brethren, if you are going to make the surrender to God. We want to know if you will consider that everything has been done for you that a God could do. We want to know if you consider that all heaven—just think of it!—all heaven has been poured out to you in one gift, with Jesus Christ. When God gave His Son He gave with Him the richest treasures of heaven. It is yours, if you will cooperate with Him. He gave all heaven; all heaven He gave in that one gift. All heaven is at our command. All heaven we may claim. When the minister goes forth to labor he can say, "I go in the strength of the God of Israel. I have no confidence in self. I have no confidence in my finite ability, but I have a standing promise from

One who says, 'I am with you I, even unto the end of the world.'" You have no lack of power then. What more assurance do you want? "If he abide in me, and my words abide in you, ye shall ask what ye will, and it shall be done unto you" (John 15:7) Do you believe it? Do you believe the promise?

We have been so earthly; we have been talking of earthly things; we have had our conversation upon common and earthly things until eternity has been dropped out of our reckoning. Shall we bring it in? God help us that we may arouse as we never have done before. I tell you, it is an individual work. Do not look at another and say, "They have defects in character; they are thus and so." "What is that to thee? Follow thou me." I speak of Peter. Said the Lord Jesus Christ, "What is that to thee? Follow thou me." (John 20:22) He told Peter what should happen to him, and then Peter says, pointing to John, "What shall this man do?" Well, now, you just keep your eye single to the glory of God. What is it to keep the eye single? What does it mean? It means that you should let the world go out of your reckoning, and let the eternal realities come in. God help us to be Christians at home.

Now I want to tell you what a saint is. A saint in heaven is just what he is in his own family at home. If he is a Christian at home he is a Christian in the church. He will be a good Christian in heaven. Now, God has placed us on trial here. How is it with you? Are you going to stand the test? He will bring circumstances around you to prove you and see whether there is any defilement of character in you. If there is any debasement, if there is any carnality, if there is any satanic tendency, He will bring you over the ground in one way, and then He will bring you over the ground in another way, and then He will test you upon one point, and then He will test you upon another. We are here to be tested and proved. What does it amount to? If you have the Spirit of Christ you will love every soul for whom Christ died. Not with a love-sick sentimentalism. Not with base affection. Nothing like that. You will love as Christ loved. You will want to carry that burden for souls, oh how carefully, that there shall not be any occasion given to the youth, or to those of mature age, that shall bring in or make occasion of their stumbling or being turned out of the way, or a channel for an impure thought. Create an atmosphere where the soul can be kept open and clean before God our Maker.

Ah, the sin of licentiousness, it is terrible! It is upon many, many that are here. They are corrupting their souls and yet they seem to think that they are Christians. Some do not know what sin is. They do not know what an offense it is to God to defile the soul-temple. But I call upon you to clear the King's highway. There are immense responsibilities that are resting upon our churches here in California where they have had the grand light of Bible truth, the precious message of truth in His Word. It is for the saving of the souls of the people. Such responsibility! It is to represent the faith you possess. It is to stand in the integrity of our soul. If you will be faithful to God, self shall be crucified. Self shall die, and Christ Jesus shall live in us, and He shall be the hope of our calling. We will represent Jesus Christ to the world. Inquire sincerely, "Am I a Christian?" If I am a Christian I am looking unto Jesus, the Author and the Finisher of my faith. In Him my hopes of eternal life are centered.

If all those that handle the Word of God, ministering to the people, will cleanse their hearts from all iniquity and all defilement, and shall come to God with clean purpose of heart, as little children, they shall see of the salvation of God. Jesus will walk in our midst. We have now the invitations of mercy to become vessels unto honor, and then we need not worry about the latter rain; all we have to do is to keep the vessel clean and right side up and prepared for the reception of the heavenly rain, and keep praying, "Let the latter rain come into my vessel. Let the light of the glorious angel which unites with the third angel shine upon me. Give me a part in the work. Let me sound the proclamation. Let me be a co-laborer with Jesus Christ." Thus seeking God, let me tell you, He is fitting you up all the time, giving you His grace. You need not be worried. You need not be thinking that there is a special time coming when you are to be crucified. The time to be crucified is just now. Every day, every hour, self is to die; self is to be crucified; and then, when the time comes that the test shall come to God's people in earnest, the everlasting arms are around you. The angels of God make a wall of fire around about and deliver you.

All your self-crucifixion will not do any good then. It must be [done] before the destiny of souls is decided. It is now that self is to be crucified—when there is work to do; when there is some use to be made of every entrusted capability. It is now that we are to empty and thoroughly cleanse the vessel of its impurity. It is now that we are to be made holy unto God. This is our work, this very moment. You are not to wait for any special period for a wonderful work to be done; it is today. I give myself to God today. What if one should go out from this meeting while he is looking forward a week, or a month, or a year before he surrenders to God, and the cars should strike him as they [did] our Sister Rowland? Are you ready to make the surrender now? You are to put away your sin right now when you see it, but do not make leeway [that] you are going to overcome by degrees; you are going to try little by little to give up sin. Now, while it is called today, heed the invitation and harden not your hearts.

Oh my soul, why not leave the cursed thing today? Sin crucified my Lord. Why not turn from it with loathing? Why not love the things that Christ loved, and hate the things that Christ hated? He has made provision ample enough for you that you can through Him be more—yea, more—than overcomers. Then what do you want? Do you want a second crucifixion of Christ? You cannot have that. You must look to Calvary. You must take the blood by faith and apply it. You must wash in it. You must be cleansed by the already shed blood of Jesus Christ. It can cleanse you to the utmost.

I love Him; I love Him for He first loved me. He has broken my heart; He has broken it, and it is not good for anything unless it is broken. Your heart is not good for anything unless it is broken. God help us that we may this very day surrender to God. There is a work to be done here. There is a work to be done in the church—a wonderful work. You are to love as you never have loved before. You are to pray to Him as you never have prayed before. You are to seek Him as you never have sought Him before. Are you going into a monastic cell as Martin Luther did to scourge yourself? The question is asked: "Shall I give my firstborn ... for the sin of my soul?" (See Micah 6:6-8) Is it burnt offerings and sacrifices that God requires? He says, "My soul is full of them." It is not that. It is a contrite heart; it is that you walk humbly, and deal justly, and show mercy. This is your work.

Take right hold of it now. Why wait any longer? Why not take God right at His word? Say, "Here Lord, I give myself away, 'tis all that I can do." If Satan comes with his hellish temptations, tell him No, there is no place in my soul for it; my soul is ravished with the love which is expressed upon Calvary; I cannot allow any of this wickedness to come into my soul; it crucified my Lord. Now brethren and sisters, we want religion; we want the baptism of the Holy Ghost. You want to be getting ready for missionaries. You do not know who may be called, but Satan wants to keep you all the time in the darkness of unbelief; he wants to keep you in the lowlands; he wants to keep you in darkness and sin. Will you break the fetters? Will you go free? Will you say, "Simply to Thy cross I cling; in my hand no price I bring"? Just myself, that is all He wants. He wants yourself—just as you are.

May God help us to look and live. May God strengthen our hearts to trust in Him. He is coming, brethren, in a little while. Here are sorrows and troubles. Here is one brother that has been suffering with rheumatism and with agony, sleepless nights. There is rest, brother; there is rest in a little while. We shall see Him as He is, and we shall be made like Him. Rest, rest in the kingdom of God. Go on a little longer; suffer a few days longer, and there is an eternity of happiness and bliss; that is what you want. The crown of righteousness is for the overcomer. Every one of you, think of this. In the morning think of it, now today I must look at that crown. I must run for it. I must run the race for it. And that crown is mine if I overcome. But if I do not overcome, and am overcome of Satan, I lose that crown; another gets it. Shall we not try to win the crown of everlasting life? If we lose heaven, we lose everything. If we gain heaven, we gain everything.

I see matchless charms in Jesus. I do not want any greater reward than He presents to us. I do not want any larger reward than that. I want to live for God, not for the world. I want the eye single to His glory. Let us every one—in the morning, and at noon, and at night—lay ourselves before God as His property, not our own, and fight the good fight of faith. Today you are not to have the faith of tomorrow. You have only faith for today; tomorrow you will find faith when that comes; so don't worry about tomorrow. It is today, Am I the Lord's? Today have I the witness of His Spirit? Today does my name come upon the lips of the great Advocate of heaven? Today am I walking in harmony with Jesus Christ and heavenly angels? The heavenly intelligences are at work to bring the light of the knowledge of the truth as it shineth in the face of Jesus Christ, to humanity.

Am I a co-laborer with Jesus Christ? What is the matter? It is because you have robbed God all through the week. You have committed robbery of God, and you have no part in His work. God help you to be converted. Some of you may be touched and say, "I don't like such straight preaching." I cannot help it if you do not. There must be somebody. "Cry aloud, spare not, lift up thy voice like a trumpet, and show my people their transgression, and the house of Jacob their sins." (Isaiah 58:1) We want your help, brethren, every soul of you.

What is the word that comes from the watchman on the walls of Zion? "The morning cometh, and also the night" (Isaiah 21:12) Both are coming. The watchman has to give the note of warning. Every watchman on the walls is to take up the note and to sound it to the people. What do the people do—just sit and gape at the watchman? They have got, in their turn, to catch the trumpet sound, then to take it up and sound it through the churches; not call, "Watchman, come here, come here," because of this note, of this warning here in our church. Give it yourself, because you are connected with God. Give it yourself, because you are the channel [of] light. Catch the words all burning from the throne of God and give them to the people. That is what you are to do. Instead of quarreling [about] who shall be the greatest; instead of dissension, instead of strife, God help you to be converted. What you want is to become as little children. I want heaven. Do you want it? We shall all see just how much we want it. We shall see just how much faith we have. For the Lord is coming and He is right at the door. We have but a little time to work, and if we let the world come in here and absorb all our attention and all our means, how can it be said of you in the judgment, "Enter ye in. Well done, good and faithful servant"? Where is your goodness and faithfulness? Was it on your farm? Was it in working with your hands? You can be faithful there, but you have something else to do. There is a world to be warned; there is a world to be saved; there is a sinner to be converted. While you are asleep the sinners are perishing; Satan is sowing his tares. You want to be wide awake in your churches. All heaven is interested for you; why not be interested for yourselves? "Open the door, and I will come in," said Christ. Will you open it? Will you let Him in? Will you be zealous and repent of your backsliding, your lack of love, your coldness, your indifference?

What we want is Jesus. What we want is His love. What we want is the elevation and ennobling of character. What we want is to die to self right here—not wait until some future period. We want to make the consecration here. Oh, I am so thankful that it is not too late for us to be righteous. I am so thankful we have a Jesus. I am so thankful that He is able to cleanse us from all sin! I am so thankful that I can hope for His blessing. I am so thankful that I can hide in Him now, and that I can accept His light and give it forth to others. May the Lord breathe upon us His Holy Spirit, and may we grow up into Christ, our living Head. We want this salvation today. We don't want to wait; we don't want to dispel Christ by our unbelief. We want to take right hold of Him because He has told us to do it; and He says—now listen, I want you to hear every word of it—"Let him take hold of my strength, that he may make peace with me; and he shall make peace with me." (Isaiah 27:5 "Come now, and let us reason together...; though your sins be as scarlet, they shall be as white as snow; though they be red like crimson, they shall be as wool." (Isaiah 1:18) Will you come? Will you believe? Will you let Him reason with you? Will you commit the keeping of your soul unto Him as unto a faithful Creator?

God grant that we may live in the light of His countenance, and at last hear Him say, "Come up higher; enter thou into the joy of thy Lord." What is that joy? Seeing sinners converted. That is joy. Let us go to work and see if you cannot help some poor, despondent soul that is crushed under the weight of discouragement. See if you cannot win some soul to Christ. You are bigger in your own eyes than you ought to be, but just see if you cannot win somebody to Christ; and as you win them to Christ you will become smaller and smaller in your own eyes, until you feel as though you were nothing. When you feel in that way, then Christ to you is everything.[22]

---

[22] This was followed by an altar call; many responded. See report in Signs, October 12, 1891; Manuscript 35, 1891; MR 900.23.

Chapter 23

Fruits of Conversion

[Sabbath morning sermon, Healdsburg, California, Camp Meeting, Sept. 19th, 1891]

"I pray for them: I pray not for the world, but for them which Thou hast given Me; for they are Thine. And all Mine are Thine, and Thine are Mine; and I am glorified in them" (John 17:9, 10).

Mark the words. It is Jesus Christ that is praying to His Father, "and all Mine are Thine, and Thine are Mine; and I am glorified in them."

Is it truth? Are we Bible believers? Is Christ glorified in us? I want you to consider this. He is speaking of the oneness and that unity that shall exist with Christ and His disciples. In that unity, in that oneness, Christ is glorified in us. Now I would have you consider how very light a matter many of us make of seeking to preserve this unity. Why, this unity with believers in and through Christ is the great strength of the church! The oneness, the love which through their faith and unity exists with God's people through faith in Christ, is a power.

How earnest, how decided, how determined should be our efforts to answer the prayer of Christ that we may have that harmony one with another for which Christ died to perfect; that we may be one with Christ; for, unless we are constantly laboring for this harmony and this unity, we shall certainly fail of answering the prayer of being one with Christ as He was one with the Father.

(You will see I have contracted a severe cold on this journey. It is very difficult for me to speak at this time, but perhaps I can make you hear. I hope I can.)

In this oneness God is glorified. In division and dissension and differences and pulling apart Satan is glorified, and all heaven looks with astonishment upon those who claim to be children of God. Have [they] not served the enemy long enough in this line? "And now," prayed Christ, "I am no more in the world, but these are in the world, and I come to Thee. Holy Father, keep through Thine own name those whom Thou hast given me, that they may be one, as we are. While I was with them in the world, I kept them in Thy name: those that Thou gavest Me I have kept, and none of them is lost, but the son of perdition; that the scripture might be fulfilled. And now I come to Thee; and these things I speak in the world, that they might have My joy fulfilled in themselves" (Verses 11-13)

Who? Believers in Jesus Christ. That they might have the joy of Christ fulfilled in us through love and unity as His disciples. What is that joy? Who for the joy that was set before Him endured the cross, despised the shame, and is forever set down at the right hand of God. What was the joy? Was it the joy that we feel when we think that we are in a very important position in this life? Is that the joy? No. What was the joy? In seeing sons and daughters brought to Jesus Christ because they have given their life to the service of Christ, of soul saving.

That is the joy that Christ had. That is our joy. And when we possess this joy we shall love souls and work for souls for whom Christ has died. You will not be in the position that you will think, "My way is right, and I will carry this through on my line"; and thus you dishonor your Creator, because Christ's prayer is against you, and you are against the prayer. Therefore how can you have His joy fulfilled in you when you have a spirit of self-exaltation and you are not at oneness with Jesus Christ?

What we want today is to be constantly studying the life of Christ and working every day of our life to answer the prayer of Christ that you may be one in His love, and work for unity. The prayer that He offered to His Father is to exercise interest and love for souls. You want in every work, in your spirit, in your thoughts, in your actions, to be cherishing the love of Christ which He has prayed might exist. You want that faith that works out your salvation after the divine similitude. Why, you tell us that by our works we are not saved! Nevertheless, you are not saved by any evil works; but you have that faith that works out a character after the divine similitude. It is a faith that works out a unity of action, brother with brother, and every hour of your life if you are standing in living connection with God. You manifest His love. It works in your home life.

There is no fretfulness seen in the home if Christ is the peace principle exercised in your soul. There is no uncourteousness there. There is no roughness or sharp speech there. Why? Because we believe and act out that we are members of the Royal Family, children of the Heavenly King, bound to Jesus Christ by the strongest tie of love—that love which works by faith and purifies the soul.

You love Jesus and you are constantly at work to overcome all selfishness and be a blessing and comfort and strength and a support to the souls He has purchased with His blood. I cannot see why we should not the more earnestly try to bring the peace of Christ right into our family, than to labor for those that have no living connection with us; but if we have religion in the home, it will extend outside of the home. You will have it everywhere. You will carry it with you to the church. You can carry it with you when you go out to your work. It will be with you wherever you shall be. What we want is religion in the home. What we need is the peace principle which shall control our spirit and our life and character after the Christlife. He has given us His example. God help us that we may walk and work intelligently to this end.

There is no virtue in your prayers to God when you get right up from your prayers and begin to speak sharp words and make yourself disagreeable in your family. When you get up from your prayers and begin to fret and to find fault with everything and with God Himself—for this has been done—your prayers don't go any higher than your head. Shall we now have that faith that works by love and purifies the soul here where this reformation means so much? Well, that is what we want; because the latter rain is coming, and we want the vessel all cleansed from its work of impurity. We want the vessel to be a vessel unto honor, fit for the Master's use. There are vessels to dishonor, and there are vessels to honor. Now we want to make our choice, and reveal we choose to be a vessel unto honor.

There is not a quarreling man—no matter if your profession is as high as heaven—nor a quarreling woman; not one that loves to talk and berate and wound and injure the souls and reputation of God's people, that will ever enter the portals of the city of God. Why? Because there would be a second rebellion in heaven. What we need now is to be students, to learn in the school of Christ to perfect a Christlike character.

"Come," says Jesus. "Come," says Christ your Saviour, "learn of Me; for I am meek and lowly in heart." His arm is extended, "Come unto Me, all ye that labor and are heavy laden, and I will give you rest." He has told you where to go. "Come unto Me," every one of you, "and I will give you rest." Do you believe it? Do we believe the word of God today? Do we believe just what He tells us? What is the matter with us, that we do not have more freedom, and that Christ is not glorified in us? It is because we don't believe Him. Every soul will act out all the faith that he has.

If we are weary, if we are heavy laden, why, then, come right to the great Burden Bearer. Say, "Here, Lord, I come just as I am. I come because I am sinful. I come because I am needy. I come because I am wholly dependent, and I want to drink in this life of the waters of life. I want to drink of the streams of salvation which flow from the throne of God."

Well, then, if you drink, how shall we know that you have been drinking? How will anyone know that you have been drinking? Will you go out and begin to kick and scold your cattle, and beat them, and bruise them? They are God's dumb animals and cannot retaliate. He made them. You must respect your cattle. Will you rise from prayer and begin to scold and fret at your children, and at the circumstances and things that transpire in your house? Will you do it? Well, what shall we think of you? We will think you are an agent of the devil, that is what; we think the thoughts that such a course of action produces. Whatever your profession, however high it may be, if the truth you profess does not have influence enough on you to change your natural heart, to convert you to be kind and courteous, and to give you a new heart and a new mind, seek the true character now.

Now what does every man and woman need? A conversion to God. That is what he needs. Then what? Why, we begin to cherish this love which Christ had. We are converted. We love one another. We see that every individual has his own individual trials. We see that every soul that we are brought into connection with knows what it is to battle with the powers of darkness if they ever overcome. "We," saith the True Teacher, "fight not against flesh and blood," but we fight "against spiritual wickedness in high places."

Well, we know Satan is against us; we know the whole confederacy of evil is united and works with the evil men and women. Satan and his angels and evil men are there manifested to attempt to deceive, to allure, and to make our lives uncomfortable and unhappy and wretched by words and actions, and is it not very poor policy for professed Christians to open the door of their house and say to the devil, come in? Many are doing this. Is it not the most wretched policy for you to give place to the devil, and then you judge [that] everybody is your enemy, and you are the enemy of everybody, and thus you talk and thus you act.

Is the joy of Christ in you? Is Christ glorified, or God glorified in you? Verily, verily, I say unto you, unless you are born again you never can see the kingdom of heaven. (See John 3:3) You may have addicted yourself to fretting and to scolding for a long while, but it has not perfected your Christian character. Now suppose you change the order of things and you begin, when Satan begins to put in the word of complaint, to find fault, you begin to sing a song, if it is the simple hymn, "I will follow Thee, my Saviour, Wheresoe'er my lot may be." Just begin to sing. Do you think that will please the devil and the confederacy of evil angels? No; they will get out of your presence as soon as possible. You have garrisoned the soul against them.

Well then, what shall we do? We shall pray more in the spirit and understanding also. We shall talk more comfortable words because the heart is converted. We will lift up the weights that are upon the souls, knowing that they are tempted of the devil and, in our turn, we will not make ourselves tempters.

Now that is what we will do when converted. You try it, and you will see what that will do for you, and you will see that you are exercising a faith that works—that works by love, which purifies the soul.

And then I will tell you what else to do. Keep the praise of God on your lips. You have had so little of it that it is a strange song. Now, we want to learn that song because in heaven the angels are constantly offering praise and thanksgiving and glory to the God of heaven. Therefore we want to catch the strain here, and heaven is much nearer to earth than we think, and we are much nearer to heaven than we imagine, because the heavenly intelligences are all through such an assembly as this.

Is that all? No. The heavenly helpers are with you in your family. Those angels want that family [to be] a sample of the family in heaven. Those angels are at work to mold, to fashion, and to make every family after the divine family. Well then, would it not be very poor policy to speak and act like sinners, to awaken an element in your family which will set them all at variance, and make them unhappy and miserable? But this work is done daily by unconverted men and women who claim to be followers of Christ. But God help us to be converted, that we may show forth the praises of Him who hath called us out of darkness into His marvelous light.

Well then, how shall we know that we have been drinking of the living streams of salvation? How shall we understand this? Oh, the heart is changed; out of it are the issues of life. The good man bringeth out of the treasure of his heart good things. Now we are to learn and are to know by their words and works who are converted. The evil man bringeth out of the treasure of his heart evil things, showing he is under the control of Satan. Every word is a seed. We are scattering it in words and actions—sowing seed—and then what will the harvest be? God help us that we may sow unto life eternal, that we may reap the precious grain in this life, and then the good works will cause souls to be converted.

I want to tell you that you have every reason to rejoice today. Christ says, "Come, come unto Me, and I will give you rest." What have we to rejoice in? That Christ is not in Joseph's new tomb, and a great stone rolled before it. Where is He? Where is Jesus? He has arisen; He has risen from the dead; He has ascended on high. He is our Advocate, and He pleads in our behalf before the Father. We have a Friend at court. Thank God, we have a Friend at court! Then offer up your petitions. The righteousness of Christ is there. The perfection of Christ is there.

You may look up and say, "Oh, I am discouraged; I am in despair; I feel so terrible," and all this! What have your feelings to do with the matter? Do tell me.

What have your feelings to do with these matters? Are they stronger than the word, the immutable word of Jehovah? Which is stronger? Is not the word of God a solid basis? Is it not the Rock of ages? Well now, what will you do? Hide in that Rock. Let your heart go out to Jesus who has bought you as His own property with the price of His sacred life-blood.

There are thousands that have been addicted to complaining; they are chronic grumblers. But all such will never enter heaven. How can you be cured? Christ tells you: "A new heart will I give you." Do they profess to believe the truth? I shall know it when there is a change in that unruly member, the tongue. "A new heart will I give thee." We shall find in the place of a stirring up by the leaven of disaffection, we shall find there are words that cement; there are words that bind together. They will not see something in everyone around them to find fault with but themselves, and expatiate upon other's evil. But they are beginning to look and say, Am I right? Have I that love, that faith that works by love and purifies the heart for the second, the latter, rain, the descent of the Holy Spirit of God?

Now, some will tell you, and they will begin to reckon, and reckon, and reckon when the latter rain is coming. I would rather that you would reckon right now whether you have brought eternity into your reckoning concerning your individual self. Consider whether you have brought eternity daily to view. If you are right with God today, you are ready if Christ should come today. What we need is Christ formed within, the hope of glory. We want that you should have a deep and earnest longing for the righteousness of Jesus Christ. Your old, tattered garments of self-righteousness will not give you an entrance into the kingdom of God, but that garment that is woven in the loom of heaven—the righteousness of Jesus Christ—will. It will give you an inheritance among the sanctified. That is what we want. It is worth more than all the worldly gain; it is worth more than all your farms; it is worth more than all the honor that finite beings can bestow upon you.

What we want to know is, Are you individually, daily preparing that you can unite with the family of heaven? Are you quarrelsome here? Are you finding fault with your household here? If you are, you will find fault with them in heaven. Your character is being tested and proved in this life, whether you will make a peaceable subject of God's kingdom in heaven.

Now let the parents go to work for their children. Don't let them hear a fretful word spoken in the house. Tell them angels are there watching over them and they must enter into no sinful practice. Tell them the heavenly intelligences are looking upon them, and don't allow a word to be spoken from your lips to educate your children in words to dishonor God. Ah, there are scores here that need to be converted on this line, and unless they are converted, they never will know what the love and joy of Christ is in the heart, and can never be translated to live with the heavenly family.

But we hope this meeting will be a time when you will surrender to God. We hope it will be a time when you will place yourself fully in Christ's love. He is coming in a little while, and when we think of it every one of you may look back and consider what your life has been. Consider how you have had the truth. Summer after summer line upon line, testimony after testimony, has come from heaven to you, and the Word, the precious Word of God—and yet, where is your reform? Where is the cleansing of the soul temple? Where is the fitting up for the finishing touch of immortality? What are you doing? Have you that faith that works, or have you that faith which does not do anything for you?

The truth of a heavenly origin converts the soul. The truth from heaven has an influence upon the human life and upon the human character that is elevating, ennobling, sanctifying, refining—making us more and more like Jesus; and thus we are changed through the sanctification of the truth from glory to glory. What is the glory? It is the character—"From character to character." And we are fitting for heaven in this life, that we may see Jesus and that we may be like Him; that we may reflect His image, and from character to character marching, marching right straight along; step by step you keep with the Leader, and He is leading you. Who is it? The Light of the world, the Truth, the Life.—all these combined, and He is leading in straight paths. You are never left without angels' care. Do you respond and seek to perfect a true righteous character? Will you be led? That is the question, the whole question of your salvation today. Will you be led?

I want to read still more. The last I read was, "And all Mine are Thine, and Thine are Mine; and I am glorified in them." Is it so? Is God glorified in you? Are you a gossiper? Are you a faultfinder? Are you suspicious? Are you jealous? Is God glorified in you? No, indeed! The devil is glorified in you, and he is wonderfully pleased with you. But what we want is to change that order by being converted to God right here and not to wait until we get off of this tent ground. What we want is to be clad with the robes of Christ's righteousness. We want to be built up in the most holy faith. We want to rejoice in Jesus Christ.

Now I read some verses further than this: "And now come I to Thee; and these things I speak in the world, that they might have"—what?—"My joy fulfilled in themselves." Well now, this is the privilege of every individual soul. The joy of Christ fulfilled in themselves. Think that this can be done; believe that it can be done. Act it; and you will find that you are brought into a purer atmosphere; you are breathing the atmosphere of heaven—not the atmosphere of hell, but the atmosphere of heaven—and when you breathe in that atmosphere, and this atmosphere surrounds the soul, all that come within the sphere of your influence are benefited and blessed.

The "joy fulfilled in themselves." What does it mean? Why, I get up in the morning, [and] I don't feel any particular joy. When I wake up, I don't feel that wonderful joy; perhaps some days, sometimes I do. But then what? Looking unto Jesus, who is the author and finisher of our faith, I begin to look up to Jesus for His presence, His light, and His love. A very simple thing. I thank God that He has kept me through the night. I am so thankful that He is a living Saviour. I am so grateful that He lives to make intercession for me; that He is not in Joseph's new tomb. He is a living Saviour and ready to bless me. Well then, I believe that He means I shall be blessed. He died for me that I might be blessed, and that His joy might remain in me, therefore I keep my mind in that channel. I educate it; I train my tongue; I train my thoughts; I train all that there is of me that I may fasten it upon Jesus Christ.

Oh, evil things come in between me and the Saviour. It is the hellish shadow of Satan. I see that shadow and darkness; shall I fall under it? Well, when I was coming in the cars in the evening and in the night season I looked at the moon, there was a whole bank of clouds it went into. Now, I thought, we will see what that moon does. I kept my eyes upon it, and soon I began to see that there was a bright, brightness coming into the cloud. The darkness of the cloud did not put out the moon nor its light, but the light kept shining. The moon in its brightness began to scatter and lighten and brighten the darkness until it rolled back and revealed the glory and light of the moon, and then its glory lighted up the clouds all around us. There is what we want to be.

Satan is not dead by any means. He is working to bring the shadow of death over your souls. Will you let him do it? Will you let him make you look at the darkness, and talk of the darkness? We are just to be like that moon. Light up all our way by faith. Through the shadow of darkness and of death Thou art the light of heaven. We are to talk of heaven and of heavenly things. We are to become more and more heavenly-minded. Now all the faith that you profess—we shall know something about it. You need not think that you can shut it up in a box like a nice perfume, and keep it there or in a bottle. But we shall know just the measure of your faith. How? By your works. By the fruits that you bear. If you have Christ abiding in your heart, you will talk Christ.

If you have Christ abiding there, you cannot fret or scold. You cannot make others unhappy and wretched and miserable. No. Because Christ is there, His joy is there, His peace is there. You want everybody to have peace; you want them to have comfort; you want them to have good hope; you want them to have courage, and you keep talking of Jesus and His love—what He has done for me. Now we lose sight of this; we lose sight of it. You look and see what Christ has done for you again and again, and the precious victories He has given you, and then as you look at things you talk of these. Don't you see, every trial sinks into insignificance in comparison with this?

Paul looked at it, and now let us hear his language—just listen to it—"I reckon that the sufferings of this present time are not worthy to be compared with the glory which shall be revealed in us." (Romans 8:18) When? At that time. "Revealed in us." Now let us make the reckoning. "I reckon," he says, Well, then, let us begin to reckon. We have reckoned long enough that the darkness is worthy to be dwelt upon. Now we reckon that the trials of this present time are not worthy to be compared with the glory. Well then, let us talk of the glory. Let us talk of what Christ is to you, what Christ is to [me]. Just talk in that way. What is He to you? A present Saviour; and if He is not a present Saviour He is not worth anything to you. You need not think He will be of any advantage to you.

Is He my Saviour? Can I lay hold upon His merits this very hour? Can I commit the keeping of my soul to Jesus Christ today? Yes. How? What assurance have I? I point you to Christ of Calvary. Can you stand under the shadow of the cross and there talk your crosses, your darkness, your wicked feelings? Can you do it? Dare you do it? You never dare to do it when standing under the shadow of the cross, because all that infinite sacrifice was made to make me love God. It was made that I might reflect the image of God in Jesus Christ. Well then, when all this sacrifice has been made for me, shall I let everybody know that it amounts to something? Shall I let the world know that Jesus, the precious Saviour, has made all this infinite sacrifice that He might be formed within, the hope of glory, and that I might rejoice in His love?

Well then, why talk darkness? Why talk rebelliousness? Why not lift yourself up in the holier, purer atmosphere? Why talk all the time that you don't feel as you want to feel? Take hold of Jesus Christ. As you feel after His hand, He takes that hand. He puts it in His; He lifts you up. Well then, be lifted up. Don't let your body, like the body of death, [remain] in darkness, [so] that nothing can lift it. Come where the light is, and let it reveal its glory—glorious beams that come from Jesus Christ through you. Talk hope; talk courage. Cease your faultfinding, and let us talk of heaven and heavenly things.

The more you do, you are shaped into the same image. Talk doubt, and you will find plenty of doubt. Talk darkness and you will find plenty of darkness and, more than that, you will have a terrible harvest to garner. You cannot afford it. Time is too precious. Every moment is golden. Every word is to be a treasure of life. Every word is to be of value to help somebody; and if you cannot, don't speak. Silence is excellent. Keep still, and, if you speak, let the law of kindness be on your lips. "By thy words shalt thou be justified, and by thy words thou shalt be condemned" (Matthew 12:37), because by your words you show whether Satan is abiding in the heart or whether Jesus Christ is abiding there.

"Behold, I stand at the door, and knock: if any man hear My voice, and open the door, I will come in to him, and will sup with him, and he with Me." (Revelation 3:20) Let us answer the knock. Let us open the door. That is our part of the business, and then the glory of God shall pervade our souls. What then? We shall be one in Christ Jesus. "I have given them Thy word; and the world hath hated them, because they are not of the world, even as I am not of the world." Well, shall we be engaged in hating one another? The world, He says, hated them. But shall we be working to annoy and make unhappy and hate one another? Is that our business? God forbid. "I pray not that thou shouldest take them out of the world, but that thou shouldest keep them from the evil."

Now, we want to be kept from the evil. "They are not of the world, even as I am not of the world. Sanctify them through Thy truth.... As thou hast sent Me into the world, even so" I also send them into the world. [It is] just as much your work to act out right in the world as it was the work of Christ to redeem. He sent you into the world. You are to be the light of the world. You are to show the distinction between the spirit of Christianity and the spirit of the worldling. You are to show the controlling influence of the power of God upon the human heart. God help us that we may be sanctified through the truth; and that sanctification shall have its influence to leaven those that are around us. Not the leaven of malice; not the leaven of jealousy; not the leaven of evil surmisings, but it is the leaven of the spirit of Jesus Christ, which is sent down from heaven, called the Holy Ghost, and that Spirit affects the heart and the character.

Now, God wants His converting power to come on this occasion. There are some that come to our meetings—they will sit all through the meetings; they have borne a few words of testimony now and then; they have gone home and done just exactly [the same as], if not worse than, before. Why? Because they had not the new heart. What is the new heart? It is the new mind. What is the mind? It is the will. Where is your will? It is either on Satan's side or Christ's side. Now it is up to you. Will you put your will today on Christ's side of the question? That is the new heart. It is the new will, a new mind. "A new heart will I give thee." Then let us begin right here.

Conversion is simple, very simple. Let us commence right here to come into the kingdom of heaven. How? As a little child. Just as simple as simple can be. You may get all your mysteries of the new birth, and you cannot make anybody understand it, or understand it yourself. But the best way for you is to give your mind to Jesus Christ. And the mind is the will to put it on, and do just as Matthew did.

The Lord Jesus came to Matthew. He was in a very unpopular business, and all the Jews looked upon them [publicans, as people] to be despised, and Christ said to Matthew, "Matthew, follow Me." Did he say, "O Lord, when I get good enough I will follow you"? Did he say, "O Lord, when I have this agony, this awful agony for my sin, then I will come"?

Well, that is what many of you are saying. No, Matthew rose up and followed Him. He was walking in the light, because he could not follow Christ unless he was walking in the light. Well then, what are we to do? We are just to believe as simply as a little child. We are to take our position on the Lord's side, and we are to be Christ's children because He wants us to be, and because He died that we might be; and will we be?

I love Jesus. I had things trouble me before I went on the cars. I was afraid the shadow would hang over me all the way; and I could not forbear as I would wake up in the night season, saying over and over, "I love the Lord; I love the Lord; I know I love Thee; Oh, I love Jesus who gave His life for me. I love the souls of all those for whom Christ has died." And thus I feel the sweet comfort of peace and hope and light and love in my heart. Well, let us educate our minds; let us educate our thoughts.

Now I am not going to hold you here, but I do want that the converting power of God should be in your midst. There is a great work to be done for many souls, but they don't see it. They don't realize it enough to go to work. Why, how, you say, can I be going to work to help myself? How can I do it? God works, and all you have to do is to cooperate with Him, and let Him work. Work in harmony with God. But He never works unless the human agent wills that He shall work, and works with Him. Then, with the human and the divine combined, we can make a glorious success. We will have the victory. Will you let Christ work on your human mind? Shall this glorious opportunity in 1891 pass over and work no decided change in our ideas and feelings? Go to work, brethren; go to work, sisters. I appeal to you to go to work.

Christ is coming, and Christ is to be revealed in you, if you will only allow His image to be revealed in you. Fall on the Rock and be broken. What did they do to Moses? They took that atom of humanity, the heavenly intelligences, and put him in the cleft of the rock, and the hand of God over the rock. Now, what you want is to be in the cleft of the rock. You want to break in pieces before God your pride, yourself, your folly, your wickedness, your dishonesty, your corruption of heart, your licentiousness, your impurity. You want to fall on that Rock, and then if the superscription of the divine plays upon you, that the love of Christ may abide with you and Jesus be in your heart.

God help you to begin the work right here; not to wait for the ministers to stir you up to a wonderful excitement. God wants intelligent Christians. He wants you to count the cost of the battle. He wants you to count whether you can war against Satan and his spiritual wickedness in high places. He wants you to see the plan of the battle, of the confederacy of evil, and then He wants you to see that angels are in the army, that the Captain of our salvation is at the head. It is they that do the warring. It is they that do the work, and we cooperate, coincide, and work with them.

Now, that is our work. Will you commence the warfare here against lust? Will you commence it against wickedness? Will you commence it against impurity? Will you be fitting up for the home in heaven above? God help you right here to be converted. You want to go from this meeting with your affection lighted up with the glory of God, saying, Hear what the Lord has done for me. He has put a new song in my mouth; even praise to our God. Well now, commence to praise God. And praise Him with heart and soul and voice. The devil doesn't want you [to], because you would be a living witness to them that you had drunk of the living waters, and he doesn't want you to praise God. Still, shall we disappoint the devil? Shall we please Jesus Christ?

Well, let us work as intelligent Christians, and may we hear the beautiful testimony from your lips, "I love Jesus, and I know that He loves me." Then the world will see [that we] have been with Jesus and have learned of Him. This is the lesson that we want you to learn in the school of Christ.[23]

[This was followed by an altar call. The response was good. See report of camp meeting in Signs, October 12, 1891.]

---

[23] Ms. 36, 1891; MR 900.38.

Chapter 24

Temperance

"Know ye not that they which run in a race run all, but one receiveth the prize? So run, that ye may obtain. And every man that striveth for the mastery is temperate in all things. Now they do it to obtain a corruptible crown; but we an incorruptible. I therefore so run, not as uncertainly; so fight I, not as one that beateth the air: but I keep under my body, and bring it into subjection: lest by any means, when I have preached to others, I myself should be a castaway." (1 Corinthians 9:24-27)

In the family circle and in the church we should place Christian temperance on an elevated platform. It should be a living, working element, reforming habits, dispositions, and characters. Intemperance lies at the foundation of all the evil in our world. We are altogether too silent upon the subject of Christian temperance. We fail to urge this subject upon Christian parents. Fathers and mothers should be invited, in the fear of the Lord, not only to abstain from all intoxicating beverages, but from tea, coffee, and flesh meat.

And I go farther. Temperance should be practiced in the cooking of the food and in the variety of dishes provided, that the mother may be spared all the labor possible. A great variety of food is not essential for the sustenance of life; instead, it injures the digestive organs, causing a war in the stomach. With the blessing of God, plain, simple food will sustain life and be the best for the entire being.

Few realize that generally more food than necessary is placed in the stomach. But the extra food eaten is a tax on the stomach and injures the whole human structure. When the stomach has too much to do it becomes weary. This weariness is felt through the entire system. The child cannot understand why he feels so tired and impatient, and [he] decides that he is hungry and must have something to eat. The real trouble is that the digestive organs have been too severely taxed and need an entire rest. But more food is eaten and the poor, wearied organs become diseased and inflamed. Dyspepsia and a diseased liver are the result.

Mothers need to be instructed on this point. Sweet cake should be kept off the table, for it is an injury to the stomach and liver. The sweets that children eat harm the life-current. By the laws of the home everything that renders the blood impure should be discarded from the table. Especially should little children be given wholesome food. They should be given no tea or coffee. Their food should not contain spices or any kind of seasoning. The plainest food is the most wholesome and keeps the temple of God in the most healthy condition.

If the peace of Christ is in the heart, plain food, seasoned by a good appetite, will be relished. We are to fulfill the command, "Whether therefore ye eat, or drink, or whatsoever ye do, do all to the glory of God." "Whatsoever ye do in word or deed, do all in the name of the Lord Jesus, giving thanks to God and the Father by Him." But how much is God brought into the thoughts of those who claim to be Christians? How much sanctified conversation is encouraged at the family board? If God were thought of when we eat and drink, the precious talent of speech would more often be employed to His glory.

Shall we not strive to avoid the sin of Belshazzar when at his sacrilegious feast he praised the gods of gold and silver? At this feast the king and his nobles drank wine out of the sacred vessels of the Lord's house. The wine confused the senses of the revelers until nothing was too sacred for them to profane. The king himself led in the blasphemy, making a display of defiant desecration.

At the very moment when the feasting was at its height, a bloodless hand came forth and traced on the wall of the banqueting room the doom of the king and his kingdom. "Mene, Mene, Tekel, Upharsin" were the words written, and they were interpreted by Daniel to mean, "Thou art weighed in the balances, and art found wanting.... Thy kingdom is divided, and given to the Medes and Persians." And the record tells us, "In that night was Belshazzar the king of the Chaldeans slain. And Darius the Median took the kingdom."

Little did Belshazzar think that an unseen Watcher beheld his idolatrous revelry. But there is nothing said or done that is not recorded on the books of heaven. The mystic characters traced by the bloodless hand testify that God is a witness to all we do and that He is dishonored by feasting, reveling. We cannot hide anything from God. We cannot escape from our accountability to Him. Wherever we are and whatever we do, we are responsible to Him whose we are by creation and by redemption.

God has given to every man his work. We may all be laborers together with Him. Parents, you have in the Scriptures the expression of the will of God. He has declared that there are only two parties in our world, the obedient and the disobedient. And although we are fallen human beings, yet we may stand on vantage ground. Christ took human nature upon Him that humanity might touch humanity and divinity lay hold upon an infinite God.

God has given us reasoning powers and talents of perception that we may distinguish between good and evil. This we may do if we refuse to yield to the temptations of Satan, who is playing the game of life for every soul. But if we stupefy our faculties by the use of narcotics, we cannot distinguish between right and wrong, between the sacred and the common. The sin of this lies at our own door. We have given our powers into Satan's keeping, and habits that are selfish and impure bind us as with chains of steel.

But God is longsuffering, full of mercy and forbearance, and even though a man be in abject slavery, if he turns from his wickedness and confesses his sins, placing himself under the guardianship of God, he will find help. Provision has been made for every soul to be saved. Those who receive Christ and believe in Him as their personal Saviour will receive everlasting life.

Christ loves every soul. He gave His life to save man. "If ye keep My commandments," He says, "ye shall abide in My love, even as I have kept My Father's commandments, and abide in His love. These things have I spoken unto you that My joy might remain in you, and that your joy might be full." "All power is given unto Me in heaven and in earth." Christ died on the cross to draw all to Him, and He would have us joyful in that joy which He alone can give, the joy of obedience.

"This is My commandment, that ye love one another." To love God supremely and our neighbor as ourselves is the fulfilling of the law. Christ has a treasurehouse full of precious gifts for every soul. "Greater love hath no man than this, that a man lay down his life for his friends." Then Christ tells us who are His friends: "Ye are My friends if ye do whatsoever I have commanded you." The work of sanctification consists of a cheerful performance of daily duties, in perfect obedience to the commandments of God. A failure to cooperate with Christ in the great work of redemption is a failure that all eternity cannot supply.

A man is received by God just as soon as he realizes that he has nothing in himself that will gain salvation. He must surrender himself as a willing servant to the One who gave His life to redeem him. When he loses all confidence in anything he has done or can do to save himself, when he gives himself up to be saved by Christ, he shows that he appreciates the sacrifice made in his behalf, that he has confidence to commit the keeping of his soul to God. Such a one can say in faith, "I know that He will keep that which I have committed unto Him against that day."

It is our duty to render implicit obedience to the divine injunctions. Our faith must grasp the mercy and forgiveness of our sins. Then, believing that our sins are pardoned, we are no longer to walk in the path of transgression, but yield ourselves to the will of God. Every day that we fail to do God's will we rob Him who has said, "Ye are not your own. For ye are bought with a price; therefore glorify God in your body, and in your spirit, which are God's."

As we go on step by step, trusting, believing, receiving the end of our faith, which is the salvation of our souls, the way will be made plain to us. But even though we may not always be able to tell why we are called to do this or that, we are to obey without questioning. Abraham was called to leave his Father's home. He could not see the future, but by faith he went into a strange country, not knowing whither he went. He was fully assured that God knew and that all he had to do was to watch for divine guidance and move in obedience to the commands of God.

We are not to lean upon man. God is to be consulted. All our trust is to be placed in Him. But to walk by faith and not by sight does not mean that we are to close our eyes and see nothing. We must open our eyes as wide as possible, but they must be directed to the Saviour. If we continue to look to Him, He will guide us into all truth. He is the Alpha and the Omega, the author and finisher of our faith.

"In all thy ways acknowledge Him, and He shall direct thy path." This is the promise. God must be consulted at every step. He would not have us trust in human beings, who need themselves to walk carefully before God. Let him that thinketh he standeth take heed lest he fall. If we look to humanity we shall obtain human help, but if we ask for divine guidance we are safe in the assurance that God is leading us.

The eyes of Abraham's understanding were not closed when he decided that the best thing he could do was to separate from Lot, although he had been to him as a father. But contention and strife he could not endure, even among the herdsmen. He could not have his peace of mind disturbed by unpleasant differences. Separation was painful to him, but it must be.

Abraham gave Lot the choice of where he would go so that afterward Lot should not be tempted to think that in the separation Abraham had his own interest in view. Lot chose a beautiful location near Sodom. The land of his choice possessed every natural advantage, but he failed to investigate the morals and religion of the Sodomites. We have on record his after-history. The time came when he had to flee from the corrupt city, which was dark with crime of every stripe and type. He was permitted to warn his daughters and sons-in-law, but they would not heed this warning any more than they had heeded his instruction. They mocked at his faith in God, and they perished in the destruction of Sodom. This is a lesson for us all. We should move carefully in the selection of homes for our families. We should seek the help of the Lord in the training of our children and their choice of a lifework. Every family should constantly look to God, trusting in Him to guide aright. Sharp discrimination is necessary in order to avoid following a wrong course for the sake of worldly gain.

The Lord's will is to be our will. God must be made first and last and best in everything. We are to be as teachable as a little child, moving carefully and with entire trust in God. Our eternal interests are involved in the steps we take, whether we move heavenward toward the city whose maker and builder is God, or earthward toward Sodom's beautiful attractions.

God does not consult our opinions or preferences. He knows what human beings do not know—the future results of every movement—and therefore our eyes should be directed to Him and not to the worldly advantages presented by Satan. Satan tells us that if we give heed to him we shall reach great heights of knowledge. "Ye shall be as gods," he said to Eve, "if you eat of the tree forbidden by God." The test given to Adam and Eve was very light, but they could not bear it. They disobeyed God, and this transgression opened the floodgates of woe on our world.

God's commands are to be obeyed by all. "This do," the Eternal One declares, "and thou shalt live." But notwithstanding that men and women have before them the history of the fall, showing them that disobedience in little things is the same in God's sight as disobedience in larger things, God's commandments are ignored and ridiculed.

The danger signal is lifted in God's Word, showing us that all who transgress God's law are under the death penalty. If the Lord were to visit the lawless transgressor with immediate punishment, men would be afraid to do the evil which is now done in our world. Those whom no entreaties or warnings will deter from following their own opinions would turn from their sins.

But although men have not discrimination to see it, yet the punishment for sin is just as certain as if it were extended when the sin was committed, unless the one who sins repents and turns to God. The longsuffering and forbearance of God will be appreciated by those who repent, and God will save them from sin. But those who continue to disobey will receive punishment which is proportionate to their rebellion against the God of heaven.

Many disregard the light and opportunities granted them by God, and stubbornly follow their own way. Thus did Belshazzar. Although God had revealed Himself in honor and majesty to Nebuchadnezzar, Belshazzar closed his eyes to the light and chose his own course. Daniel declared to him: "O thou king, the most high God gave Nebuchadnezzar thy father a kingdom, and majesty, and glory, and honour: and for the majesty that He gave him, all people, nations, and languages, trembled and feared before him: whom he would he slew; and whom he would he kept alive; and whom he would he set up; and whom he would he put down. But when his heart was lifted up, and his mind hardened in pride, he was deposed from his kingly throne, and they took his glory from him: And he was driven from the sons of men; and his heart was made like the beasts, and his dwelling was with the wild asses: they fed him with grass like oxen, and his body was wet with the dew of heaven; till he knew that the most high God ruled in the kingdom of men, and that He appointeth over it whomsoever He will. And thou his son, O Belshazzar, hast not humbled thine heart, though thou knewest all this; But hast lifted up thyself against the Lord of heaven; and they have brought the vessels of His house before thee, and thou, and thy lords, thy wives, and thy concubines, have drunk wine in them; and thou hast praised the gods of silver, and gold, of brass, iron, wood, and stone, which see not, nor hear, nor know: and the God in whose hand thy breath is, and whose are all thy ways, hast thou not glorified." (Daniel 5:18-23)

This history is written for our learning, that we may not do as did this idolatrous king. Abraham's character was in every way the opposite of that of Belshazzar. Abraham's practical obedience to the Lord's commands revealed a sure growth in spiritual knowledge, and every additional test was a renewal of the trust reposed by God in him. In mind and purpose he was one with God, and to him God revealed future events. "Your father Abraham rejoiced to see My day," Christ declared. "He saw it, and was glad." "If any man will do His will, he shall know of the doctrine, whether it be of God."

But Belshazzar lifted himself up against the Lord. "Thou ... hast not humbled thine heart, though thou knewest all this; but hast lifted up thyself against the Lord of heaven." "Because sentence against an evil work is not executed speedily, therefore the heart of the sons of men is fully set in them to do evil." Too often the patience and forbearance of God makes transgressors bold and unimpressible.

It is time for the message of God's forbearance to be proclaimed to win men to repentance; and it is just as verily time for men to be warned that there are limits to God's forbearance. Men may advance, as did Belshazzar, in presumption and defiance, until they pass the boundary. Blasphemy may be so developed as to exhaust the patience of the longsuffering God.

We are living in a time when there are multitudes who have no fear of God. The age is marked with a depravity extremely offensive to God. Ministers and church members engage zealously in the work of making void the law of God. They have reduced the holy precepts to a dead letter. The time is coming when God must vindicate His glory before the transgressors of His law.

Christ gave His life to establish forever before the heavenly universe, before the unfallen worlds and before a fallen world, the immutability of the law of God. But the religious world has put the Lord of heaven to open shame. They refuse to receive His law as the rule of this life, and because of this disregard, the world is becoming as it was before the flood. Then, as now, the people were eating and drinking, planting and building, marrying and giving in marriage, in utter forgetfulness of God. The flood came and destroyed them all. Thus shall it be in the day when the Son of man is revealed.

In the midst of mirth, feasting, and forgetfulness of God, the command will go forth for the sword of the Lord to be unsheathed, that an end may be put to the insolence and disobedience of men. The prayers of God's people have ascended, "It is time, O Lord, for Thee to work; for they have made void Thy law." These prayers will erelong be answered. When men pass the limit of grace, God must let the world see that He is God.

The time has nearly come when transgression will no longer be tolerated, when God will interfere to repress the overflowing tide of iniquity.

At this time what will be the course of those who claim to fear God and respect His commandments? Will they be carried away by the apparently overwhelming power of the tide of evil? Will they allow themselves to be tempted by the scorn thrown upon God's law, to think that it makes no difference what day they keep? Shall they not give heed to God's word: "Ye shall keep the Sabbath therefore; for it is holy unto you: every one that defileth it shall surely be put to death: for whosoever doeth any work therein, that soul shall be cut off from among his people. Six days may work be done; but the seventh is the Sabbath of rest, holy to the Lord: whosoever doeth any work in the Sabbath day, he shall surely be put to death. Wherefore the children of Israel shall keep the Sabbath, to observe the Sabbath throughout their generations, for a perpetual covenant. It is a sign between me and the children of Israel forever: for in six days the Lord made heaven and earth, and on the seventh He rested, and was refreshed." (Exodus 31:14-17)

Will not all say that the Lord's word is positive and must be obeyed? The law of God will become more and more precious to us as we see the result of transgression upon the characters of the disobedient. If we are led by the Spirit of

Christ, our estimation of the value and sacredness of the law of Jehovah will increase in proportion as we see it despised and trampled on by unholy, profligate feet. Our language will be, "They have made void Thy law: therefore I love Thy commandments above gold; yea, above fine gold."

This is the sanctification to which those attain whose love of God's law increases as the contempt of transgressors increases. There is need for this increased confidence in the law, for fraud, violence, and crime are rapidly increasing. Men show their hatred of God by fighting against His law which He has pronounced "holy and just and good." Liquor saloons are established in every city. These are death traps, and those who establish them, seeking to accumulate gain at the cost of poverty, misery, and woe, provoke the Lord of hosts to their destruction.

God gives to all a period of probation but men can reach a point where they can expect from God nothing but indignation and punishment. This time is not just now, but it is fast approaching. The nations will advance from one degree of sinfulness to another. The children, educated and trained in transgression, will add to the evil entailed on them by parents who have no fear of God in their hearts.

Already the judgments of God have begun to fall upon the world in various calamities, that men may repent and be converted to truth and righteousness. But the candle of those who harden their hearts in iniquity will be put out by the Lord. They have lived only for themselves, and death must come to them.

When the limit of grace is reached, God will give His command for the destruction of the transgressor. He will arise in His Almighty character as a God above all gods, and those who have worked against Him in league with the great rebel, will be treated in accordance with their works.

In his vision of the last days Daniel inquired, "O my Lord, what shall be the end of these things? And he said, Go thy way, Daniel: for the words are closed up and sealed till the time of the end. Many shall be purified, and made white, and tried; but the wicked shall do wickedly: and none of the wicked shall understand; but the wise shall understand. ... Blessed is he that waiteth, and cometh to the thousand three hundred and five and thirty days. But go thou thy way till the end be: for thou shalt rest, and stand in thy lot at the end of the days." (Daniel 12:8-13) Daniel has been standing in his lot since the seal was removed and the light of truth has been shining upon his visions. He stands in his lot, bearing the testimony which was to be understood at the end of the days.

"And at that time shall Michael stand up, the great prince which standeth for the children of thy people: and there shall be a time of trouble, such as never was since there was a nation even to that same time: and at that time thy people shall be delivered, every one that shall be found written in the book. And many of them that sleep in the dust of the earth shall awake, some to everlasting life, and some to shame and everlasting contempt. And they that be wise shall shine as the brightness of the firmament; and they that turn many to righteousness as the stars for ever and ever. But thou, O Daniel, shut up the words, and seal the book, even to the time of the end: many shall run to and fro, and knowledge shall be increased." (Daniel 12 :1-4)[24]

---

[24] Manuscript 50, 1893, September 1893; MR 900.33.

Chapter 25

Keep the Commandments

[Sermon at Williamstown, a suburb of Melbourne, Victoria Sunday, 4:00 p.m., February 11, 1894]

"For God so loved the world, that he gave his only begotten Son, that whosoever believeth in him should not perish, but have everlasting life." (John 3:16) Suppose that we had not another promise in all the lids of the Scripture. Is not this enough to condemn every soul that has not a living faith in a personal Saviour? Whosoever believeth in Him. He gave His only begotten Son that whosoever—and that whosoever means you and me; it means parents and children. For whom did Christ die? Was it for a select few? It was for the whole world, the world that was fallen because of transgression.

Adam and Eve became sinners because of transgression, and now the Lord has given to the world His only begotten Son. That He might abolish the law? That law that Adam transgressed? Do you read it thus? I do not. Well then, what was the matter with Adam? Adam ventured to transgress one prohibition of God which was the test that God gave to man to try his loyalty and obedience. There was nothing in the fruit of the tree of knowledge that was dangerous in itself, but the danger was in Adam and Eve listening to Satan and venturing to transgress. Here was Eve listening to the voice of the tempter. His words were contradicting the words of God that death was the penalty of transgression. Satan says, "Ye shall not die." God says, "If ye eat of it ye shall die." Whom shall we believe?

God declares that He came not to destroy the law or the prophets. Why, if God could have changed or altered one precept of His law to meet man in his fallen condition, Christ need not have left the royal courts; He need not have laid off His kingly crown and royal robe, and yielded up His position as Commander in the heavenly court. He gave up all. For our sakes He became poor. Why? That we through His poverty might be made rich; that man should have another test of his loyalty and be brought back to obedience to the law of God. This infinite sacrifice was not to be made to immortalize sin.

It is the privilege of every sinner to ask his teacher what sin really is. Give me a definition of sin. We have one in (1 John 3). "Sin is the transgression of the law."

Now this is the only definition of sin in the whole Bible. We are going to read it to you right out of the Book, so that you need not have the idea that it is not in the Bible, that it is another Bible that we preach to you. We will just read it out of the good Book, and we will begin at the beginning of the chapter. "Behold, what manner of love the Father hath bestowed upon us, that we should be called the sons of God." That is our privilege.

"Therefore the world knoweth us not, because it knew him not." Now this knowledge does something for us. It is faith in Jesus Christ that is the living, working element. What does it do? "And every man that hath this hope in him purifieth himself, even as he is pure." Now there are a good many who have this faith tied on the outside, but it needs to be in them, a living, working element in the soul. It needs to be Christ enthroned in the heart. Well, "every man that hath this hope in him purifieth himself, even as he is pure." Wonderful, wonderful! By beholding Christ, by talking of Him, by beholding the loveliness of His character, we become changed. Changed from glory to glory. And what is glory? Character—and he becomes changed from character to character. Thus we see that there is a work of purification that goes on by beholding Jesus.

If the enemy makes us believe his presentations and assertions, we begin to behold another character. We will entertain his suggestions, and put him in the place of God. God is the one that we are to believe. We are to live on every word that proceedeth out of the mouth of God. Here the enemy brought in a lie, and man believed it. What we are to do is to purify our souls by obeying the truth, and we are to educate ourselves in a certain faith. What is that certain faith? It is the faith that works by love to purify the soul from every idol that we have enthroned there. We cannot afford to entertain an error because it has been handed down from generation to generation till it has come down to our time. What we want is truth, and we want it on every point.

As we listen to the words of Christ we will get truth. It is light; it is the way we are to travel to reach the heaven of eternal rest. It is the truth, and let us hang our helpless souls upon it. Not upon the minister, for you will find this a broken reed. Whom shall we hang our souls upon? Upon Him whose arm is strong to save to the utmost all that come to Him. How shall we come? Well, we will read a little farther: "Whosoever committeth sin transgresseth also the law: for sin is the transgression of the law." This is away down this side of the crucifixion of Christ. Is not His law there? "God [had] no law to govern in heaven the angelic host, and on earth the inhabitants of the earth!" Did He ever mean that such a statement should come from human lips? Never, never. This is the reason that the earth has fallen to the depths that it has. For this reason it is that the souls of parents and children are in danger. For this reason we read of robbery and murder and the depravity that everywhere comes to our notice.

We want to understand the character of sin. "Whosoever committeth sin transgresseth also the law: for sin is the transgression of the law." Where there is no law there is no sin. What kind of world have we? What kind of world is it that will people heaven in their lawlessness? A people that will enter in through the portals of the city and have another world just as we have it here?

Christ died, not to immortalize sin, not to perpetuate transgression, but He died as the only hope for the transgressor; to make a perfect sacrifice and offering; and there was not an angel in heaven that could do that work. Not one of the angelic throng would be accepted as an offering but Jesus Christ. He that was one with the Father, and was in the express image of His person. He was full of grace and truth, and when He came to our earth He found transgression everywhere. And He found that the traditions and customs of men were taught as—what? The commandments of God. They had the truth mixed with such a mass of error that it was brought down to the very dust. He came to teach the truth in its purity and tear away the error enveloping the commandments of God. He showed the true character of the law of Jehovah.

In the sermon on the mount He showed its far-reaching claims. He presented it in a manner that the people had never heard before, for the scribes had dwelt upon technicalities. And the great principles, what are they? The first four and the last six commandments.

The lawyer asked, "What may I do that I may inherit eternal life?" What did Christ tell him? He said, "What of the law? How readest thou?" and put the burden right upon the law. The Jews had sent him to Christ hoping they could find something whereby they could catch Christ in His words. The question was put on the lawyer's lips by the scribes and the Pharisees, but, said Christ, "What saith the law and the prophets? How readest thou?" (See Luke 10:26) Thou shalt love the Lord with one-quarter of your heart? No. One-half of your soul? That is all we can expect from those who are serving Christ and mammon. Two-thirds? No. "Thou shalt love the Lord thy God with all thy heart, and with all thy soul, and with all thy mind, and with all thy strength." (Mark 12:30) All there is of us. "And thou shalt love thy neighbor as thyself." (Vers. 31)

That is for every one of you to take hold of, for it is of great consequence to us whether we are striving for the crown of immortal glory or whether we are having a form of godliness without the power. The forms, traditions, and customs of men making void, as Christ charged upon them, the commandments of God.

Have you a tradition that has come down through the ages? Have you such a tradition? Will the baptism sanctify it and make it whole, that by observing it you may save your soul from death? Will it do it? No, decidedly not. Christ says, "I am the true witness. I am Alpha and Omega, the beginning and the end, the first and the last." (See Revelation 1:8) "Blessed are they that do his commandments, that they may have right to the tree of life, and may enter in through the gates into the city." (Revelation 22:14) I want to be there. I want to see the King in His beauty. The King that died a victim on Calvary's cross for me, that I should not be found, when he comes in power and great glory to be admired of all them that believe, under the bondage of sin.

We must see in Christ a perfect representation of the law of Jehovah. He came to this earth to remove every vestige of excuse from every mortal living on the earth to deride the character of God. What is His law? An expression of His character; a transcript of His character. Jesus came that everyone that would believe in Him, everyone that would repent of their transgressions and accept of the righteousness of Christ, could come back to their loyalty; everyone upon whom the light shone.

But what if my father did not know that the seventh day was to be kept as the Sabbath? Every soul that has lived in every age is accountable for the light that has shone upon his pathway. When the light comes it tests their character and proves their loyalty. If you see that all these years you have been trampling upon the commandments running all through the Bible, then determine that you will do so no longer. It is those that obey that will be blessed of God. He says that He will bless your children and your lands and all that you lay your hand unto. Do you think that Satan is going to allow this without making a struggle for the mastery?

He is determined that he will be master. When in heaven he said, "What need have the angels of any law?" "Why hast thou fallen from heaven, O Lucifer?" Because he wanted to be equal with Christ, and when he fell he brought many of the angels with him. They took his side. The enemy is working just as sharply and decidedly now as he worked upon the minds of Adam and Eve in Eden. The people are gathering under his banner, and he is encircling them with his power. But everyone that sees that the law of God is changeless in its character will decide on the side of Christ. If God could have changed one precept of His law to meet fallen man, then Jesus Christ need never have come to our earth to die.

Did Christ die to let loose the whole of humanity to worship idols instead of God, when the commandment said, "Thou shalt worship the Lord thy God, and him only shalt thou serve."? "And the Lord made the heaven and the earth," and what then? "And rested the seventh day and sanctified it," and gave it to you to observe as God's memorial—a memorial that He is the living God that created the heavens overhead and the earth upon which we stand. (See Exodus 20) He made the lofty trees, and put the covering upon every flower. He gave to each one its tints, and the Lord of heaven made man and gave him the Sabbath. What for? For all the posterity of Adam. It was a gift to all his posterity.

If man had always obeyed the fourth commandment there never would have been an infidel in the world, because it testified that the Lord made the heaven and the earth, the sea and all that in them is; wherefore the Lord blessed the Sabbath day, and hallowed it. (See Exodus 20:11)

And because the children of Israel went down into Egypt, they lost the knowledge of God. Moses went to bring them out with a strong arm, and the Lord told Moses to say, "I am sent unto thee. Let my son go that he may serve me." (See Exodus 4:23) Afterwards he says, "Reprove them because they have not kept my Sabbath." And he brought them to Sinai, and the law of God was spoken from the Mount. There God through His son, Jesus Christ, was the Founder of the whole Jewish economy. The sacrifices typified the wonderful Antitype. Jesus Christ was to come and give His life that He might set man free from Satan's claims, that He might unlock the prison houses and bring forth those that plead for a glorious immortality. When type met Antitype in the death of Christ, what was done? What need was there for any more sacrificial offerings? Type had met antitype. No more need for any sacrificial offerings, because the great antitypical offering had been made to save every transgressor of the law if they would believe on Jesus Christ as their Saviour and return to their loyalty. Then every sin and transgression would be forgiven.

Christ in the mount proclaimed the far-reaching principles of the law of God to be carried out in every transaction of life. I worship the true and living God. His hands are over His creative works. Can you wonder that the devil wants to make void the law of God, the standard of His character? It will be the standard in the judgment when the books shall be opened, and every man judged according to the deeds that are done. And the names are written—what does He say?—"Engraven upon the palms of my hands." The marks of the crucifixion have engraven them. They are His property, and you are God's by creation and by redemption. Then we want to know whether you are giving your whole heart to Him, whether you are serving Him with all the power and strength of your intellect; for on these great principles hang all the law and the prophets. The first four commandments define man's duty to His Maker—supreme love to God; the last six define the duty of man to his fellow man. What do we give to Satan when we concede the point that the law of God needs to be taken away? We give the whole creative universe a defective God, a God that made a law and it was so defective that He had to take it away. That is all Satan wants. Can we afford to be working on any side but that of God?

Can we afford to say, My father did not keep the commandments, and I think he was right? Well, if your father lived today, and he was a Christian living according to every ray of light, when the light came that the law of God was being transgressed, he would on his knees inquire, is this so? And then he would have said, "Children, we have made a decided mistake. We have been keeping an institution that has not a single syllable for its sanctity in the Word of God. I am sorry that I have not been a man of the Bible before. I am sorry that I have not seen the precious light of truth. Now it has come to me and I am responsible for it, I do not want to be found a lawbreaker but a subject of the King. I want to hear Him say to me, 'Sit ye on my right hand.' 'Blessed are they that do his commandments, that they may have right to the tree of life, and enter in through the gates into the city.'" (See Revelation 22:14)

He will teach them the truths of the Scriptures as we have never seen them before, and it will take all eternity to understand the word that has been crowded out of the mind by false teachers. God has been made of no effect by their tradition. But He will give us increased light, and wipe all tears from our eyes.

I want to say this to you because we have all been transgressing the law of Jehovah. Live up to every ray of light that you have received. Your eternal interests are involved here, and that is why I say, "Cherish every ray of light." On your knees ask Christ to impress your heart by His Holy Spirit, and turn not away from His law.

We read that many of the priests believed on Jesus, but it stopped right there. They did not confess Him because they were afraid of being turned out of the Sanhedrin. Are there any here today who say, "Do you think that if I had lived then I would have united with those that cried 'Crucify Him'?" Well, prove it by obeying the light of today. You are not responsible for those that with hoarse voice cried out when Pilate said, "Who shall I deliver unto you?" Who do you suppose it was that led those minds to say that? It was Satan, and when men reject light, when they grieve the Spirit of God, there is somebody ready to pick them up. It is the prince of darkness in our world striving for every soul, and we do not want to file under his banner. We want to stand under the blood-stained banner of Prince

Emmanuel.

In the judgment, when we stand around the great white throne, what evidence will be presented for the law of God? The victim of Calvary's cross testifies that God could not change His law, but that He "so loved the world that he gave his only begotten Son" in order to give man another trial to see if he would keep the commandments. This will decide our destiny for eternity, because if we are obedient children here we will be obedient children there. He will not take those to heaven who have no respect for the law. He has a law to govern in heaven. But God will not force anyone to keep the commandments, because every soul is elected to be saved if they will obey the light that falls upon their pathway.

We want parents to awake from their lethargic sleep. Awake and see that at this time you must put on the beautiful robe of Christ's righteousness. "Buy of me," He says, "gold tried in the fire that thou mayest be rich, and white raiment that thou mayest be clothed." (See Revelation 3:18) What was the matter with Adam and Eve? They saw that they were naked. The covering of God was not enveloping them. God says, "Buy of me." Well, what? Buy of Me My righteousness. "Buy of me gold tried in the fire, and white raiment that thou mayest be clothed." Are you clothed with it, or are you transgressing the commandments of God by your traditions and by the maxims of men?

The righteousness of God never covers a soul all polluted with sin. John says, "Behold the Lamb of God that taketh away the sin of the world." (John 1:29) Will you let Him take it away? You cannot bear your own sin. Christ says He will take your sin if you lay hold of the merits of a crucified and risen Saviour. Christ came and suffered for our sins "that whosoever believeth on him should not perish, but have everlasting life." (John 3:16) Believe on Him as One upon whom the sins of the whole world are laid that man might have another trial. That trial we are having today. Shall it be that Christ shall not have died for us in vain? Shall we give to the world the evidence of the character of God because of our rectitude in keeping His commandments? May God help us to be loyal servants of His.

How careful we are with all our property. You are very careful to keep all the laws of the land, and to see that your deeds are made right. Be as careful that you get a deed [the following two lines have been over-typed and are not readable]. Those who have been careless regarding the law will lose heaven. We do not want to lose the place in the world that is to be purified—Abraham's farm.

You are heirs of God and joint heirs with Christ to riches that will be imperishable. Christ says, I go to prepare a place for you that where I am. There ye may be also." (See John 14:2, 3) Then we will be with Christ until the city of God comes upon the earth and we will take possession of our home. We will build houses and inhabit them, and plant vineyards and eat the fruit of them. Heaven is worth something to us. We want you to have a place in the earth made new. That is why we have been talking so plainly to you today. We want to tell every one of you who have been sinning against the law of God, Repent of your transgressions and come to Jesus for mercy, and He will abundantly pardon. He will cleanse you from every stain of sin.

You will be the happiest people while you know that you are not in conflict with the law of God, and there is a crown laid up for every one of you. We have only touched on a few points of the truth, but we want you to be doers of the Word of God, that when He comes your house will not fall because it will be founded upon a Rock. The one built upon the sands will be swept away.

May God help us to keep all His commandments, that we may cast our glittering crowns at His feet. He will forgive every one of our sins if we come to Him with contrition, and then we can sing the song of Moses in the city of God.[25]

---

[25] MR 900.10.

Chapter 26

Eternal Life

[Sermon at Prahran, a suburb of Melbourne, Victoria, Australia Sunday, 4:00 p.m., February 18, 1894]

(John 17:2, 3 quoted) Here is the greatest knowledge and the most essential for every individual to know. You may, every one of you, put forth all your efforts; you may expend money; you may go to the highest institutions of learning to obtain an education, and yet if you do not feel the necessity of being acquainted with God and Jesus Christ whom He hath sent, all the knowledge that you obtain cannot give you eternal life.

We have traveled extensively and seen many going from place to place, from east to west, to Europe and back again, and traveling over the world. What were they after? They wanted to prolong their life. We saw one poor human being suffering in distress, such distress. A large tumor on his head, increasing till it bowed his head down to his breast. He believed in Jesus, but he said, "Give me something to prolong my life." Even in suffering and distress, such a tenacious hold on life. He wanted life. We tried to talk with him about the life which measures with the life of God. We tried to talk with him about that life which runs parallel with the life of Jehovah. It is a life without sigh and without sin, a life without bereavement, without infirmities, without affliction, and with no fear of death. What a life that is! Well, here are the conditions whether you shall have that life or not: This is life eternal, to know the true and living God and Jesus Christ whom He hath sent.

Why then is the world not filled with the glory of God? Why do you not find human beings that are making it their aim and object to know God and to know Jesus Christ whom He hath sent? Why do you not see the instruction coming from parents to children? Why has it not been in past generations that the instruction has come from parents to children, and thus children have been trained and disciplined and educated so that the first lessons they shall teach their children will be lessons of God and Jesus Christ whom He hath sent? They must know this or they will never know what eternal life is.

How wicked it is for parents by precept and example to show by their conversation and practice that this world absorbs all their mind. Who gave you your mind? Why, it was God. He gave you your intellect and He gave you that mind that it should be educated, that it should be trained, that it should be disciplined. He alone can do it.

When parents give the lessons to their children from their babyhood, should it not be God and Jesus Christ whom He hath sent? And when the words of life, the lessons of Jesus Christ are familiar to their own mind, the treasures of the heart are molded by the treasures of the God of Heaven, and they are teaching their children to know God and Jesus Christ whom He hath sent. Not to know Him as children have been taught in generations back—that He is a spy upon them and that God is a stern judge. No, you do not want to teach them that. You want to weave love into your own character, and you want to bring it into the character of your children. You want true Christian courtesy in your own life, and you want to bring it into the lives of your children. You want it in the lives of your children. You want to keep before them that they are living in the sight of God, that they are living in the sight of Jesus Christ.

Cherubims and seraphims, angels and archangels, are watching the battle that is going on in this life. Between whom? The Prince of life and the power of darkness. And what does God do? He shows us how we must do, how we must conduct the battle. He left the royal courts, laid aside His royal robe, and clothed His humanity with divinity. He became a man among the sons of men, and here He walked the world as what? A representative of the love of God, an example that we may study, a character that we may imitate every phase of, that we may see that He did not live to glorify Himself, but He lived to point to God. He came to live the law of God, because Satan was bringing his power to bear upon men, and his lying fallacies were all the time pressing upon them.

You cannot keep the law. No. It is impossible for man of himself to keep the law. He cannot do it. But what can he do? Lay hold by living faith of the righteousness of Jesus Christ, and present to the Father the righteousness of Christ; and the fragrance of His character is brought into his life. Here Satan is dethroned; he is emptied out of the house, and the vacuum is supplied by the righteousness of Jesus Christ. Christ sits enthroned in the human soul. Christ never wars against Christ.

Christ says, "If ye abide in me and my words abide in you, ye shall ask what ye will and it shall be done unto you." (John 15:7) Then it is plainly expressed what His will and work are, in the fourteenth chapter of John and the twelfth verse. It is believing on Jesus Christ who is able to save you to the utmost. He came to this world to bring fallen man moral power, that he might keep the commandments of God and be a partaker in the divine nature, overcoming the corruption that is in the world through lust. It is the privilege of every one of us.

God has done so much for us in giving His only begotten Son that whosoever believeth on Him should not perish but have everlasting life. We are persons of hope. We may every one lay hold on the hope that is set before us. "He that believeth on me, the works that I do shall he do also" (John 14:12), and He says, "I kept My Father's commandments." The Pharisees said when the disciples rubbed the ears of corn as they went through the wheat fields, "He has broken the Sabbath." Could they have fastened that upon Him, then what? They would not have had to get false witnesses to speak against Him. They would have condemned Him as a Sabbath-breaker. But He said, "Ye do not know what this means, I will have mercy and not sacrifice" (See Matthew 9:13), or ye would not have condemned the guiltless.

Who dares to say that Christ is a Sabbath-breaker? He made the Sabbath Himself. He is the one that spoke the law from Sinai. He is the one who was enshrouded in the pillar of cloud, and therefore He said, "Ye are ignorant of the Scriptures and of the power of God." Why? Because they covered it all up with their maxims and traditions which had been handed down from rabbi to rabbi, and repeated and enlarged till the specifications of the law of God were buried in a mass of rubbish, and till the people were not certain that they were keeping the law, for the law is the transcript of the Father's character.

If the law could have been abolished, Christ need not have died, but He came, the only begotten Son, to die and suffer for the human family. Now He says, "Ye that believe in me the works that I do shall they do also, and greater works than these shall these do because I go to my Father; and whatsoever ye shall ask in my name that will I do, that the Father may be glorified in the Son." (See John 14:12, 13) Please tell me, if you can, why you are so weak and helpless. Why, as professing Christians, are we so mixed and mingled with the world till we lose sight of eternity, till we lose sight of Jesus Christ, and till we lose sight of the Father?

Why, I ask you, are there so many families destitute of the Spirit of God? Why are there so many families that have so little of the life and love and likeness of Jesus Christ? It is because they do not know God. If they knew God, and if they would behold Him by faith in Jesus Christ who came to our world to die for man, they would see such matchless charms in the Son that they by beholding would become changed into the same image. Now you see the wrong of conforming to the world.

We have a brief lifetime to live here, and we know not how soon the day may come when the arrow of death must strike our heart. We know not how soon the time may come when we shall have to give up the world and all interest in the world. Have we individually become acquainted with God, the governor of heaven, the law giver, and Jesus Christ whom He hath sent into the world to represent Him?

The world could not bear Him. Just three years and a half of public ministry and then they got rid of Him. The heavenly vine was taken and transplanted on the other side of the wall. There the heavenly boughs hang over this side of the wall by the Holy Spirit. The Holy Spirit was given to man and here the communication is to be kept up between heaven and earth, between God and man. The communication is to be preserved lest man be overcome of the world. Christ says, "I have overcome the world." Why? On our behalf. That you may overcome as He overcame. Then our work is to seek God with all our hearts that we may find Him.

Do not be afraid to be found on your knees acknowledging God as your Father. Acknowledge your dependence upon God. Acknowledge that you are acquainted with His power, that you want a vital connection with the God of heaven. "Well," you say, "they misinterpret me, and if I am in the world I must be of the world." No, that does not necessarily follow. Christ says, "Ye are the light of the world." (Matthew 5:14) "Let your light so shine that they may see your good works" (see Matthew 5:16), and let them see that you are turning your eyes upon heaven. But it is not the fashion, and I am so sorry that it is not the fashion.

Moses lifted up his hands toward heaven when Israel and the opposing power were in warfare. Before all Israel he stood with his hands uplifted toward heaven. As soon as they began to drop the enemy gained the victory, and every time his hands were uplifted toward heaven the forces of Israel gained the victory. So Aaron and Hur stood on each side and held his hands toward heaven as a symbol, signifying that he was laying hold of the God of heaven as they must do. They must stretch their arms toward heaven. Christ is their helper.

Here we are in a world that is unfavorable to right and truth. What shall we do? We must put our whole business into the business of serving God. "Seek ye first the kingdom of God and His righteousness; and all these things shall be added unto you." (Matthew 6:33) You have a God who says, "If ye keep my commandments I will bless you in your fields, and flocks, and herds, and vineyards, and all that you put your hand unto." The God of heaven has placed a benediction upon them that keep the commandments of God. Shall we stand as a peculiar people of God, or shall we trample upon the law of God and say it is not binding? God might just as well have abolished Himself. In the law every specification is the character of the infinite God.

What are we to do? Study the Scriptures. Search the Scriptures. See whether you are obeying the law of God and the standard of his righteousness. Tell your children that you have disregarded the law of God. Tell them you feel as Ezra did. Here was Josiah, so sorry to think that the law had been lost, and that they had been careless and heedless of it. They bring it before him. There stands up one that reads it, and the people weep and mourn because they have not kept the law. But rejoice that you have the law now. We will keep it. Bring your offerings and gifts, and offer praise to God with your tears and mourning. That is just what we want to do.

If the light of the law of God comes to us and we see intelligently that we have been transgressing it, we can say, "Now I understand how it is that we have been in darkness and uncertainty. Now we will lay right hold of the commandments of God and we will keep them and live, 'for the law of the Lord is perfect, converting the soul.'" Why should God abolish a perfect thing? We want to use our intelligence to a purpose, and send back joy and rejoicing that you have found out that you were not loyal servants of the Lord of heaven, but that you would be. You would not have it go up to the judgment that you were transgressing the law of God, and putting Christ to an open shame before the world. Thinking good but not practicing will not answer.

We want Christ and His obedience and we want to drink in of the Spirit of God. I want to be like Him. I want to practice His virtues and be a doer of the Word. And what did He say on the Mount? "Think not"—on their startled ears fell the words, their very thoughts unrolled before them—"think not that I am come to destroy the law of the prophets: I am not come to destroy, but to fulfill." (Matthew 5:17) He came to fulfill every specification of the law. "Till heaven and earth pass, one jot or one tittle shall in no wise pass from the law, till all be fulfilled." (Vers. 18) I want you to take this. It is the word of God. You will hear from the word of men that the law is abolished and that it is not binding upon men. And they act just so. But you cannot afford to work against God. "Ye are laborers together with God." (1 Corinthians 3:9) I would rather be a laborer with God than to be laboring counter to Him. I see in Him matchless charms.

"But," you say, "the law cannot save anybody." No, we are free through Christ, living in obedience to the law, through the merits and righteousness and virtues of His character. And when we lay hold of Him by living faith, what shall we do? Keep the commandments of God and His law as the apple of your eye. These are the words of inspiration, "Keep them and live." You do not have anyone touch that part of your eye. You know how painful it is.

Do you want to know just what to do? Say, "I rejoice that I have found out how defective I am, and I am going to overcome sin and be a victor; for He says," To him that overcometh will I grant to sit with me in my throne, even as I also overcame, and am set down with my Father in his throne." (Revelation 3:21) Will you overcome as Christ overcame? Shall we have the victory? Jesus Christ is our Saviour.

We have a great work to do. Not to tell them that there is no law. No law to govern heavenly and human intelligences? Whoever picks that up is in Satan's army and you cannot afford to be there. I beseech you to seek the Lord with all your heart that you may find Him to be precious to your soul. Jesus died that you might have salvation, that you might go on, not linking hands with the world, not that you might know more and more of the world, but that you might know God and Jesus Christ whom He hath sent.

The law cannot save you, but it is the standard of character, and to represent the character of Jesus Christ you must live the law, for He lived the law in our world. Paul says, "I have taught them from house to house, repentance toward God and faith toward our Lord Jesus Christ." (See Acts 20:20, 21) This is the way. We behold Him for the perfection of His character and then we see the defects in our own character. Do you stand before God and say, "Cleanse us and change us"? You should flee to Jesus Christ and lay hold of the divine merits of the Son of God, and then you are washed from the defilements and stains of sin. There is not a stain in the character because God is enthroned in the heart and Christ does not war against Christ. Christ does not war against the Father. "I and the Father are one." He was in the express image of the Father's person, and we want to express the character of Jesus Christ.

We must claim His sufficiency. Christ has died for us. Satan says, "You are a sinner and cannot make yourself any better." Yes, I am a sinner, and I need a Saviour, and I lay hold of the merits of Jesus Christ to save me from all transgression. We wash in the fountain that has been prepared for us, and we are cleansed from all the defilement of sin.

There is a matchless loveliness in Jesus Christ. I love Him because He first loved me. We want the purity that there is in Jesus Christ, and He will save to the utmost all who come to Him. Then you see what Christ suffered for us. Are we willing to be partakers of His sufferings? He says if we are we will be partakers of His glory.

How much have you suffered for Christ's sake? Are you willing to be partakers with Him in His suffering? If you are, He will cooperate with you and you can cooperate with the heavenly intelligences to bring the lost sheep back to the fold. There are souls that are perishing out of Christ, and what we want is to bring God's lost sheep back to Christ. May God help us to know what we must do. Christ loves us because we are helpless and dependent.

We are lost without Christ, but God has given us something to bring us back to our loyalty. We want the deep moving of the Spirit of God on our hearts. We want to walk in the light as God is in the light and then we shall not walk in darkness. We shall have songs of praise and rejoicing, for we can tell the story of the love of Jesus toward man. He died on Calvary that we should not perish in our sin. Then cease from evil and follow on to know the Lord. Oh, the light and love and preciousness that there is in Jesus Christ! He will encircle us in the arms of His mercy and He will love us freely.

God grant that we may seek the perishing and bring them back to the fold of God. We want to see sinners converted, and we want to seek to expel sin from the world. God will deliver us and we may represent the character of Jesus Christ who died for the sins of the whole world. Let us, everyone, learn of Jesus. Take His yoke. Love Him because He first loved you, and we shall have a most precious victory by and by. He will open the gates of the city of God and bid us come in. He will welcome us and give us a heavenly benediction. To all who have tested their obedience that they will obey the law of God, He says, "Well done thou good and faithful servant, enter thou into the joy of thy Lord." What is that joy? The joy of seeing sinners converted. They will be brought to Jesus Christ and this is His joy. We have been partakers with Jesus Christ. "Laborers together with God." And thus we see that we can indeed be partakers of His glory, which shall be given to every faithful child of God.

Let us take the robe of His righteousness woven in the loom of heaven. There is not a thread of humanity in that robe. It is the robe of Christ's righteousness. Let us put it on right here. We want life. We want to give the example of what Christ is and what we may be. Oh, that we might manifest God to a fallen world. We may be purified so that we may wear the robe of Christ's righteousness, and the crown of immortality. God grant that this may be our lot; for Jesus loves us with a love that is infinite. He does not want that one of us should perish, but that everyone may have that life that measures with the life of God. God grant that we may secure that blessed inheritance.[26]

---

[26] Ms. 12, 1894; MR 900.11.

Chapter 27

Seeking Heavenly Treasures

[Sermon Sunday afternoon, October 28, 1894, Campground, Ashfield, N.S.W.]

[My text is] Matthew, sixth chapter, commencing at the nineteenth verse: "Lay not up for yourselves treasures upon earth, where moth and rust doth corrupt, and where thieves break through and steal: but lay up for yourselves treasures in heaven, where neither moth nor rust doth corrupt, and where thieves do not break through nor steal: for where your treasure is, there will your heart be also."

Now, this is a very important matter to us. Who is the speaker? It is Jesus Christ. Who is He? The only begotten Son of God. Who is He? Our Saviour; One who left the royal courts of heaven, laid aside His high command in heaven, and clothed His divinity with humanity. He came to our world that humanity might touch humanity, that His long, human arm might encircle the race while His divine arm grasps the throne of the Infinite.

For our sakes He became poor, that we through His poverty might become rich. What kind of riches? It was not the riches of this earth, but it was the eternal riches, the knowledge of God communicated through Jesus Christ. He consents to become man's substitute and surety; He engages to bear the penalty of the debt which man had incurred by transgression. It is He that loved us, and so loved us that He offered His life as a living sacrifice to bear the sins of a guilty world, that man should have a second probation, that man should be tested and proved and tried to see whether he will stand under the blood-stained banner of Prince Emmanuel or whether he will choose to stand under the banner of the prince of darkness.

Has He not an interest in His purchased possession? Is He not intensely interested that the people for whom He has suffered so much should be successfully carried through the warfares and conflicts of this life, that they may have that immortal inheritance that He has given His life to purchase for the human family? Then has He not a right to speak in warnings, in instruction? What weight do these words of the Son of the infinite God have with the human family? He tells you that which is for your present and eternal good.

"Lay not up for yourselves treasures upon earth, where moth and rust doth corrupt, and where thieves break through and steal: but lay up for yourselves"—you are working for yourselves, cooperating with God who has laid out the plan whereby you can work successfully through His grace for yourselves, to secure your own eternal happiness in the kingdom of glory. "Lay up for yourselves treasures in heaven, where neither moth nor rust doth corrupt, and where thieves do not break through nor steal: for where your treasure is, there will your heart be also."

Christ has bought our hearts. Christ has bought the human intelligence. Christ has bought the reasoning powers; and Christ has entrusted us with capabilities and with powers. He does not want that we should let these powers and capabilities be employed merely in the common things of earthly substance, and lose sight of the eternal. (See 1 Corinthians 6:19, 20) He came to our world when Satan appeared to have the human race under his control.

The Lord Jesus made our world. Everything was made by Christ. Here Christ through God created our world, and He engaged before the foundation of the world that if man that was created and in Eden should transgress the law of God, He would take the penalty of their transgression upon Himself. And He did this. Then has He no right to instruct His subjects what to do, that they shall not miss the eternal reward?

Who, I ask you of this congregation, will absorb brain, bone, and muscle for the acquisition of merely temporal advantages? Christ gave His life that we might not perish. "For God so loved the world, that He gave His only begotten Son, that whosoever believeth in Him should not perish, but have everlasting life."

Our precious Saviour has made the world, and when He came into the world He found the great usurper there, and He came into the world that He might contest with him the possession of this earth. Therefore the battle, the conflict, was carried on right here in this world, and here He tells us that it is for our eternal interest to lay up for ourselves a treasure in the heavens. You ask, How can I do it? In Christ. When the Householder went away from His house, He gave to every man talents, to some five, to some two, and to another one. And these talents He gave them direction to employ in His service, He gave to some the property of means, to others ability, intellect—all God's gifts. We could not have any of it unless it came through Jesus Christ.

Then He tells you to use these talents to His glory. Improve them. How shall we improve them? As God gives me light, as God gives you light, as He has given you His precious Word. It is full of hidden treasures. He wants you to explore, work the field, and you will find the treasures, and you will sell everything that you might buy the field that contains the treasure. There are the jewels of truth that are to be searched for as hidden treasures.

As you find them, what then? Why, you find that there is truth, beautiful truth, jewels of truth, riches of truth, and you accept them. What do they do? They bind you by the golden links to the eternal God, for Jesus Christ came that He might link finite man with the infinite God, and connect earth that has been divorced by sin and transgression from heaven. What riches, what treasures, what love, are here revealed! It is impossible, yes, it is impossible, to conceive of the love of God that is bestowed upon fallen humanity. Well, He tells you, "Lay up for yourselves treasures in heaven. "Will you do it? "Ye are," says Jesus, "the light of the world"—if you become rich in heavenly treasure, in the knowledge of the true God. You are to search for it, search that Book, the Word of God, and then you are to diffuse to others the knowledge that you have obtained. Impart the heavenly gift.

"Oh," says one "I must attend to my farm; I must attend to the interests of my family. I cannot afford to be here, giving my interest and time and money in order that I may win souls to Jesus Christ." Well, this shows that you do not appreciate the heavenly Gift. It shows that you do not appreciate and value the human families that Christ has estimated of such cost that He came into the world to suffer and become a man of sorrows and acquainted with grief. [He was] wounded for our transgressions, bruised for our iniquities, the chastisement of our peace was upon Him, and with His stripes we are healed.

Only think of it! No one could bear the stroke of God's justice but His only beloved Son. He came in the express image of His Father's person, one with God. He thought it not robbery to be equal with God. The plan is laid out. You are not to occupy brain, bone, and muscle to the acquisition of the things of this life, and invest not in the treasures of heaven. He wants all that there is of man. He wants the whole heart.

The question is asked by the lawyer that came to Christ, "What shall I do to inherit eternal life?"—this very inheritance that He had been presenting to him. Well now, there stood the frowning Pharisees; there stood the rabbis; there stood the priests and the rulers of the synagogue, and they hoped to catch something from the answer that they could use, that they might condemn Christ, the world's Redeemer, the mighty Healer, the greatest Teacher that the world ever knew. Christ read their heart and their purposes, and what did He do? He turned back upon the lawyer himself the labor of answering that question. He said, "What is written in the law? How readest thou? And he answering said, Thou shalt love the

Lord thy God with"-nine tenths of your heart? Two-thirds? One-half? One quarter?—"thou shalt love the Lord thy God with all thy heart, and with all thy soul, and with all thy strength, and with all thy mind." (Luke 10:25-27) This takes intellect; this takes reason; this takes education, ability; and it takes all there is of man.

But just as soon as some enter college and get a little bit of knowledge they think they know more than God. And you hear of the higher critics. Who is the Higher Critic? It is the Lord God of the universe, who has spread the canopy of the heavens above us, and has made the stars and called them forth in their order; that has created the lesser light, the glory of the moon, to come in its order and to shine in our world. And the higher critics come in. Who are they? Poor, finite man on probation to see if he will be loyal and true to God that he can stand under the blood-stained banner of Prince Emmanuel, and that he can become a child of God and an heir of heaven. Talk of the critics, the higher critics. We have God; we have his Word in its simplicity.

Jesus might have opened to the world door after door of the mysteries of science, and gratified the inquisitive mind; but did He do it? He had one object before Him, as we should have in following His example. It is to bring to the human family the divine knowledge of the Christ of God, to teach them how they may save their souls, and that they may have that life that measures with the life of God.

The salvation of man was to Him everything. He takes the world by the hand, and He places it in its proper position, subordinate, while He brings eternity that has been lost from their reckoning, in view. He leads you to behold the threshold of heaven flooded with divine glory, flushed with the glory from the throne of God, and He tells you it is for you. He tells you to strive for that inheritance that poverty cannot strip from you. He tells you to seek for that kingdom that hath foundations, that city whose builder and maker is God. That is the eternal treasure; that is the immortal inheritance. I want it.

I long for it; yes, and I am willing to spend to the last that which I shall accumulate, that I may recover souls that are ready to perish. All the value there is in money to me is to invest it in the treasures of God, that He may have meat in His house, that when missionaries are called to lift the standard in the places that know not God He shall not find an empty treasury because men spend God's money for liquor and tobacco—ten, twenty, a thousand times more in eating and in drinking these things that are taking the underpinning out from their house, which are obliterating the image of God in man, which are creating disease and infirmity and imbecility, and shortening the existence of men years, that they might [not] use their God-given life to the glory of God. Why, it is God's money. He has seen fit in His providence to open the way before me that I could have a little of His money to use for His treasury, and to carry the truth to the people that are ready to perish.

He wants us to do what? "We are laborers together with God; ye are God's husbandry, ye are God's building." (1 Corinthians 3:9) And that is what we are in the world for—not to eat and to drink and to attend horse races, and to use the holidays in idling and in gratifying self; and if we have a shilling, get on the cars and go somewhere to have a good time. There are souls to be saved. There are youth to be educated by our precept and example. The Lord is coming. The end of all things is at hand, and it is time now, as the end of all things is at hand, that we commence the work for youth; that we begin to see what we can do to gather souls to Jesus Christ. There is poverty around us; there is distress; there are the naked to clothe, the hungry to feed; and those that are thirsting for the water of life and hungering for the bread of salvation, we want to give it to them.

I will read a little farther. "The light of the body is the eye: if therefore thine eye be single [your discernment is of that character that it is single], thy whole body shall be full of light." (Matthew 6:22) Do you think you will find men that are smoking tobacco, introducing a poison into their system, when nature makes the most tremendous effort to expel the intruder that it almost dies in the conflict, and if that was the terms of eternal life you would think it was a very hard condition. But it is not, thank God.

But who has instituted this? It is the devil that wants the brains of man. He wants to cobweb your faculties and your thinking forces, and he wants to send disease between the fluids and the solids of your body, that you shall not have health, and that you shall be in the slavery of a perverted appetite, an appetite which has no foundation in nature and the most difficult to break from because the enemy has woven his threads all about you to bind you to the habits which will ruin both soul and body.

Not an unclean thing is to enter the kingdom of God. I want you to think of this; and those that benumb their senses, paralyzing their reasoning by intoxicating drinks, I want you to consider they have sold their reason to the devil, and he takes possession of them soul and body; and you know what he does with them; you know that it is the attributes of Satan that walk right out in these men. Shall we make an attempt to save men? Shall we educate our children from their very babyhood to self-control? Shall we teach them the blessed, precious name of Jesus? Shall we sing to them the heavenly songs? Shall we teach them to imitate the graces of Jesus Christ?

I was riding with an Englishman, and we were in Texas. My husband was then living. We were laboring there in Texas; and [this Englishman] was smoking his pipe. My husband said, "What do you think, friend, did Christ give you an example of using your pipe? Did He lay down this example for you?"

"Oh," he groaned, "I never regarded it in that light. No, no," said he, "I throw this pipe away; I will never touch it again. To think of the Redeemer of the world going through the streets smoking a pipe, making a chimney of His nose! No, I never could do that again." It seemed his sensibilities were shocked. But here, see, the devil had invented it. What for? To consume money so that the poor should not be clothed; so that the needy and the distressed might suffer for the want of food and care and house; so that the gospel should not be carried to all parts of our world.

Well, here is God's money. How much better to say, Here I see that man eating his house in liquor, eating the very substance which should go to his family, in smoking. Now you are taking this portion which my brother uses, or my brethren, and you are putting it into God's treasury. And then there is a meetinghouse to be built; here is a church to be organized; here is a company sending the Macedonian cry, "Come over and help us." In our cities you could send scores of laborers and support them in the field if man would only sacrifice the idol of tobacco.

Professed Christians stand off in their slavery and say, I can't overcome it. No, I cannot, but through Jesus Christ you can overcome; through the merits of the blood of Christ you can sweep away this deadly evil which is corrupting our earth and corrupting our youth. And parents are giving their appetites and passions as an inheritance to their children; and they are weaker in moral power than they themselves are to resist the contaminating influence that is upon our earth.

What account will fathers have to give in the judgment? What account for the habits of liquor drinking? What accounts for the habit of tobacco using, the money consumed in lessening physical, mental, and moral power that belongs to God? All of it has been purchased by an infinite price, the price of the Son of God. You do not realize the necessity of sending light to those that are in darkness because your eye is not single to the glory of God. Your whole body is full of darkness, and you treat yourself as a slave, a slave to grant to taste and appetite that which is unwholesome and unhealthy, and which is destroying vitality.

"But if thine eye be evil, thy whole body shall be full of darkness. If therefore the light that is in thee be darkness"—if you are not observing the truth of God's Word above everything in the earth, and if you are not investing the talents that He has given you, put them out to the exchangers. Let light shine forth from you. The Master is going to require an account of you, and your whole body is full of darkness. You consume means on your body that ought to be given to the treasury of God, and you stand forth in your God-purchased nobility of character that is standing in the sight of God, written in the books of heaven as a man—a man that will overcome every pernicious habit and every pernicious practice. Now He says, "How great is that darkness."

No man can serve two masters. If tobacco is your master, if it has brought all your forces under the control of the pernicious appetite, it is your master and you are its slave. How then can you serve your tobacco and your God, sending up the fumes of tobacco before you go into the prayer meeting so that your mind is so confused that you do not know what you are about? Why? Because the stimulant of tobacco and the stimulant of the Holy Spirit of God never combine to give meaning to inspiration in the meeting that you may give the testimony clear from the courts of heaven that God wants you to give.

"Ye are my witnesses," says God, and God wants us by precept and example to represent Christ in our world. He represented the Father, and He left the work in our hands to attend to the needy and the distressed, and to have something to help them that they may have the blessing of relief, the necessities of suffering humanity. But if we use it up unwisely, imprudently, He will say, "Thou wicked and slothful servant, why did not you take My talent, why did you not put it out to the exchangers? Why did not you use My gift that you could double it for My service?" God wants us to win souls for Him; and then what? You are to begin to work with the talent which God has lent you, and then [use] every gift there is to the praise of heaven.

Oh, I am so thankful for a Saviour! I am so thankful for One that is mighty in power, that will help in every emergency. "Lo," He says, "I am with you always, even unto the end of the world." Well now, if we have Christ at our right hand to help us—how much can He help that man that is so devoted to the smoking of his pipe that he can think of nothing else? God help us to cleanse the soul temple of its impurity. God help us that we may give to God an offering that is untainted physically, mentally, and morally. Well, "no man can serve two masters: for either he will hate the one, and love the other; or else he will hold to the one, and despise the other. Ye cannot serve God and mammon." You see, the problem is weighed with God, and He tells the result. He requires all there is of you.

When the lawyer asked a decided question, Christ let him answer that; and what does Christ say after He had declared, "Thou shalt love the Lord thy God with all thy heart, and with all thy soul, and with all thy strength, and with all thy mind"? He added, "And thy neighbor as thyself." Here is [summarized] the first four commandments, which reveal the duty of man to his God. Here he must give supreme worship to God; and the next is to love his neighbor as himself. Who keeps the commandments? Who keeps them? Oh, that God would help us to see how many of us are commandment breakers, and are robbing God of the gifts, the precious gifts He has given us!

Jesus came to bring moral power to man that he might overcome every sin, that he might become conqueror through Christ. Man cannot do it of himself, but Jesus brings moral power to combine with man's human effort, that man may stand victor, on vantage ground with God. May the Lord help us that we may possess that grace and divine power, [and] be partakers of the divine nature, that we may overcome the corruption that is in the world through lust.

"Therefore I say unto you, Take no thought for your life, what ye shall eat, or what ye shall drink; nor yet for your body, what ye shall put on. Is not the life more than meat, and the body than raiment?" (Matthew 6:25) Should we not educate and train our children that to preserve health, to preserve themselves with a sound mind in a sound body, is of more consequence than the gratification of adornment, or the gratification of such a variety of food and such endless preparations for the table, the spices, the pickles, the condiments, the wine, the beer drinking, and the desserts? I want to know what is the necessity of all these things?

The cook has no time to read her Bible. You say, I hire the cook. And has not the cook any soul as well as you? The cook has a soul to save, and you want to educate and train that cook to seek God in the morning, to seek Him at night, and to live so she can have a chance to read her Bible. With all the wonderful preparations for man's appetite and taste and passions for the varieties of his life, people rob God of His service. They have no time to go to their neighbors and to teach them right in the shadow of their own doors how they may love Jesus and how Jesus loves them.

This is what we are in the world for—on trial to see if we will be fit for the courts above, to see if God can honor us to become one of the heavenly family in the kingdom of glory. If we are so selfish here that we have no interest for one another to make them obedient, and to bless them with the good things that He has provided for us in this life, how will we manifest anything like unselfishness in the kingdom of glory? How will we do it? We would be wanting to snatch the crown from another's head because it is more brilliant than ours. Another would become jealous, and we should have as bad a time as when Satan set up that work in heaven of rebellion against God.

Therefore the Lord has given man a probation, and we will work out our characters as the artist takes [an image] upon the polished plate. As he takes the features of the one that wants his picture produced, the God of heaven is taking the character of every human soul of us. That character is going up to heaven, and it is produced there; it is recorded there in the book what traits of character we manifest. If we manifest the attributes of Satan, it is that character that can find no place in the heavenly courts above.

Well then, how shall we occupy our time here? As pilgrims and strangers. You have a home. Thank God for that. There are many who have none. Make that home just as pleasant, just as nice as you can, but not extravagant. You can make things very nice and very tasteful with few things. By exercising taste you can make a beautiful home. Then will you sit down and enjoy it? Here are youth who have no home. Here are orphans with no father or mother, without a home. Here is the example of horse racing and holidays, and the tobacco devotees, and the world is full of excitement and corrupting influences that are making the people as the inhabitants of the earth before the flood, whom God swept away by the waters of the flood, and as Sodom that fire came from heaven and consumed.

Now, there is work for every one to do. God calls for the talents that He has lent you, and He wants you, in the place of devoting money and time for expensive dress and for expensive adornments and for expensive houses merely for visitors, to do something different from that. They come in and you show them all about the little things that you have to take their attention. [You are] professed Christians, but never speak of Jesus; and God says to you, What saw they in thine house?

Did they see you imparting the light and knowledge of Him? Did they see you bring up your children in the nurture and admonition of God? Did they see you preparing those little ones for the crown of immortal glory? Will you place their hands in the hands of Jesus Christ? Will you educate them to meet the standard of the world, to do as the world does, to practice the maxims [of], and to follow the fashions of, this degenerate age, which are ever changing, and its mouth is always swallowing money, money, money? The poor are suffering for food, and there are youth that you could educate and train.

Our houses should be made pleasant to our children. Remove the drapery that would shut out the sunlight and the pure air of heaven lest they tarnish the beautiful pictures and the carpets. Let them tarnish them. Had they not better tarnish these than have the children obtain a street education, and imbibe the appetites and the passions of this degenerate age, which tarnish the soul and may produce a scar which can never be effaced?

Here are the human beings. The probabilities and the possibilities are before them of working out a character for the future, immortal life, so that the Lord can say, "Well done, thou good and faithful servant: thou hast been faithful over a few things, I will make thee ruler over many things." (Matthew 25:21) Oh, will not that fall on the ear like the sweetest music? "I was hungry, and ye fed me; I was sick and in prison, and ye visited me; I was naked, and ye clothed me."

Jesus was abiding in the heart and in the mind. They were serving Him so perfectly that they have no idea that they have done anything wonderful. They don't know what they have done. "Inasmuch," said Jesus Christ," as ye have done it unto one of the least of these My brethren, ye have done it unto Me." I want the tobacco devotees to reckon up every week how much they devote to their idol-god tobacco. I want the liquor drinkers to reckon up what they spend for wine, brandy, and strong drinks, and then see the sum you might expend on God's purchased possession.

Jesus gave His life that these precious souls might have eternal life. "We are laborers together with God." What sacrifice will you make? What self-denial will you practice? It may be self-denial for a time, but in the end it is the greatest blessing to soul, body, and spirit that you can experience. We have a duty to humanity. We are bound before God, if we possess eternal life, to show that we appreciate the value of the sacrifice which Christ has made, and that is to purchase heaven, that we may glorify His name upon the earth, and that we may win souls to the cross of Calvary, that we may win souls to teach them how to give their hearts to Jesus Christ, that we may represent Jesus Christ as Jesus Christ represented the love of the Father. This is our business in the world.

We are not here to please ourselves. And then our families, our children—don't say to them as I have heard many mothers say, "There is no room for you in the parlor. Don't sit on that sofa that is covered with satin damask. We don't want you to sit down on that sofa." And when they go into another room, "We don't want your noise here." And they go into the kitchen, and the cook says, "I cannot be bothered with you here. Go out from here with your noise; you pester me so, and bother me." Where do they go to receive their education? Into the street.

Fathers and mothers, you have an awful responsibility lying at your door. What has made the drunkards? They are made at home. It is the neglect of teaching the children the commandments of God when they rise up and when they sit down, when they go out and when they come in.

What are the commandments of God? They are the ten holy precepts, the royal law, the holy law of God, which is the standard of character, which every soul present must meet in the judgment, notwithstanding it may be proclaimed from the pulpits of the day that God has no law. Now who believes it?

Every nation has a law; but the God of heaven has given us His law to represent His character, and there it stands. There is not one of the precepts done away. They stand immutable and eternal. "The law of the Lord is perfect, converting the soul." Why should anyone want to change a perfect thing? You cannot get anything more than perfect, and the law of the Lord is for us to respect and reverence and obey.

And if the inhabitants of the world had obeyed the law of God instead of hearing reiterated from the pulpits that God has no law, that God has no commandments; and if the parents should educate their children as Christ enshrouded in the billowy cloud gave the direction to Moses to give to Israel, we should not hear of the thefts, the robberies, the murders, and our jails be filled, the prisons filled with criminals because of the crime and wickedness that prevails in our world to such a fearful extent. Now we would say, Let us love God and keep His commandments, for this is the whole duty of man.

Well, I will read a little farther. I want to take up some other points, but we shall have to leave them for another discourse. A few thoughts more, and I will close.

"Which of you by taking thought can add one cubit unto his stature?" Now just as though God that places you in this world could not carry you through this world. If you are diligent, if you are patient, if you try, if you do what is fitted for you to do, and are colaborers with God, He says, "Which of you by taking thought can add one cubit unto his stature?" God works for you all the time. God Himself is taking care of you. "And why take ye thought for raiment? Consider the lilies of the field, how they grow; they toil not, neither do they spin: and yet I say unto you, That even Solomon in all his glory [could not be compared with one of these] was not arrayed like one of these."

He has been telling about raiment. Now, that God that puts the tints and the color upon all these things, can He not provide for us suitable clothing and comfortable clothing, neat and warm clothing? We need not practice extravagance. There are other ways for our clothing than that. Now He says, "Solomon in all his glory was not arrayed like one of these. Wherefore, if God so clothe the grass of the field, which today is, and tomorrow is cast into the oven, shall He not much more clothe you, O ye of little faith?" Well now, why not trust Him who made the beautiful lilies of the valley?

In America we have the fresh water lilies. These beautiful lilies come up pure, spotless, perfect, without a single mar. They come up through a mass of debris. I said to my son, "I want you to make an effort to get me the stem of that lily as near the root as possible. I want you to understand something about it."

He drew up a handful of lilies, and I looked at them. They were all full of open channels, and the stems were gathering the properties from the pure sands beneath, and these were being developed into the pure and spotless lily. It refused all the debris. It refused every unsightly thing, but there it was developed in its purity.

Now, this is exactly the way that we are to educate our youth in this world. Let their minds and hearts be instructed who God is, who Jesus Christ is, and the sacrifice that He has made in our behalf. Let them draw the purity, the virtue, the grace, the courtesy, the love, the forbearance; let them draw it from the Source of all power.

When God gave Jesus, He gave us all the riches and treasures of heaven in one gift, and He says, Impart these riches to everyone that needs them. Then let us come and ask Him. Ask, and ye shall receive. Teach your children to pray from their very babyhood; teach them to lift their little voices to God in prayer. He is their Maker; He is the One that can make their hearts happy; He is One that can give them contentment; He is One that can give them virtue; He can reshape even the tendencies that have been transmitted to them by unwise parents.

God help us to feel the weight of our responsibility. Take the youth, if you have none of your own, adopt them. I had children of my own, but I did not stop there. I was traveling nearly all over the world, and yet I gathered into my house—"I have a house," I said, "and children shall come in and enjoy it." And I adopted child after child, and I brought some of them up to womanhood and manhood, and God has helped me in the work. When I could gain a victory (when children laid down the stubbornness of their natural tempers) not by beating them, I tried a better plan—to gain their confidence—and then I could do anything with them; and God has helped me in the work. No soul that I have taken in to train and educate has made me regret it. They have given their hearts to Jesus, and we have tried to point them to the Lamb of God that taketh away the sin of the world.

I love Jesus. I love those that are found in His image, and I want to do everything in my power to help them. Next month I shall enter upon my sixty-seventh birthday, and yet I expect to issue many books yet; I expect to bear my testimony in other countries besides this, and, God helping me, I shall seek to let the light shine for others that they may see the way that they can enter the strait gate, and have eternal life. May God help us to help our children. God help us to help our neighbors. God help us in the church to let more light shine nigh and afar off to go into the byways and the highways and point souls to Jesus Christ, and show them how they can believe in God, and have His righteousness imputed to them by taking Jesus Christ as their personal Saviour.

And now I would say to every one of you, if I have introduced into this little address any ideas that you will work upon, I shall feel that I am abundantly paid; and if I have helped to point the eye to Jesus Christ, I will praise Him for that. You want to educate your children to praise God. You want to educate them to bring their little offerings to God. You want to educate them not to make themselves a center and a core, and all the gifts of the parents be lavished upon the children. God's cause calls for money. God's cause calls for means that you may carry the light into the regions that are beyond. And then I beg of you, for Christ's sake, to let the treasury be supplied that God may have meat in His house.[27]

---

[27] Manuscript 43a, 1894; MR 900.42.

Chapter 28

"Walk in the Spirit"

"If we live in the Spirit, let us also walk in the Spirit. Let us not be desirous of vain glory, provoking one another, envying one another." (Galatians 5:26)

Many are deceiving their own souls, because that while they assent to the truth they fail to become sanctified through the truth. To have a right religious experience it is essential not only to have an intelligent idea as to what is the theory of truth, but the heart and mind must be trained, and the habits must be in harmony with the expressed will of God. The Word, the requirements of God, must be studied; for if we weave into our experience incorrect principles, we shall cherish false ideas as to what constitutes a Christian, and shall not be found obeying the voice of God. We cannot spiritually discern the character of God, or accept of Jesus Christ by faith, unless our life and character are marked by purity, by the casting down of imaginations and of every high thing that exalts itself against the knowledge of God, and bring into captivity every thought to the obedience of Christ.

It is sin that has dragged down and degraded the faculties of the soul; but through faith in Jesus Christ as our Redeemer we may be restored to holiness and truth. All who would learn of Christ must be emptied of human wisdom. The soul must be cleansed from all vanity and pride, and vacated by all that has held it in prepossession, and Christ must be enthroned in the heart. The constant strife in the soul that results from selfishness and self-sufficiency must be rebuked, and humility and meekness must take the place of our natural self-esteem.

I am pained beyond measure when I see men and women professing the name of Christ yet manifesting not the spirit of Christ, for I know that they are dwelling in fatal delusion. Many are satisfied with a mere semblance of religion, and they have no experimental knowledge of the virtues of Christ, no vital connection with Jesus. They listen to the most searching presentation of truth, but make no application of the truth to their own souls, because they are clothed with a garment of self-righteousness. Every salutary impression is warded off with the thought that they are Christians, and that the close, searching appeals are not meant for them.

The most solemn message from the great Teacher through His delegated servants is lost upon them, because they do not see the need of any such warning or appeal. They have not come to the point of realizing that they are sick and in need of a physician. Christ said, "They that are whole need not a physician, but they that are sick."

Solemn conviction of sin will lead individuals to tremble at the word of God, and surrender their ways, their ideas, and their will to God. I tremble when I see so many who feel perfectly contented. They will admit that they have little experience in religious things, and when given an opportunity to gain an experience they do not advance, because they do not feel their need; and so the matter ends where it began, for they do not seek divine enlightenment with true contrition of soul.

It is only at the altar of God that we kindle the taper with holy fire. It is only the divine light that will reveal the littleness, the incompetence, of human ability, and give clear, distinct views of the perfection and purity of Jesus Christ. It is only as we view His righteousness that we hunger and thirst to possess it, and ask in earnest prayer, in humility and simplicity, as a little child asks an earthly parent for some good thing, that God will grant unto us our heart's desire. Such prayer is heard and answered. The Lord is more willing to give the Holy Spirit to them that earnestly desire it than are earthly parents to give good gifts to their children. Christ has promised the Holy Spirit to guide us into all truth and righteousness and holiness. The Holy Spirit is not given by measure to those who earnestly seek for it, who by faith stand upon the promises of God. They plead the pledged word of God, saying, "Thou hast said it. I take Thee at Thy word."

The Comforter is given that He may take of the things of Christ and show them unto us, that He may present in their rich assurance the words that fell from His lips, and convey them with living power to the soul who is obedient, who is emptied of self. It is then that the soul receives the image and superscription of the divine. Then Jesus Christ is formed within, the hope of glory.

"Take heed therefore unto yourselves, and to all the flock, over the which the Holy Ghost hath made you overseers, to feed the church of God, which He hath purchased with His own blood." (Acts 20:28) Those who are called to be shepherds of the flock of God are called to be laborers together with God. The Lord Jesus is the great Worker, and He prayed to His Father that His followers might be sanctified through the truth. If we are doers of the word of God, we shall understand that we cannot retain any sinful habit, or indulge in any crooked or guileful way. His truth, His word, must be brought with divine power into our hearts, and we must purify our hearts by obeying the truth. We must renounce all the hidden things of dishonesty, all craftiness and satanic wiles. We must be where we shall be enabled to discern the snares of him who lieth in wait to deceive. Sin must be sensed in its true, hateful character, and expelled from the soul.

All who preach the word in verity and truth can afford to be fair in its presentation. We are not to be deceitful in any way, not handling the word of God deceitfully. We are to let the cross of Christ stand in prominence in all our teaching. We are not to hide the gospel, or cover the cross of Christ with ornamental roses, and thus make the preaching of it of no effect. Let no one shun the cross of self-denial.

Make the instruction plain as to what it means to be a Christian. "If any man will come after Me," said Jesus, "let him deny himself, and take up his cross daily, and follow Me." "He that eateth My flesh, and drinketh My blood, dwelleth in Me, and I in him." Food is the substance of which we partake that our bodies may be strengthened and built up. In like manner we are to feed upon that which will build up spiritual nature. Jesus said, "It is the spirit that quickeneth; the flesh profiteth nothing: the words that I speak unto you, they are spirit, and they are life."

Our bodies are composed of that upon which we feed, so our spiritual life will be composed of that upon which we feed. If we feed on Christ by thinking of Him, by obeying His words, we are built up in Him, and grow in grace and in the knowledge of the truth unto the full stature of men and women in Christ Jesus. "Receiving a kingdom which cannot be moved, let us have grace, whereby we may serve God acceptably with reverence and godly fear."

As God works in us to will, we are to cooperate with God, manifesting a determination like that of Daniel to do the will of God. Teachers of the word of God are not to keep back any part of the counsel of God, lest the people shall be ignorant of their duty, and not understand what is the will of God concerning them, and stumble and fall into perdition. But while the teacher of truth should be faithful in presenting the gospel, let him never pour out a mass of matter which the people cannot comprehend because it is new to them and hard to understand. Take one point at a time, and make that one point plain, speaking slowly and in distinct voice. Speak in such a way that the people shall see what is the relation of that one point to other truths of vital importance.

Every man who becomes a teacher must also become a learner, and daily sit at the feet of Jesus. It is impossible for anyone to rightly divide the word of truth unless he earnestly seeks wisdom from on high that he may understand what is taught in the Scriptures. The Holy Spirit must attend the word spoken to the heart.

It will be difficult to create prejudice in the hearts of those who are seeking for truth as for hidden treasure if the speaker will hide himself in Christ, for he will then reveal Christ, not himself.

"And He gave some, apostles; and some, prophets; and some, evangelists; and some, pastors and teachers; for the perfecting of the saints, for the work of the ministry, for the edifying of the body of Christ: till we all come in the unity of the faith, and of the knowledge of the Son of God, unto a perfect man, unto the measure of the stature of the fullness of Christ." (Ephesians 4:11-13) But though God has set these different laborers in the church, there is to be no neglect on the part of one in the performance of duty.

Let no one neglect to give faithful and plain instruction upon tithing. Let there be instruction as to giving to the Lord that which He claims as His own, for the commendation of the Lord will not rest upon a people who rob Him in tithes and offerings. There will be need of often setting before the people their duty on this matter, that they may render unto God His own. Let the one who first presents the truth be faithful in presenting this matter, and let him who follows up the interest also make plain the requirement of God on tithing, that the people may see that in all points the laborers are teaching the same truth, and are of one mind in urging them to yield obedience to all the requirements of God.

But let laborers have discretion, and not give strong meat to those who are as babes; feed them with the sincere milk of the Word. In no case mingle your own spirit and ideas with the truth and cover up the precepts of God by traditions or suppositions. Let the people have the truth as it is in Jesus, and do not mingle it with decoctions of your own devising; for your presentation of truth will taste so strongly of self that it will disgust the hearers.

Be able to say with Paul, "I kept back nothing that was profitable unto you, but have showed you, and have taught you publicly, and from house to house, testifying both to the Jews, and also to the Greeks, repentance toward God, and faith toward our Lord Jesus Christ. ... I take you to record this day, that I am pure from the blood of all men. For I have not shunned to declare unto you all the counsel of God." (Acts 20:20, 21, 26, 27) There is most earnest work to be done, in order that you may so search the Scriptures that you may be able to declare unto those with whom you meet the whole counsel of God.[28]

---

[28] Ms. 39, 1895; MR 900.46.

Chapter 29

Camp Meeting Message on True Education

In the night season some things were opened before me in reference to the work and the school that will soon be opened in this locality. The light given me was that we must not pattern after the similitude of any school that has been established in the past. We must study the Word of God critically as the great lesson book, in order to know what the school may become under the receiving and doing of the Word of God. Unless we are guarded, we shall experience those hindrances to the spiritual education that have retarded the work of our schools in America by misapplication and miscalculation of the work most essential.

When Christ was working in our world, He had but few followers, and those whom He called His disciples were, by the maxims and customs of the scribes and Pharisees, constantly kept back from the advancement they might have made in supplying their great want and becoming efficient in usefulness. Through the rabbis, customs had come down from generation to generation, and these were made all-essential, even of more force than the Ten Commandments. Thus the precepts of men were taught and dwelt upon as of more value than a "Thus saith the Lord."

I have been warned that the teachers in our school should not travel over the ground that many of the Battle Creek teachers have gone over in their experience. Will ministers and teachers bear this in mind? Popular amusements for students were brought in there under a deceptive garb. Satan approached as an angel of light, and he worked most actively. If he could obtain the sanction of the teachers in the school at the great heart of the work, every school established would follow in its tread. The leaven of evil introduced and sanctioned at Battle Creek would spread the properties introduced to all with whom it had any connection.

The Lord has thought it essential to give reproof, correction, and instruction in righteousness on many things in regard to the management of schools among Seventh-day Adventists. All the light that has been given must be carefully heeded. No man or woman should be connected with our schools as educators who have not had an experience in obeying the Word of God. That which the Lord has spoken in the instruction given to our schools is to be strictly regarded, for if there is not, in some respects, an education of altogether a different character in our schools than has been given in Battle Creek, then we need not go to the expense of purchasing land and erecting school buildings.

In every school Satan has tried to make himself the guide of the teachers who instruct the students. It is he who has introduced the idea that selfish amusements are a necessity. Students sent to school for the purpose of receiving an education to become evangelists, ministers, and missionaries to foreign countries should not have received the idea that amusements are essential to keep them in physical health, when the Lord has presented before them that the better way is to embrace in their education manual labor in the place of amusements. These amusements, if practiced, will soon develop a passion that gives disrelish to useful, healthful exercise of mind and body. Such exercise makes students useful to themselves and others.

This education, in felling trees, tilling the soil, erecting buildings, as well as in literature, is the very education our youth should each seek to obtain. As soon as possible a printing press should be connected with our school, in order to educate in this line. Tent making also should be taken hold of. Buildings should be erected, and masonry should be learned. There are also many things which the lady students may be engaged in. There is cooking, dressmaking, and gardening to be done. Strawberries should be planted, plants and flowers cultivated. This the lady students may be called out of doors to do. Thus they may be educated to useful labor. Thoughtful, necessary work is essential for all to have to prepare them to be missionaries. Bookbinding also, and a variety of trades should be taken up. These will not only be putting into exercise brain, bone, and muscle, but will also be gaining knowledge.

The greatest curse of our world in this our day is idleness. It leads to needless amusements merely to please and gratify self. The students have had a superabundance of this way of passing their time. They are now to have a different education, that they may be prepared to go forth from the school with an all-round education. We are to keep before the school the development of the useful arts, acquiring adaptability and talents to be employed to be co-laborers with God. This kind of knowledge will open to them doors of welcome for foreign fields, and the building of plain, simple homes will be essential.

The proper cooking of food is a most essential acquirement, especially where meat is not made the staple article of diet. Something must be prepared to take the place of meat, and these foods must be well prepared so that meat will not be desired. Culture on all points of practical life will make our youth useful after they shall leave school to go to foreign countries. They will not then have to depend upon the people to whom they go to cook and sew for them, or build their habitations. And they will be much more influential if they show that they can educate the ignorant how to labor with the best methods and to produce the best results. This will be appreciated where means are difficult to obtain. They will reveal that missionaries can become educators in teaching them how to labor. A much smaller fund will be required to sustain such missionaries, because they have put to the very best use their physical powers in useful, practical labor combined with their studies, as essential acquirements in education. And wherever they may go, all that they have gained in this line will give them a welcome and standing room. If the light God has given were cherished, students would leave our schools free from the burden of debt, because they can be useful and their help is of value.

It is also essential to understand the philosophy of medical missionary work. Wherever the students shall go, they need an education in the science of how to treat the sick, for this will give them a welcome in any place, because there is suffering of every kind in every part of the world. Sanitariums are to be established, and thus the body is to be brought into existence which is essential for health.

The education given in our schools is one-sided. Students should be given an education that will fit them for successful business life. The common branches of education should be fully and thoroughly taught. Bookkeeping should be looked upon as of equal importance with grammar. This line of study is one of the most important for use in practical life, but few leave our schools with a knowledge of how to keep books correctly.

The reason that today so many mistakes are made in accounts is not because those in charge of them are dishonest but because they have not a thorough knowledge of bookkeeping. They are not prompt in making a faithful, daily estimate of their outgo. These mistakes have placed them in the ranks of dishonest men when, designedly, they are not dishonest. Many a youth, because ignorant of how to keep accounts, has made mistakes which have caused him serious trouble. Those who have a living interest in the cause and work of God should not allow themselves to settle down with the idea that they are not required to know how to keep books.

Education, true education, means much. The time devoted in school to learning how to eat with your fork in place of your knife, is not the most essential. These little matters of form and ceremony should not occupy time and strength. Those students who are at first somewhat coarse and awkward will soon overcome this. If the teachers are themselves courteous and kind and attentive, if they are true in heart and soul, if they do their work as in the sight of the whole universe of heaven, if they have the mind of Christ and are molded and fashioned by the Holy Spirit, they will behave, not in a simpering, affected manner, but as ladies and gentlemen of solid worth. And if students have before them the teachers' example of propriety, they will day by day be educated in proper manners.

To establish our school in Cooranbong, in this out-of-the-way place, seemed surprising to some. It has required some hard work to make a beginning. If the work is well begun, it will cost time and money. But a thing begun right is half done. It is the first steps that cost, but in holding what is already gained they will make a continual advance in the right direction. All are not wise to see this. (But children managed at home to receive the proper ideas that true education takes brain, bone and muscle.) [Handwritten Interlineation]

By the blessing of the Lord the work has been started, and on these grounds now the help of everyone is needed. The students must be taught how to begin. The educators must be men and women who have had experience, can patiently instruct, and who will lead the students in the right way at every step they advance. Teach Bible manners; teach purity of thought and the strictest integrity. This is the most valuable instruction that can be given. Keep Jesus, the Pattern, ever before your students by your example. This will act a prominent part in restoring the moral image of God in those under your charge. Teachers, you have no time, no duty, to teach students the forms and ceremonies of worldly customs of this age of corruption, when everything is perverted to outward appearance and display. This must never find a place in our school. Good, wholesome, sensible words always spoken politely are essential. This reform is not to be brought in as non-essential.

All religious exercises are to be treated with the greatest solemnity and reverence. The teaching given should be of a higher class, of a more sacred and religious character, than has been given in schools generally. Human nature is worth working for, and it is to be elevated and refined. There is a work which God alone can do for those who are deficient. They must be fitted with the inward adorning which is in the sight of God of great price. But the teachers can cooperate with God. Through the grace of God in Jesus Christ, which bringeth salvation and immortality to light, teachers may cooperate with God, and His heritage may be educated, not in the minuteness of etiquette, but in the science of salvation and godliness, and this will prepare the sons and daughters of God to be finally transformed by the finishing touch of immortality, and in heaven they will carry forward more thoroughly the education begun in the school here below. We shall be learners through all eternity.

Every student should aspire to obtain a fitness by the inward adorning of a meek and quiet spirit, which is in the sight of God of great price. Therefore all should in this life make diligent use of every opportunity and privilege to obtain all the knowledge possible for a qualification for that higher life in the future world.

God requires of every youth the full development and cultivation of all his powers. Every faculty of mind, soul, and body, is to be taxed to the highest to understand the Word of God, and have a correct knowledge of the people and their manners, who are chosen the elect of God, and who will receive the "Well done" from the lips of their Master, and compose the family of God in heaven. This is work that everyone can do. Some are incapable of managing or organizing, but these can cooperate in this school below with those who have a talent for this important work.

The teachers are to educate the youth to realize that if they receive Christ and believe on Him, they will be brought into close relationship with God. He gives them power to become the sons of God, to associate with the highest dignitaries in the kingdom of heaven, and to unite with Gabriel, with cherubim and seraphim, with angels and the archangel. (Revelation 22:1-5, quoted)

In His teaching our Saviour did not encourage any to attend the rabbinical schools of His day, for the reason that their minds would be corrupted with the continually repeated, "They say," or "It hath been said." The Lord can do more with minds that have no connection with schools where infidel authors are perused. These lesson books He reaches out His hand to remove, and in their stead places the Old and New Testament Scriptures. Those who will search the Scriptures for themselves, because it is the Word of God, who are willing to dig for the truth as for hidden treasures, will receive for their prize that wisdom which cometh alone from God. If they will not rely upon their own smartness, and not trust in their own inventions and their supposed fruitful minds, if they will give the working of the mind into the Lord's hands, and yoke up with Jesus Christ, they will not take steps where Jesus does not lead the way.

The aim of life should be to obey the call of Christ, "Follow me." Those whose minds are kept pure and uncrowded with too many small items, who will let their mind give its strength to those things that will be received not from their standpoint but from the light that God has given, will be continually gaining in knowledge. And this knowledge will direct them in straightforward channels. By their aftersight they will be able to give thanks to God that they have studiously chosen to know and understand what saith the Lord to His servant.

The Word of God is to be studied and taught. Converse with God through the medium of His Word. Thus our characters will be transformed. The ideas and habits once thought essential will be changed. God's Word is to be our lesson book. It is through the medium of this Word that we are to learn all about that better country, and the preparation essential for everyone to obtain an entrance into the kingdom of God, and come into possession of eternal life. That Word obeyed cheerfully and willingly, will ennoble your whole being in this life.

(Galatians 4:6-10, quoted) The observance of holidays in this country is a great evil. We want not to give sanction to the days and many traditions that are brought in. We need not pay any heed to them.

We all need to understand more and still more perfectly the life of Christ. He was the perfect image of God. He came to our world the great Teacher, and He will educate all who will be educated.

Whoever longs for honor and distinction will find that the standard of virtue and holiness, strictly, steadfastly, adhered to as revealed in the Word of God, will place him as a wise man among the most noble advisers and counselors; for God's Word will elevate a man. His Word, if obeyed, will sanctify and refine and ennoble the entire man. There will be no cheap timbers brought into the structure of character-building. The natural, inherited tendencies, if erratic, will be, by the obedient, corrected by the Word; they will not be cherished as virtues and imitated by learners who will, in their turn, educate others, thus transmitting and perpetuating faulty sentiments that should never see the light of day. We are to be impelled by pure, disinterested motives, having no prejudices or preferences to strengthen, no set notions or ideas that Christ has never taught. Truth sanctifies the hearer, the mind, the will, for they are, if obedient, partakers of the divine nature.

The direction has been given to the students in the school of Christ: "As newborn babes, desire the sincere milk of the word, that ye may grow thereby." (1 Peter 2:2) This is indeed eating the flesh and drinking the blood of the Son of God. (John 6:54-66, quoted)

There are many who have no greater depth of faith and spiritual perception than had the disciples who forsook their Lord because their limited comprehension could not discern His words. The feeding upon the divine Word of God is the divine element which the soul needs in order to secure a healthy development of all its spiritual powers. In all our schools this Word is to be made the essence of education; it is this that will give sanctified strength, wisdom, integrity, and moral power, if it is brought into the experience. It is not the words of worldly wisdom, it is not the maxims of men, not the theory of human beings, but it is the Word of God.

We shall have to guard against the steadfast holding to ideas and maxims that have been presented us as essential from a human standpoint. Every soul who would be successful in warring the good warfare can be so only on one condition—that he "receive with meekness the engrafted word, which is able to save your souls." (James 1:21) Those who have dug deep for the hidden treasure will find their reward in the precious veins of valuable ore, and these will make them wise unto salvation. All the wiles and subtleties of Satanic agencies cannot beguile you from the position of steadfast self-denial if you are carefully following the example of your Saviour. You will meet the enemy's treacherous advances with the words, "Get thee behind me, Satan." (Luke 4:8)

Our time is precious. We have but few, very few, days of probation left us in which to qualify ourselves for the future eternal life. We are not to devote these precious moments to forms and ceremonies, or cheap, superficial education. Think deeply before you speak. God designs that we shall keep the mind in pursuit of something tangible, something that we will not leave behind in this world, but that we can take with us into the higher school. The minds of the youth need the Word of God for instruction, that they may be "thoroughly furnished unto all good works." (2 Timothy 3:16, 17) The teachers will need to be very simple when teaching from the Scriptures. The students must be given "precept upon precept; line upon line, line upon line; here a little, and there a little." (Isaiah 28:10) Do not leave the slightest impression on the minds of your students that they are restricted and forced to wear a yoke of restraint that is unnecessary.

Strive to understand thoroughly every passage that you read. Fix one verse in mind, and after you have studied it prayerfully yourself, trying to understand thoroughly every word expressed, present that verse to the students. It is of little advantage to skim over the surface of the Scriptures. If we would understand fully the words of Christ, thought must be brought into the searching of the Scriptures. We should open the Scriptures with great reverence, and not in a slothful, lazy manner. The word of Christ is spirit and life to the receiver. The words of Christ to the Pharisees were, "[Ye] search the Scriptures; for in them ye think ye have eternal life; and they are they which testify of me." (John 5:39) They were searching the Scriptures for evidence of Christ's appearing, gathering up every evidence in regard to the manner in which they supposed He would come, while Christ was in their midst, and they did not discern Him by the use of faith. "Ye will not come to me, that ye might have life," He said. "I receive not honor from men," He said to the opposing Pharisees, (Verses 40, 41; Verses 42-47 quoted).

In this our day, as in Christ's day, there will be a misreading and misinterpreting of the Scriptures. If the Jews had studied the Scriptures with earnest, prayerful, humble hearts, their searching would have been rewarded with a true knowledge of the time, and not only the time, but also the manner, of Christ's first appearing. They would not have ascribed the glories of the second appearing of Christ to His first advent. They had the testimony of Daniel; they had the testimony of Isaiah and the other prophets; they had the teaching of Moses; and here was Christ Himself in their midst, and still they were searching the Scriptures for evidence in regard to His coming. They were doing to Christ, at the same time, the very things that it had been prophesied they would do. They were so blinded that they knew not the time of His visitation, or what they were doing. Thus they were fulfilling the Scripture.

Many are doing the same thing today, in 1897, because they have not had experience in the testing message comprehended in the first, second, and third angels' messages. There are those who are searching the Scriptures for proof that these messages are still in the future. They gather together the truthfulness of the messages, but they fail to give them their proper place in prophetic history. Therefore such are in danger of misleading the people in regard to locating the messages. They do not see and understand the time of the end, or when to locate the messages. The day of God is coming with stealthy tread, but the supposed wise and great men are prating about "higher education" which they suppose originates with finite men. They know not the signs of Christ's coming, or of the end of the world.

The evidence of the soon coming of Christ is right upon us, and many of us are asleep. We do not half gather up the important truths that are for our admonition, upon whom the ends of the world are come. If we did receive and believe the Word of God, we should be farther in advance spiritually than we are today. Iniquity abounds everywhere, and the love of many has waxed cold. Unless we understand the importance of the moments that are swiftly passing into eternity, and make ready a people to stand in the great day of God, we shall be registered in the books of heaven as unfaithful stewards. The watchman is to know the time of the night. Everything is now clothed with a solemnity that all who believe the truth should feel and sense. They should act in reference to the great day of God. The plagues of

God are already just upon the world, and we need to be preparing for that great day. We have not time now to spend in speculative ideas, or in hap-hazard movements. We should fear to skim the surface of the Word of God. When the light shines in our hearts, we shall, by all our words and works, live in accordance with that light, understand the words of God, and make it our spiritual, daily food, as represented by Christ as eating His flesh and drinking His blood. Then we will be prepared to teach the Word of God as we never have done before. We must sink the shaft deeper in the mines of truth. All the little things of life are but a mote now. Those that pertain to eternity are of great consequence.[29]

---
[29] Ms. 41a, 1896. (Written Dec. 20, 1896, from "Sunnyside," Cooranbong, N.S.W.); MR 900.24.

Chapter 30

The Ministry

[Sermon by Ellen G. White, August 30, 1898, a portion of which appears in Evangelism]

(Colossians 1:25-29, quoted)

The ministry is a sacred office. Christ crucified is the power of God unto salvation to all who will believe. A Saviour lifted up—a Saviour full and complete to all who accept Him—is the science of salvation. The subject is never exhausted. It is always fresh; for today Christ is a living Intercessor before the Father in the heavenly courts. Christ, the propitiation for the sins of the world, is a living subject instinct with divinity, and always fresh and new.

It is through His merits, through an example of suffering, that the chosen disciples of Christ are fitted for every work of ministry and for every trial and discouragement in this work. Looking unto Jesus—His self-denying life, His sacrifice, His humiliation in their behalf—they are ready to follow in His footsteps, to endure the cross, despise the shame, and go without the camp bearing His reproach. The Holy Spirit makes them one with Christ, their divine Leader. The truth enthroned in the heart sanctifies the soul, and the power and grace of God within manifests itself in the life as the power and wisdom of God.

Christ promised His followers, "If I go away, I will send another Comforter, that He may abide with you forever." (cf. John 14:16) With this divine endowment the human agent is qualified to work in Christ's lines. Christ continued, "He shall teach you all things, and bring all things to your remembrance, whatsoever I have said unto you." (Verse 26)

Individually living the life of Christ, His followers become living working agencies. They possess the character of Christ. They have the love of Christ, His faith, His hope, His oneness with the Father. They lean on Christ as their only staff and sufficiency. They are Christ's living witnesses. By their words, their spirit, their true courtesy, their influence, by their every action, they testify of Christ. A power goes out from these human agencies, bearing the testimony that they are laborers together with God, that they have communion with their Saviour.

The preaching of the Word is not to be undervalued. The work for the salvation of souls is a sacred, holy work. Says the prophet, "How beautiful upon the mountains are the feet of him that bringeth good tidings, that publisheth peace; that bringeth good tidings of good, that publisheth salvation; that saith unto Zion, Thy God reigneth." (Isaiah 52:7)

What honor is conferred upon men in that they may be laborers together with God, His messengers, to proclaim as did the forerunner of Christ, "Behold the Lamb of God, which taketh away the sin of the world." Lift up the risen Saviour, and say to all who will hear, Come to Him who has loved us and died for us. Let the self-denial, the compassion, the great love wherewith Christ has loved us in purchasing us with His own life, be unfolded before men. The science of salvation is to be the burden of every sermon, the theme of every song. Let it be poured forth in every supplication.

Let nothing be brought into the preaching of the Word to supplement Christ, the Word and power of God. Let His name, the only name given under heaven whereby we may be saved, be exalted in every discourse, and from Sabbath to Sabbath let the trumpet of the watchmen be given a certain sound. Christ is the science and eloquence of the gospel, and His ministers are to hold forth the word of life, presenting hope to the penitent, peace to the troubled and desponding, and grace and completeness and strength to the believing.

Encouragement should be given to the precious lambs of the flock. Said the Majesty of heaven, "Suffer the little children to come unto Me, and forbid them not; for of such is the kingdom of God." (Mark 10:14) He does not send those children to the rabbis. He does not send them to the Pharisees. He says, The mothers who have brought their children to Me have done well. "Suffer the little children to come unto me, and forbid them not; for of such is the kingdom of God."

Then let the mothers accept the invitation, and lead their children to Christ. Let the ministers of the gospel take the children in their arms and bless them. In the name of Jesus let words of tenderness and love be spoken to the little ones, because Christ took the lambs of the flock in His arms and blessed them.

Our expectation is from God who in the crucified One, has given us rich and powerful truths and weighty arguments to move the hearts of men. The simple prayer indited by the Holy Spirit will ascend through the gates ajar, the open door [of] which Christ has declared, "I have opened, and no man can shut." (cf. Revelation 3:7) Those prayers, mingled with the incense of the perfections of Christ, will ascend as fragrance before the Father, and answers will come. The Holy Spirit will descend, and souls will come to a knowledge of the truth. Sinners will be converted, and their faces turned from the world and earthly things toward heaven. The Sun of righteousness will inspire them with motives for action, and they will realize that they are witnesses for Christ.

We are to be judged according to the deeds done in the body. "By thy words thou shalt be justified, and by thy words thou shalt be condemned." (Matthew 12:37) The watchmen are not to slumber and sleep in their important mission. They must not only preach, but minister, educating the souls who have turned from error to truth, by personal labor, by precept and example teaching them that "denying ungodliness and worldly lusts, we should live soberly, righteously, and godly, in this present world; looking for that blessed hope, and the glorious appearing of the great God and our Saviour Jesus Christ: who gave His life for us, that He might redeem us from all iniquity, and purify unto Himself a peculiar people, zealous of good works."

Ministers of God, great is your responsibility to go forward in Christian experience and righteousness, from light to still greater light, walking conscientiously, striving to reach a high and exalted standard. As the powers of darkness with intense activity work from beneath, the agencies of God should be more and more vigilant in cooperating with the divine, in giving the trumpet a certain sound. In earnest tones, distinct and startling, they are to proclaim the righteousness of the law, that no watchman may fail to catch the sound of alarm, and in their turn sound the warnings coming from heaven. All must be aroused from their lethargy to wakeful, earnest, watching for souls as they that must give an account.

Light, increased light from heaven, is waiting to be imparted to those who will walk and work in the light which they already have. There is to be quick and earnest thought, talent, and tact displayed in enterprises that will communicate light to those who are near and afar off. Careful consideration should be made of every way that is not the way of the Lord. No sleepy watchman must be tolerated. Under their leader the principalities and powers and rulers of the darkness of this world are at work.

Because it has been so difficult to arouse from their lethargy the many who have long professed to know the truth, spiritual wickedness in high places has increased. Men have taken their stand to hedge up the way of the Lord's army of workers. They have taken souls unaware and led them into strange paths. May the Lord show these men who have long been hindrances, who, whenever opportunities have presented themselves, have placed a stumbling block in the way of others, [by] whose side they have worked, and make diligent work of repentance. They have weakened the hands of others, and given the enemy every advantage.

Time, precious time, has been lost. Golden opportunities have passed by unimproved, because of a lack of clear spiritual eyesight and wise generalship to plan and devise ways and means to frustrate the enemy and preoccupy the field. These men think they have been doing a very wise work, but the Judgment will show what has been the character of their warfare and what has been lost to Christ through their maneuvering. Let us now wake up. There is earnest work to be done. If we will draw nigh to God, He will draw nigh to us.

Slumbering watchmen, what of the night? Do you not know the time of night? Do you feel no burden to lift the danger signal and give the warnings for this time? If you do not, come down from the walls of Zion, for God will not entrust you with the light He has to give. Light is only given to those who will reflect that light upon others. "We all, with open face beholding as in a glass the glory of the Lord, are changed into the same image from glory to glory even as by the Spirit of the Lord."

Lift the standard. The minister of the gospel must not give all his attention to sermonizing. The church of God must be kept in order. There is ministering to be done. The sick are to be visited. Men and women are to be educated after the divine model. "It is high time to awake out of sleep: for now is our salvation nearer than when we believed. The night is far spent, the day is at hand: let us therefore cast off the works of darkness, and let us put on the armor of light."

The grace of Christ received in the soul will work as an educator. The trust received in the heart will purify the soul. The religion of Jesus Christ never makes the receiver coarse and rough and uncourteous. Truth is delicate and elevating. It acts as a refiner. It sanctifies the soul. The constant influence of truth trains the soul after Christ's pattern, and molds and fashions the character for the courts above. It is a grand principle which must be brought into the daily practical life.

There is no danger of belittling the mind by giving attention to the little things of life with which we have to do. Any negligence of acts of politeness and tender regard on the part of brother for brother, any neglect of kind, encouraging words in the family circle, parents with children and children with parents, confirms habits which make the character unChristlike. But if these little things are performed, they become great things. They increase to large proportions. They breathe a sweet perfume in the life which ascends to God as holy incense. An angel presence is in the home. Love is manifested in kindness, gentleness, forbearance, and longsuffering.

The man who accepts the position of being [a] mouthpiece for God should consider it highly essential that he present the truth with all the grace and intelligence he can, that the truth may lose nothing in his presentation of it to the people. Those who consider it a little thing to speak with an imperfect utterance, dishonor God. God is not glorified when His servants, in holding forth the word of life pitch their voices to a high key, and talk in loud, unnatural tones. By so doing they abuse the organs of speech. God enjoins us, "Be ye therefore perfect, even as your Father which is in heaven is perfect." (Matthew 5:48) "Whom we preach, warning every man, and teaching every man in all wisdom; that we may present every man perfect in Christ Jesus." (Colossians 1:28)

The apostle Paul could say: (Acts 20:18-20, quoted)[30]

---

[30] Manuscript 107, 1898; MR 900.30.

Chapter 31

The Will of God Concerning You

Through the apostle John God sends the message to His people in these last days: (Revelation 3:15-18, quoted)

As a people we are in danger of being separated from the Sun of righteousness. We are to be sanctified to God through obedience to the truth. Our conscience must be purged from dead works to serve the living God. Sanctification means perfect love, perfect obedience, entire conformity to the will of God. If your lives are conformed to the life of Christ through the sanctification of mind, soul, and body, our example will have a powerful influence on the world. We are not perfect, but it is our privilege to cut away from the entanglements of self and sin, and go on unto perfection. "We all with open face, beholding as in a glass the glory of the Lord, are changed into the same image from glory to glory, even as by the Spirit of the Lord."

Christ in His prayer to the Father, said: (John 17:15-23, quoted)

These are grand and uplifting truths. Great possibilities, high and holy attainments, are placed within the reach of all who have true faith. Shall we not anoint our eyes with eyesalve, that we may discern the wondrous things here brought before us? Why do we not with persevering earnestness, work out this prayer, advancing onward and upward, reaching the standard of holiness? We are laborers together with God, and we must work in harmony with one another and with God, "for it is God which worketh in ... [us] both to will and to do of his good pleasure."

When I was a child," Paul said, "I spake as a child, I understood as a child, I thought as a child: but when I became a man, I put away childish things." (1 Corinthians 13:11) How many men there are who have grown to man's estate, but have not outgrown their childhood, who bring the defects of their child-life into their religious experience. "Brethren be not children in understanding: howbeit in malice be ye children, but in understanding men." (1 Corinthians 14:20)

The Lord takes no pleasure in seeing us spiritually weak. "God, who commanded the light to shine out of darkness, hath shined in our hearts, to give the light of the knowledge of the glory of God in the face of Jesus Christ. But we have this treasure in earthen vessels, that the excellency of the power may be of God, and not of us." We have conflicts and trials to meet, but we need not fail or be discouraged. The apostle says, "We are troubled on every side, yet not distressed; we are perplexed, but not in despair; persecuted, but not forsaken; cast down, but not destroyed; always bearing about in the body the dying of the Lord Jesus, that the life also of Jesus might be made manifest in our body." (2 Corinthians 4:8-10)

It is the supposed little sins that will exclude us from heaven. We cannot carry with us a part of our sinful selves, that sensitiveness which is always ready to be hurt and cry out. Our refusal to let self die and our life be hid with Christ in God, will leave us in unbelief and transgression of the law. The gospel has not abolished the law, or detracted one tittle from its claims. It still demands holiness in every part. There is no such thing as making the law void through faith in Christ. The law is the echo of God's own voice, giving to every soul the invitation, Come up higher; be holy, holier still.

If we would press forward to "the mark for the prize of the high calling of God in Christ Jesus," we must show that we are emptied of all self, and supplied with the golden oil which through the two golden pipes is communicated by the two anointed ones who stand by the Lord of the whole earth. God is dealing with us through His grace and providence. From eternity He has chosen us to be His obedient children. He gave His Son to die for us, that we might be sanctified through obedience to the truth, cleansed from all the littleness and cheapness of self. As a people, we are far behind. A personal work is needed, a personal surrender of self. We are to be controlled by the Holy Spirit. "Ye are the light of the world. ... Let your light so shine before men, that they may see your good works, and glorify your Father which is in heaven." God can only be honored when we who profess to believe in Him are conformed to His image. We are to represent to the world the beauty of holiness, and we shall never enter the gates of the city of God until we perfect a Christlike character. If we, with trust in God, strive for sanctification, we shall receive it. Then as witnesses for Christ, we are to make known what the grace of God has wrought in us.

The greatest disquietude we can have is uncertainty. The acceptance of the blessings of God brings righteousness and peace. The fruit of righteousness is quietness and assurance forever. We must have simplicity and Godlike sincerity. We must have that wisdom which cometh from above. Our Christian experience must be animated by piety, and instinct with the divine life.

You strike too low, my brethren. Set your mark high. Let your works be in harmony with the works of Jesus Christ. It is the privilege of all to grow up to the full stature of men and women in Christ Jesus. "This is the will of God, even your sanctification." (1 Thessalonians 4:3) Is it your will also? With intensity of desire, long after God; yea, pant after Him, as the hart panteth after the water brooks. Press to the mark of the high calling of God in Christ Jesus.

Why do not all who have named the name of Christ put on Christ? Why do they not awake from their indifference, arouse from the lukewarm state, their self-satisfied condition? God's people must have a fixed purpose. They will never be holy until they put all the energy of their being into the work of conforming to the will of God.[31]

---
[31] Ms. 38, 1899; MR 900.18.

Chapter 32

Talk Faith and Move Forward

[The closing address presented at the Australasian Union Conference session, Cooranbong, N.S.W., July 23, 1899]

"These words spake Jesus, and lifted up His eyes to heaven, and said, Father, the hour is come; glorify Thy Son, that Thy Son also may glorify Thee: As Thou hast given Him power over all flesh, that He should give eternal life to as many as Thou hast given Him. And this is life eternal, that they might know Thee the only true God, and Jesus Christ whom Thou hast sent. I have glorified Thee on the earth: I have finished the work which Thou gavest Me to do" (John 17:1-4)

While we know Christ in one sense, that He is the Saviour of the world, it means more than this. We must have a personal knowledge and experience in Christ Jesus, an experimental knowledge of Christ, what He is to us, and what we are to Christ. That is the experience that everyone wants. Now, I cannot have it for any of you, nor can you have it for me. The work that is to be done for us, is to be through the manifestation of the Holy Spirit of God upon human minds and human hearts. The heart must be purified and sanctified.

I need not tell any of you that it is so, because you know it. Not one of us needs to feel a doubt as to where we are, or to think, "I wish I knew where I stood before God," but, by living faith, we must sink ourselves in God; and when we do that, His life will shine upon us. There is not a particle of need of our being in a state of inefficiency and coldness.

What is the matter with us? "If any of you lack wisdom, let him ask of God, that giveth to all men liberally, and upbraideth not, and it shall be given him." It shall be given him. There are no "ifs" nor "ands" about it. "But let him ask in faith, nothing wavering." (James 1:5, 6)

You pray, and ask God for wisdom, strength, and efficiency, and feel you must have them. But perhaps, right after that prayer, it will seem as though a hellish shadow of Satan was cast right athwart your pathway, and you see nothing beyond. What was that? Why, the devil wanted to obscure your faith in that cloud. But there is no necessity for you to do that. Is feeling to be our criterion, or is it to be the word of the living God? Are we to sink our faith in the cloud? That is what Satan wants us to do. But we should not give him so much pleasure as that. What are we going to do?

I have had that cloud settle upon me at times, but I knew that God was there just the same. Since this conference began, I have hardly been able at times to sit up. When I came to the meeting first, I came by faith, and I didn't know as I could say anything. I had been in such terrible sickness that I could hardly tell my own name. But I said, I shall go; I am going to put myself in the channel of light, and there I am going to remain; then I shall expect the Lord to help me. (I have a great deal of talking to do with the Lord in the night, and I always know He will help me.) When I came in here I was so weak I did not know if I could speak or not. But you know how He gave strength to me, and the last time when I read that long paper to you, He gave me strength, and I thank Him that I had strength to do it. I have been astonished at the measure of strength given me.

"Ask in faith, nothing wavering." Don't let one single suggestion of the devil come in. It is to be "nothing wavering. For he that wavereth is like a wave of the sea." (Verse 6) The Lord will do great things for us if we will only show our trust in Him.

I remember when I was in Switzerland, the darkness of the enemy came over the pathway when I was trying to do a work for God there. I wanted them to do a special work in erecting some buildings, and I tried every way to bring them around. Finally, after standing there so long, and I could do no more, the meeting closed, and I went in my room. I said, I will take right hold of the promises of God, and those promises are "yea, and amen," and I believe they are mine.

Well, I said, "Lord teach me what to do in this emergency, for I am not going to give this up, or waver in the matter at all." Now, the Lord helps them that are of one mind, and it had seemed that there were as many different minds as there were different people. We wanted a school building and a meeting place.

While I was praying, I said, "I put my trust in Thee. Thou wilt keep that which I have committed to Thee. Thou must strengthen my faith." I kept holding right on; and as I prayed it seemed that the sweet Spirit of God just went right through the room, wave after wave, and every particle of unbelief or anything like it was brushed away, and we carried every point; and so the building was put up.

What we want is that faith that will not let go, a faith that will not fail or be discouraged. I know your faith is to be tried, and I know the banner of truth has got to be lifted in places all around here. "Why," says one, "how can we do all this if the Lord is coming so soon?" Why, the Lord can do more in one hour than we can do in a whole lifetime, and when He sees that His people are fully consecrated, let me tell you a great work will be done in a short time, and the message of truth is to be carried into the dark places of the earth, where it has never been proclaimed.

When we first came to Melbourne I was very sick. Some of you know something about that. I had to be propped up with pillows, and they would carry me in their arms up into their hall, and there I would speak to the people. But all the time I had the presence and blessing of God. It was a most precious time to me.

When we come to the hardest places, we may know that all heaven is interested and will bear us up, if we will not fail or be discouraged. Cling to the mighty One. Do not talk unbelief at all, because the more you talk unbelief the more unbelief you will have; and the more you talk darkness, the more darkness you will have; and the more you talk light, the more light you will have; and the more you talk faith, you will have faith.

I want to read a few more verses. (Verses 14-19, quoted) The truth of God must sanctify the whole man, body and soul. It is not the truth to you unless you practice it.

Our precious Jesus gave up all heaven to come to this world that He might sanctify us through the truth. Will we be sanctified? In His life and example, His lessons and His words, there was the sanctification of the Spirit of God. Sanctification was upon Him for us. God Himself worked through humanity, just as humanity must work through humanity. That is why He took humanity upon Himself that He might teach humanity how to work for itself. He took humanity that He might experience death in our behalf, that we might have life and immortality through His life and death.

"Neither pray I for these alone, but for them also which shall believe on Me through their word." (Verse 20) Now, that prayer of Christ's is for us that we may be sanctified through the truth. "That they all may be one; as Thou, Father, art in Me, and I in Thee, that they also may be one in us: that the world may believe that Thou hast sent Me." (Verse 21) Get out the coldness from your heart; get out the evil surmisings; get out every bad thought; and let the Lord Jesus take the throne of the heart and reign there.

"And the glory which Thou gavest Me I have given them." (Verse 22) The character that God gave Him, He has given us. "That they may be one, even as we are one: I in them, and Thou in Me, that they may be made perfect in one; and that the world may know that Thou hast sent Me, and hast loved them, as Thou hast loved Me." (Verse 22, 23)

Can we take that in? It is a wonderful thing, that God loves them that believe on Him as He loves Christ Himself. We are made one with God, and we want that oneness. We want to seek Him earnestly for the faith once delivered to the saints, and we want the spirit of the Third Angel's message. We want to realize that the end of all things is at hand; that speech is a talent; and that faith is the gift of God; and we must work and pray that God may preserve that faith.

You must put your foot right on the Word, and say, I believe; I will believe; I will press to the mark of the prize, and everything that hinders me shall be swept away; I will not allow anything to interpose between my soul and God.

No, the dark shadow of Satan will come right across our pathway if we let our faith sink into it. But we must do as the eagle does when he is in the cloud and bewildered in the fog. He does not go one way and another as though distracted, but presses upward through the cloud, until he comes into the light above. And so we should press upward beyond the hellish shadow of Satan, when he tries to eclipse the rays of light that come from God.

Now, we want the life of Christ in our hearts to make us one, and there will be united action. We must press to the mark of the prize of the high calling which is in Christ Jesus our Lord; and what we need is that living, active faith that takes God at His word. We must have it, and God will let us have it if we will.

We must not be discouraged. We want to get rid of unbelief; we do not want to talk it, or act it, or think it, but press forward to the mark of the prize of the high calling that is in Christ Jesus our Lord. I feel anxious, because I know that the time has come when God's people should put on their beautiful garments. "Arise, shine; for thy light is come, and the glory of the Lord is risen upon thee." It is the word of infinite power that He wants you to eat and drink. He wants you to eat His flesh and drink His blood, and then the power of God will be in your midst. Then the voice will be touched with a peculiar power.

After the passing of the time in 1844, I remember we were a sorrowful little company. There was a little boy who had twenty-five cents, and he threw it into the mud puddle, because he said he would not need it, for the Lord was coming. And afterward he was seen hunting in the mud puddle for his twenty-five cents. I thought, How many of us would do just like that. There was one brother who had been out praying with others, and he began to say in a loud voice, "Great, great, great is the Lord; and greatly to be praised." I think he repeated that over many times, and his face was shining. Before he finished, the power of God was upon us.

While it is true that we were disappointed, yet we had the blessing of God.

"And at that time shall Michael stand up, the great prince which standeth for the children of thy people: and there shall be a time of trouble, such as never was since there was a nation even to that same time: and at that time thy people shall be delivered, every one that shall be found written in the book." (Daniel 12:1) Let everyone inquire, "Is my name written there?" Do not think about your brethren and sisters for fear they are not ready, but think about yourself. You want to know where you are, and to know that Christ is formed within, the hope of glory. You want to be constantly singing, and when you do that you will stop your criticizing. If you are beholding Him, you will not have time for anything else. And if you see His face, it will be reflected in your face, and all this mourning and groaning is dishonoring God, for "whoso offereth praise, glorifieth God."

You are going to have trials in your churches because there are murmurers and complainers and faultfinders there. Go straight ahead and be cheerful. And when Brother Irwin and Brother Haskell return to America, they are going to have trials there. Do not let your head be cast down, or feel discouraged, but go forward, firm in Jesus Christ, keeping your eye fixed on the crown of life which Christ, the righteous judge, shall give you in that day.

Just keep praising God, and when the devil tempts you, sing. When Christ was a child He was tempted in every way, and what did He do? He sang psalms, and praised God, and there was music in His voice. And there was an impression made upon the hearts and minds of those who heard Him. He wants you to have heaven in view, and heaven is a good deal nearer than you think. God's holy, anointed ones are right by you, and here is His church, the greatest object of His love that it is possible for Him to have. He is watching over every one of us.

I love Him because He first loved me. I love Him because He gave His life for me. And God forbid that I should be a coward. When the children of Israel went out to fight, God told them to sing, and as soon as they began to sing, their enemies fled, for they saw the whole army of heaven before them. They were afraid of their destruction and fled. God wants us to vanquish the enemy. Let us pray as we never prayed before. We do not pray half enough. We ought to pray and have regular praise meetings together. May God bless you, and may the Spirit of God be with us.[32]

---

[32] Manuscript 93a, 1899; MR 900.31.

Chapter 33

Words to Students

I am glad to see so many students here this morning. Students, you may have the best and wisest teachers to be found in our world, but they cannot make your heart ready to receive the Lord. You must do this work for yourself. Your teachers cannot think for you or act for you. The question each student should ask himself is, Am I determined to develop a character which God can approve? You may give yourselves up to float with the current, or you may struggle bravely onward and still onward. Ask yourselves, How can I conduct myself so that I shall be approved by God? The approval of God is worth more than all else in our world. If you will set your mark high, if you will make the most of your opportunities and privileges, wherever you are, whatever your position, you will be given strength and courage to persevere. You will not be wanting in bright, keen ideas. We have the precious Word of God to give us encouragement, and if we are determined to keep ever before us the fear of God—the beginning of wisdom—we shall be learners in the school of Christ.

You may set for yourselves a low standard. You may cling to cheap, common ideas. But if you do this, you will leave the school cheap and common. You may make up your mind that while in school you have not a moment to lose, that this is a time large with important results; and that therefore you must improve every opportunity presented to you. Doing this, you will go from school purer and holier for your stay.

What may come in a few months from now is impossible to say. You may never have another opportunity to attend the school in Cooranbong. But now, just now, at the very beginning of this school year, seek God with the whole heart, and He will be found of you. Our God watches over the children of men. And the angels of light—thousands upon thousands of them—what are they doing? What is their work? "Are they not all ministering spirits, sent forth to minister for them who shall be heirs of salvation?" (Hebrews 1:14) Constantly the battle between the army of Christ and the army of Satan is going on. The angels of God are round about us as a wall of fire. We need them, for Satan is always seeking to cast his hellish shadow between us and God. But God's angels press back the powers of darkness; Satan cannot hurt us if we trust in the Lord.

God has a church in the world, and this church is nearer to His heart than anything else in this earth. He holds communication with His church. He gives individuals ability and talents, and imparts to them of His Spirit, that they may be the guardians of His church, to watch over the interests of His people. These are His stewards, and He has placed some of them in this school, to watch over the youth who may attend. Students, when you see that they have a kindly interest in you, respond to it for Christ's sake. Place yourselves on the right side. Be determined that you will not be found under the black banner of the prince of darkness, that you will fight under the blood-stained banner of Prince Emmanuel.

Christ has given you talents, and these talents He expects you to improve. To one He gives ten talents, to another five, and to another one. He gives to each according to his several ability. If the man with one talent will improve that talent to the utmost of his ability, he will be given other talents. To these, as they are faithfully improved, will be added others. Thus the talents continually increase. But supposing a man has only one talent and gains only one? If his work has been in proportion to his ability, he will be just as surely rewarded as the man who gains a larger number of talents.

Those who make the most of their opportunities, who place themselves in right relation with God, will be rewarded even as was Daniel. We read of him, "Daniel purposed in his heart that he would not defile himself with the portion of the king's meat, nor with the wine which he drank: therefore he requested the prince of the eunuchs that he might not defile himself. Now God had brought Daniel into favour and tender love with the prince of the eunuchs. And the prince of the eunuchs said unto Daniel, I fear my lord the king; … for why should he see your faces worse liking than the children which are of your sort? Then shall ye make me endanger my head to the king." (Daniel 1:8-10) "Prove thy servants, I beseech thee, ten days," Daniel said, "and let them give us pulse to eat, and water to drink. Then let our countenances be looked upon before thee, and the countenance of the children that eat of the [portion of the] king's meat: and as thou seest, deal with thy servants. So he consented to them in this matter, and proved them ten days. And at the end of ten days their countenances appeared fairer and fatter in flesh than all the children which did eat the portion of the king's meat."

God gave Daniel and his companions "knowledge and skill in all learning and wisdom: and Daniel had understanding in all visions and dreams. Now at the end of the days that the king had said he should bring them in, then the prince of the eunuchs brought them in before Nebuchadnezzar. And the king communed with them; ... and in all matters of wisdom and understanding, ... he found them ten times better than all the magicians and astrologers that were in all his realm."

Babylon was at this time the greatest kingdom in the world. God permitted Daniel and his companions to be taken captive that they might take to the king and nobles of Babylon the knowledge of Him, the only true God, the Creator of the heavens and the earth.

God brought Daniel into favor with the prince of the eunuchs because he behaved himself. He kept before him the fear of the Lord. His companions never saw in his life anything that would lead them astray. Those who had charge over him loved him because he carried with him the fragrance of a Christlike disposition. You may say, But I have not a good disposition. If in the past your disposition has been bad, now is the time to seek to make it good. The term is just about to commence. Begin now to obtain the victory over self. God will help you.

No one need place himself where he is out of touch with everybody else, where he fancies that no one will care, no matter what he does or says. Students, each one of you has a different disposition, a different mind. The work of your teachers is necessarily very hard. You can make it harder by giving way to selfishness. You may help them by working together in harmony.

God cooperates with human effort. Daniel might have said, Of course, I must eat as the king commands. But instead, he resolved to obey God, and God began at once to help him. So when you are determined that you will obey the divine command, God will cooperate with you, making you witnesses of which heaven approves. Christ says, "Be ye therefore perfect, even as your Father which is in heaven is perfect." (Matthew 5:48) This is your work—to gain perfection of character. Set your mark high, and then be determined to reach it. If a fellow-student asks you to go contrary to the rules of the school, answer him with a decided No. Say, I will have no part in this matter. The fear of God is before me. I love God, and I will keep His commandments. Act in this way, and you will receive brain-power. God will strengthen you as He strengthened Daniel.

I want to begin to do my talking at the beginning of the school year, because as I shall speak to you from time to time, I do not want you to feel that I have heard of your wrong course, and am hitting at you. I want to stand right by your side. I want to help every one of you. I present you before God in my prayers. I want you to take hold with me. How? "Let him take hold of my strength," God says, "that he may make peace with me; and he shall make peace with me." (Isaiah 27:5) Daniel not only made peace with God, in making peace with God he made peace with one who knew not God.

Help your fellow-students to cooperate with God. Help them to cooperate with the prayers which I have heard rising in their behalf. As God's people bow before Him, they pray that His angels may watch over the students in this school.

Students, you know not in what position you may be placed. God may use you as He used Daniel to take the knowledge of the truth to the mighty of the earth. It rests with you to say whether you will have knowledge and skill. God can give you skill in all your learning. He can help you to adapt yourselves to the line of study you shall take up. Place yourselves in right relation to God. Make this your first interest. Gather up right principles, noble principles, uplifting principles. Then when visitors come to the school, they will be impressed that the students are receiving the right education. God desires you to be witnesses for Him. He desires you to draw in right lines. As you do this, he will give you skill and wisdom and understanding. You will advance step by step, for God does not want you to stand still. He wants you to run in the way of His commandments, constantly moving forward and upward.

God is connected with the threads of our existence. He knows every thought of the heart, every action of the life. Then strive to live in harmony with Him. Seek to reach a high standard. Your teachers will help you, heavenly angels will help you, and, more than that, Christ will help you. The Prince of life is more interested than anyone else in your salvation. You can do Him honor by showing that you appreciate what He has done for you. You can glorify Him and make the angels glad by revealing in your life that He has not died in vain. Be determined that opposite your names in the books of heaven shall be written the word, Overcomer. Then all discontent and unhappiness will vanish. Your hearts will be filled with peace and joy in the Holy Spirit.[33]

---

[33] Ms. 13, 1900; "Words to Students." Feb. 2, 1900; MR 900.4.

Chapter 34

The Christian Life

[Sermon by Mrs. E. G. White in the Tabernacle, April 14, 1901, General Conference session, Battle Creek, Michigan.]

"Lay not up for yourselves treasures upon earth, where moth and rust doth corrupt, and where thieves break through and steal. But lay up for yourselves treasures in heaven, where neither moth nor rust doth corrupt, and where thieves do not break through nor steal. For where your treasure is, there will your heart be also.

"The light of the body is the eye: if therefore thine eye be single, thy whole body shall be full of light. But if thine eye be evil, thy whole body shall be full of darkness, If therefore the light that is in thee be darkness, how great is that darkness." (Matthew 6:19-23)

Christ is the light of the world. In all that we do, let us walk in this light. In the Word of God our work is laid out before us. Let us not think that the Lord has given us talents to use in whatever way we please. Our talents are given us to hold in trust for Him. Our money is His. In its use we are to remember that Christ gave His precious life that we might have a probation in which to make a suitable preparation for the future life. "Ye are not your own; for ye are bought with a price: therefore glorify God in your body, and in your spirit, which are God's." (1 Corinthians 6:19, 20)

This present life is our time of test and trial. God placed Adam and Eve in the beautiful garden of Eden, saying to them, "Of every tree in the garden thou mayest freely eat." But there was one prohibition. "Of the tree of the knowledge of good and evil, thou shalt not eat of it; for in the day that thou eatest thereof thou shalt surely die." (Genesis 2:16, 17) God wished to test and try the beings He had made, to see if they would be loyal and true to Him.

In this prohibition Satan saw a chance to misrepresent God. Disguised as a serpent he came to Adam and Eve, saying, The reason God has forbidden you to eat of that fruit is because He knows that if you do eat of it, you will be as gods. You will become wise. And they did become wise—wise in knowing the evil which God meant them never to know.

After Adam and Eve had yielded to the tempter, the covering of light, their garment of innocence, was taken from them. "The eyes of them both were opened, and they knew that they were naked; and they sewed fig leaves together, and made themselves aprons." In the past they had been glad to see their Creator when He came to walk and talk with them. Now in their sinfulness they were afraid to meet Him. Hearing the voice of God in the garden, they "hid themselves from the presence of the Lord God amongst the trees of the garden. And the Lord God called unto Adam, and said unto him, Where art thou; and he said, I heard thy voice in the garden, and I was afraid, because I was naked and hid myself." "Who told thee that thou wast naked?" God asked. "Hast thou eaten of the tree, whereof I commanded thee that thou shouldest not eat?" Then Adam did that which it is natural for all human beings to do. He threw the blame on someone else. "The woman whom thou gavest to be with me," he said, "she gave me of the tree, and I did eat." (See Genesis 3:7-12)

God told Adam that because of his disobedience the ground should be cursed. "In sorrow shalt thou eat of it all the days of thy life; thorns also and thistles shall it bring forth unto thee.... In the sweat of thy face shalt thou eat bread, till thou return unto the ground; for out of it wast thou taken; for dust thou art, and unto dust shalt thou return." (Genesis 3:17-19)

The floodgates of woe were opened upon our world. All nature must feel the effects of sin. But God did not leave Adam without a ray of hope. He gave him the promise which ever since has brightened the pathway of the faithful. He said to the serpent, "I will put enmity between thee and the woman, and between thy seed and her seed; it shall bruise thy head, and thou shalt bruise his heel." (Genesis 3:15)

Good and evil are set before us. Which are we choosing? Are we serving and glorifying self, losing sight of the light of the world, or are we denying self and following the Redeemer? Christ is the propitiation for our sins. Laying aside His royal robe and kingly crown, He stepped from His high command, and clothed His divinity with humanity. For our sakes He became poor, that we through His poverty might be made rich. (See 2 Corinthians 8:9)

To us has been given the privilege of laying up treasure in heaven. This we may do by following Christ. He came to our world to demonstrate to the universe that man, his eyes fixed upon God, can be an overcomer. Thus was fulfilled the promise that the seed of the woman should bruise the serpent's head. Christ humiliated Himself to stand at the head of humanity, that we might be heirs to an immortal inheritance in the kingdom of glory.

When Christ came to John for baptism, John refused to baptize Him, saying, "I have need to be baptized of thee, and comest thou to me?" "Suffer it to be so now," Christ said, "for thus it becometh us to fulfil all righteousness." (See Matthew 3:14, 15) Provision has been made that when man repents and takes the steps requisite in conversion, he shall be forgiven. When he is baptized in the name of the Father, the Son, and the Holy Ghost, these three great powers are pledged to work in his behalf. And man on his part, as he goes down into the water, to be buried in the likeness of Christ's death and raised in the likeness of His resurrection, pledges himself to worship the true and living God, to come out from the world and be separate, to keep the law of Jehovah.

When Christ bowed on the banks of Jordan and offered up prayer to heaven, it was in our behalf that He prayed. And as He prayed, the heavens were opened, and the glory of God like a dove of burnished gold rested upon Him, while from the highest heaven was heard a voice, saying, "This is my beloved Son, in whom I am well pleased." (Matthew 3:17) This is heaven's pledge in behalf of humanity. Christ's prayer was offered for us. We are accepted in the Beloved. What an incentive this should be to us to strive earnestly and perseveringly to please our Saviour, to live so that He shall not have died for us in vain!

Think of the possibilities and probabilities before us. We can have all the strength of heaven; for when God gave Christ to our world, He gave all heaven. The Saviour's long human arm encircles the race, while with His divine arm He grasps the throne of the Infinite. We are sinful, but Christ is sinless, and through Him we may stand on vantage ground with God. "God so loved the world that he gave his only begotten Son, that whosoever believeth in him should not perish, but have everlasting life." (John 3:16) There is no excuse for any man or woman to lose eternal life. Everyone can gain heaven, but God will not force anyone to accept the provisions He has made. God forces no one to obey. Neither does He place anyone in a position where he will be tempted above that he is able to bear.

We have everything to be thankful for. Never ought Christians to move along like a band of mourners in a funeral train. God does not require this of His followers. He does not ask them to spread sackcloth and ashes under them. "Is it such a fast that I have chosen?" he asks; "a day for a man to afflict his soul? Is it to bow down his head as a bulrush, and to spread sackcloth and ashes under him? Wilt thou call this a fast, and an acceptable day unto the Lord?" God tells us what kind of a fast He has chosen. "Is not this the fast that I have chosen? To loose the bands of wickedness, to undo the heavy burdens, and to let the oppressed go free, and that ye break every yoke?" This is the fast he wishes us to observe. "Is it not to deal thy bread to the hungry, and that thou bring the poor that are cast out to thy house? When thou seest the naked that thou cover him; and that thou hide not thyself from thine own flesh?" (Isaiah 58:5-7) In these words our duty is outlined. God shows us where we should place our treasures. As we follow in the path of self-denial and self-sacrifice, helping the needy and suffering, we shall lay up treasure before the throne of God.

The advantage this will be to us is shown in the following words:

"Then shall thy light break forth as the morning, and thine health shall spring forth speedily; and thy righteousness shall go before thee; the glory of the Lord shall be thy rereward. Then shalt thou call, and the Lord shall answer; thou shalt cry, and he shall say, 'Here I am'." (Isaiah 58:8, 9) Here is shown action and reaction. As we impart the goods the Lord has lent us in trust, we receive more to impart, and blessing comes to us. As we take hold upon Christ as a personal Saviour, we are enabled to do "all things."

Christ is not dead. He has proclaimed over the rent sepulcher of Joseph, "I am the resurrection and the life" (John 11:25). Satan has thrown his dark shadow across our pathway, but let not our faith falter. Rather, let it cleave through the shadows to the place where Christ sits as our Intercessor. Satan is trying to hide the light of heaven from us, but he cannot do this if we will cling to the mighty One. Call upon the Lord, and He will answer, "Here am I." Cooperate with God in striving against the enemy. Put on the Lord Jesus Christ, and be determined that you will be temperate in all things.

Remember that there is a world to save. We are to act our part, standing close by the side of Christ as His co-laborers. He is the head; we are His helping hand. He designs that we, by doing medical missionary work, shall undo the heavy burdens and let the oppressed go free. Let us not close our eyes to the misery around us or our ears to the cries of distress which are continually ascending. Christ is the greatest missionary the world has ever known. He came to uplift and cheer the sorrowing and distressed, and in this work we are to cooperate with Him.

Intemperance is seen on every side. What are you doing to overcome it? What are you doing to baffle the efforts of the enemy? Are you standing for the right as did Daniel in the courts of Babylon? He was tempted, but he would not swerve from the principles of right. He refused to partake of the food and wine from the king's table, and requested that he and his companions be allowed a simpler diet. His request was granted, and ten days' trial revealed that the Hebrew youth possessed health and fairness of countenance which were not possessed by those who had eaten of the food from the king's table. Let us be Daniels in this world of temptation and trial, standing steadfastly for the right because it is right.

"No man can serve two masters: for either he will hate the one, and love the other; or else he will hold to the one, and despise the other. Ye cannot serve God and mammon." (Matthew 6:24) If you center your thoughts upon the world, you will be worldly; you cannot help but be. But if you weave into your life the principles of heaven, keeping your attention fixed on Christ, you will be prepared for association with the angels. Remember that God wants you to bring Christ into your business transactions just as surely as into the house of prayer. He wants us to bear the testimony that in a world corrupted by sin, human beings can live untainted by worldliness. He wants us to show that we are standing under the bloodstained banner of prince Emmanuel. He does not tell us that the path to heaven is a smooth one. He takes us to an eminence and shows us the powers of darkness arrayed against us. But He tells us that more than men are in the army fighting on the side of right. "Be of good cheer," he says, "I have overcome the world." (John 16:33)

After assuring us that we cannot serve two masters, Christ says, "Take no thought for your life, what ye shall eat, or what ye shall drink; nor yet for your body, what ye shall put on. Is not the life more than meat, and the body than raiment." (Matthew 6:25) What we need is the robe of Christ's righteousness. Christ says that He will take away our sins, and cover us with His righteousness.

Fathers and mothers, God has placed the younger members of His family under your care. Are you fitting them to live that life which measures with the life of God? Are you teaching them by example to hide the life with Christ in God, to believe in Him, to love Him? God said of Abraham, "I know him, that he will command his children and his household after him, and they shall keep the way of the Lord, to do justice and judgment." (Genesis 18:19) Now, as then, this is what God requires from parents. He wants them to educate their children in such a way that when they go forth into the world, they will resist the temptations which beset them on every side.

Parents, God desires you to make your family a sample of the family in heaven. Guard your children. Be kind and tender with them. Father, mother, and children are to be joined together with the golden links of love. One well-ordered, well-disciplined family is a greater power in demonstrating the efficiency of Christianity than all the sermons in the world. When fathers and mothers realize how their children copy them, they will watch carefully every word and gesture.

Educate your children from their babyhood to be cheerful and obedient. Teach them to help you. Tell them that they are a part of the firm, and that you need their help, so that you will be spared to care for them. "Oh," say some mothers, "my children bother me when they try to help me." So did mine, but do you think I let them know it? Praise your children. Teach them, line upon line, precept upon precept. This is better than reading novels, better than making calls, better than following the fashions of the world. We shall go through this life but once. We cannot afford to fail of reaching the goal for which Christ has told us to strive.

Do you teach your children to pray? It pays to be a praying household. The world is given up to horse racing and games. Are you teaching your children to run with patience the race for the crown of life? Those who run in the races of this world are temperate in all things, knowing that if they succeed they must keep the powers of the body in the best condition. How important, then, that those who are running the race for immortality be temperate in all things, that they may serve God acceptably.

Close the windows of the soul earthward and open them wide heavenward. If you let the bright beams of the Sun of Righteousness flood the soul temple, you will not be cross or irritable in your home. If you put away from you tobacco and liquor and all that tends of intemperance, the Lord will help you to be cheerful and serene. He does not want us to live on the flesh of animals. He has something better for us—fruits and grains. He wants us to be strictly temperate. He wants us to teach our children to be temperate, to practice self-denial.

Let us make straight paths for our feet, lest the lame be turned out of the way. If we allow our children to associate with evil companions, they will by beholding become changed. They will lose the sense of repulsion to evil. Let us do all in our power to keep them from the evil that is in the world. Some years ago, while rowing on Lake Goguac with my husband, we saw a beautiful lily. I asked my husband to get it for me, and to pluck it with as long a stem as he could. He did so, and I examined it. In the stem was a channel through which flowed the nourishment best suited to the development of the lily. This nourishment it took, refusing the vileness with which it was surrounded. It had a connection with the sand far below the surface, and from there drew the sustenance which caused it to develop in its loveliness.

Christ says, "Consider the lilies of the field, how they grow; they toil not, neither do they spin: and yet I say unto you, That even Solomon in all his glory was not arrayed like one of these." (Matthew 6:28, 29) No artist can produce the beautiful tints which God gives to the flowers. "Wherefore, if God so clothe the grass of the field, which today is, and tomorrow is cast into the oven, shall he not much more clothe you, O ye of little faith?" (Matthew 6:30)

Nature is our lesson book. Christ used the objects of nature to impress truth on the minds of His hearers. Let us point our children to these things. When they are impatient and fretful, take them into the garden, and teach them the lessons found in the flowers and fruits.

"Therefore take no thought, saying, What shall we eat? Or, What shall we drink? Or Wherewithal shall we be clothed? ... for your heavenly Father knoweth that ye have need of all these things. But seek ye first the kingdom of God and his righteousness; and all these things shall be added unto you. Take therefore no thought for the morrow: for the morrow shall take thought for the things of itself. Sufficient unto the day is the evil thereof." (Matthew 6:31-34)

Let us do all we can to show our children that there is a heaven to win and a hell to shun. Let us teach them to strive for everlasting life. And remember that you will not help them by scolding. This stirs up the worst passions of the human heart. Make home pleasant. Be kind and gentle, but at the same time, be firm, requiring obedience. I have brought up children who by others were pronounced incorrigible. I never struck them a blow. I won their love and their confidence. They knew that I would ask them to do nothing but what was for their happiness. I did not whip them, knowing that this would not make them righteous. Prayer was my strength. Bring your children up in the admonition of the Lord, and you have fitted them to work in the church, you have fitted them to go forth into missionary fields, you have fitted them to shine in the courts of the Lord.

Parents, do not try to follow the ever-changing fashions of this degenerate age. It does not pay. At the last day God will ask you, "What have you done with my flock, my beautiful flock?" (See Jeremiah 13:20) How will you answer Him if you have betrayed your trust? For Christ's sake I beseech you to guard your children. Do not be cross or hasty. Give them happy things to think of.

Christ gave His life for our children and for us, because He desired us to form characters after the divine similitude, that we may enter in through the gates into the holy city, and hear from the divine lips the benediction, "Well done, good and faithful servant, ... enter thou into the joy of thy Lord" (Matthew 25:23). Do you not want to hear these words? Strive with all the power God has given you to gain the crown of everlasting life, that you may cast it at the feet of the Redeemer, and touching the golden harp, fill all heaven with rich music. God help you to gain eternal life, that you may see His face.[34]

---

[34] Ms. 31, 1901; MR 900.3.

Chapter 35

The Student's Privelege

[Portion of an address given at the opening of the Fernando, California, school, Oct. 1, 1902]

I am glad to see so many here this morning. Students, I desire to say to you that the prosperity of the school depends largely upon your endeavors. Your teachers will do all that they can to help you. They will try to show you what you must do to inherit eternal life. They will try to show you how to become conversant with the living principles of truth, that you may stand before God and men on vantage ground. Will you cooperate with your teachers? Will you strive earnestly to become useful men and women? Christ is waiting to help you, and He is an all-powerful Helper. When God gave Him to our world, He gave all heaven. He placed in His hands every power, every facility of heaven, to give to those who receive Him. Christ came to our world to give us an example of what we may become, to show us that we may live a perfect life. He says to us, "Lo, I am with you I, even unto the end of the world." (Matthew 28:20)

Students, you are here to obtain an education that will help you to stand by the side of Christ in unselfish service. This is the highest education that you can possibly obtain. The Word of God declares, "Ye are laborers together with God." "Work out your own salvation with fear and trembling. For it is God which worketh in you both to will and to do of His good pleasure." (Philippians 2:12, 13) As you stand firm for God, filled with courage and perseverance, constantly revealing self-denial, angels from heaven will come into this school. They will keep guard over you. Your health will be precious in God's sight, because you keep His commandments.

Do not let self-assertion mingle with your work. Remember the lesson that Christ gave to His disciples when they were contending as to who among them should be the greatest. Placing a little child in the midst of them, He said, "Except ye be converted, and become as little children, ye shall not enter into the kingdom of heaven. Whosoever therefore shall humble himself as this little child, the same is greatest in the kingdom of heaven." (Matthew 18:3, 4)

In your school work, do not spend time in learning that which will be of little use to you in your after life. Instead of trying to gain a knowledge of foreign languages, strive first to speak the English language correctly. Be sure to learn how to keep accounts. Gain a knowledge of those lines of study that will help you to be useful wherever you are.

Remember constantly your need of a union with Christ. United with Him, you will bring into your work the fragrance of His character, and your well-ordered life will be a blessing to your teachers and your fellow-students. The sanctifying presence of God will be with you as you seek to do His will with a sincere desire to glorify Him.

Among these students there are those who have come here to prepare themselves for missionary work. May the Lord help you and bless your efforts. The number of our missionaries is not half large enough. The fields are white, ready to harvest, but the laborers are few. God is waiting to endow you with power from on high, that you may go forth to work for him.

There will come to you many opportunities to help one another. Not all are able to grasp ideas quickly. If you see that a fellow-student has difficulty in understanding his lessons, explain them to him. Be patient and persevering, and by-and-by his hesitancy and dullness will disappear. He will gain courage and strength to endure trial. And in the effort to help others, you, too, will be blessed. God will give you power to advance in your studies. He will cooperate with you in your effort to help your fellow-students, and in heaven the words will be spoken of you, "Well done, good and faithful servant."

Let two or three students meet together, and ask God to help them to be missionaries in this school, a blessing and a help to their fellow-students. The lives of such ones will exert a powerful influence for good on those who scoff at religion.

Let your faith be pure and strong and steadfast. Bring all the pleasantness you can into the school, Let gratitude to God fill your hearts. Remember the words, "Whoso offereth praise glorifieth God." (See Psalm 50:23) When you rise in the morning, kneel at your bedside and ask God to give you strength to fulfill the duties of the day and to meet its temptations. Ask Him to help you to bring into your work Christ's sweetness of character. Ask Him to help you to speak words that will draw those around you nearer to Christ.

Live in this world to some purpose. If you waste the life that God has given you, when Christ comes to gather His children home you will have no place in the mansions that He is preparing for those that love Him.

God wants you to receive the wisdom that He has for you. He wants you to be

Bible students and Bible believers, living in obedience to the words, "Thou shalt love the Lord thy God with all thy heart, and with all thy soul, and with all thy strength, and with all thy mind: and thy neighbor as thyself." (Luke 10:27) Then He can bestow on you the power of His truth. Then He can mold and fashion you after the divine similitude. Living in conformity to Christ's will, you will be changed into His likeness. You will grow up into Him, and at last the pearly gates of the holy city will for you swing back on their glittering hinges, and you will enter to hear the words, "Blessed are they that do His commandments, that they may have right to the tree of life, and may enter in through the gates into the city." (Revelation 22:14) In your hands will be placed a golden harp and, touching its strings, you will join with the redeemed host in filling all heaven with songs of praise to God and to His Son.

Students, do your best. This is all that God asks of you. He who has given His life for you will aid you in your efforts to win eternal life. God wants you to have a far more exceeding and eternal weight of glory. Obey Him and in this school His salvation will be revealed. I want to meet you all around the throne of God. Learn here the lessons God desires to teach you, and you will join in the song of triumph in the heavenly courts.[35]

---

[35] Ms 125a, 1902; "The Student's Privilege." Portion of an address given at the opening of the Fernando, California, School, Oct. 1, 1902; MR 900.6.

Chapter 36

Word to Students

[A Talk given by Ellen White at the opening of the Fernando School, October 1, 1902]

I am indeed glad to see so many here this morning. Students, will you remember that the prosperity of the school depends in a large degree on your endeavors? Will you remember that you are to help to make the school a success? Your teachers will find their task difficult as they try to understand for themselves and to help you to understand what the Word of God means and what its requirements comprehend. Will you resolve not to make the work of your teachers harder by your perversity? I plead with you as Christ's purchased possession to help your teachers and your fellow-students by being so closely connected with God that into this school heavenly angels can enter and abide. Let everyone see what he can do to bring into the school sunshine and sweetness. Let everyone manifest that conformity to God's will that brings His rich blessing.

Students, you are here to fit yourselves to enter the higher school. You are here to obtain a knowledge of God, to learn how to obey His commandments. Obedience is our life in this world, and it will be our life in the world to come. And remember that a knowledge of God and of Christ is the sum of all science. God teaches us to count all things but loss for the excellency of the knowledge of Christ Jesus our Lord. To know God and Christ--this is eternal life. Incorporated with the life, this knowledge fits us for heaven. And all other knowledge, however high or broad, unless charged with it, is valueless in God's sight.

You have been bought with a price--and what a price! Who can measure the line let down from heaven for the saving of the subjects of sin. Who can compass a love that is as broad as eternity? Think of the sacrifice that Christ made for you. He stepped down from His high command, and came to this world with the treasures of heaven, that every human being might have power to reach the standard set before him in God's law. Clothing His divinity with humanity, He came to stand at the head of the human race, in our behalf to live a perfect life, that He might know how to help us in our conflict with sin. Through His sacrifice, human beings may reach the high ideal set before them, and hear at last the words, You are complete in Him, not having your own righteousness, but the righteousness that He wrought out for you, Your imperfection is no longer seen; for you are clothed with the robe of Christ's perfection.

After His baptism, Christ knelt on the banks of Jordan and offered prayer to His Father, And as He prayed, the heavens were opened, and the glory of God, like a dove of burnished gold, rested upon Him, while from the highest heaven there came the voice, "This is my beloved Son, in whom I am well pleased." (Matthew 3:17) Christ's prayer was offered for us, and it cleaves through every shadow that Satan casts between us and God. In our behalf the Saviour laid hold of the power of Omnipotence, and as we pray to God, we may know that Christ's prayer has ascended before, and that God has heard and answered it. With all our sins and weaknesses we are not cast aside as worthless. "He hath made us accepted in the beloved." The glory that rested upon Christ is a pledge of the love of God for us. It tells of the power of prayer--how the human voice may reach the ear of God, and our petitions find acceptance in the courts of heaven. The light that fell from the open portals upon the head of our Saviour, will fall upon us as we pray for help to resist temptation. The voice that spoke to Jesus says to every believing soul, "This is My beloved child, in whom I am well pleased."

You remember the experience of Daniel. He received wisdom and understanding because he placed himself in right relation with God. God has intelligence for you, just as He had for Daniel. He has knowledge for you that is far above all human knowledge. If you stand where Daniel stood, you will gain a progressive education, and a progressive education means a progressive sanctification. Such an education will prepare you to inherit the kingdom that from the foundation of the world has been prepared for God's faithful ones. As you strive to obtain a knowledge of God, He will commune with you as He communed with Daniel and his companions, and will give you power that will prevail.

Your teachers will do all that they can to help you. They will try to show you what you must do to inherit eternal life. They will try to show you how to become conversant with the living principles of truth, that you may stand before God and men on vantage ground. Will you cooperate with your teachers? Will you strive earnestly to become useful men and women? Christ is waiting to help you, and He is an all-powerful Helper. When God gave Him to our world, He gave all heaven. He placed in His hands every power, every facility of heaven, to give to those who receive Him. Christ came to our world to give us an example of what we may become, to show us that we may live a perfect life. He says to us, "Lo, I am with you alway, even unto the end of the world."

What are you here for? Is it to obtain an education that will help you to stand by the side of Christ in unselfish service? This is the highest education that you can possibly obtain. The Word of God declares, "Ye are laborers together with God." "Work out your own salvation with fear and trembling. For it is God which worketh in you both to will and to do of His good pleasure." (Philippians 2:12, 13) As you stand firm for God, filled with courage and perseverance, constantly revealing self-denial, angels from heaven will come into this school. They will keep guard over you. Your health will be precious in God's sight because you keep His commandments.

Do not let self-assertion mingle with your work. Remember the lesson that Christ gave to His disciples when they were contending as to whom among them should be the greatest. Placing a little child in the midst of them, He said, "Except ye be converted, and become as little children, ye shall not enter into the kingdom of heaven. Whosoever therefore shall humble himself as this little child, the same is greatest in the kingdom of heaven." (Matthew 18:3, 4)

In your school work, do not spend time in learning that which will be of little use to you in your after life. Instead of trying to gain a knowledge of foreign languages, strive first to speak the English language correctly. Be sure to learn how to keep accounts. Gain a knowledge of those lines of study that will help you to be useful wherever you are.

Remember constantly your need of a union with Christ. United with Him, you will bring into your work the fragrance of His character, and your well-ordered life will be a blessing to your teachers and your fellow-students. The sanctifying presence of God will be with you as you seek to do His will with a sincere desire to glorify Him.

Among these students there are those who have come here to prepare themselves for missionary work. May the Lord help you, and bless your efforts. The number of our missionaries is not half large enough. The fields are white, ready to harvest, but the laborers are few. God is waiting to endow you with power from on high, that you may go forth to work for Him.

I want to speak a few more words to you about helping one another. Not all are able to grasp ideas quickly. If you see that a fellow-student has difficulty in understanding his lessons, explain them to him. Be patient and persevering, and by-and-by his hesitancy and dullness will disappear. He will gain courage and strength to endure trial. And in the effort to help others, you, too, will be helped. God will give you power to advance your studies. He will cooperate with you in your efforts to help your fellow-students, and in heaven the words will be spoken of you, "Well done, good and faithful servant."

Let two or three students meet together, and ask God to help them to be missionaries in this school, a blessing and a help to their fellow-students. The lives of such ones will exert a powerful influence for good on those who scoff at religion.

Let your faith be pure and strong and steadfast. Bring all the pleasantness you can into the school. Let gratitude to God fill your hearts. Remember the words, "Whoso offereth praise glorifieth God." When you rise in the morning, kneel at your bedside and ask God to give you strength to fulfill the duties of the day and to meet its temptations. Ask Him to help you to bring into your work Christ's sweetness of character. Ask Him to help you to speak words that will draw those around you nearer to Christ.

Live in this world to some purpose. If you waste the life that God has given you, when Christ comes to gather His children home, you will have no place in the mansions that He is preparing for those that love Him.

God wants you to receive the wisdom that He has for you. He wants you to be Bible students and Bible believers, living in obedience to the words, "Thou shalt love the Lord thy God with all thy heart, and with all thy soul, and with all thy strength, and with all thy mind; and thy neighbor as thyself." (Luke 10:27) Then he can bestow on you the power of His truth. Then He can mold and fashion you after the divine similitude. Living in conformity to Christ's will, you will be changed into His likeness. You will grow up into Him, and at last the pearly gates of the holy city will for you swing back on their glittering hinges, and you will enter to hear the words, "Blessed are they that do His commandments, that they may have right to the tree of life, and may enter in through the gates into the city." (Revelation 22:14) In your hands will be placed a golden harp, and touching its strings, you will join with the redeemed host in filling all heaven with songs of praise to God and His Son.

Students, do your best. This is all that God asks of you. He who has given His life for you will aid you in your efforts to win eternal life. God wants you to have a far more exceeding and eternal weight of glory. Obey Him, and in this school His salvation will be revealed. I want to meet you all around the throne of God. Learn here the lessons God desires to teach you, and you will join in the song of triumph in the heavenly courts.[36]

---

[36] Ms 125, 1902; "Words to Students," a talk given at the opening of the Fernando School, Oct. 1, 1902; MR 900.7.

Chapter 37

The Foundation of Our Faith

[See Selected Messages, book 1, pp. 201-208, for a similar, though not identical, presentation]

At this time--the last days of this earth's history--we are to make the book of Revelation a special study. Why? Because it depicts the scenes that we are to meet. We need to understand what we are to meet, and how we are to meet it. We must know what efforts we are to make, so that, in this perilous time, we shall not be taken by the enemy's devices. We know that the last great conflict will be Satan's most determined effort to accomplish his purposes. He will come, not only as a roaring lion, but as a seducer, clothing sin with beautiful garments of light, that he may take human beings in his snare.

The Lord desires us to realize that it is of great importance that we stand in these last days upon the platform of eternal truth. Those who think that the church militant is the church triumphant make a great mistake. The church militant will gain great triumphs, but it will also have fierce conflicts with evil, that it may be firmly established upon the platform of eternal truth. And every one of us should be determined to stand with the church upon this platform.

(Revelation 1:1-3, 9-13, 17-20 quoted)

Thus Christ instructed John. It is the word of God that you will find in the book of Revelation. There are those today who call the Revelation a sealed book. But it is a mystery unfolded. We need to understand what it tells us in regard to the scenes that are to take place in the last days of this earth's history. The enemy will bring in everything that he possibly can to carry out his deceptive designs. Are they not lacking in wisdom who have no desire to understand in regard to the things that are to take place on this earth?

I am so sorry that Living Temple came out as it did, and was circulated, and the worst of it--that which struck right to my heart--was the assertion made regarding the book: "It contains the very sentiments that Sister White has been teaching." When I heard this, I felt so heartbroken that it seemed as if I could not say anything. Had I said anything, I would have been obliged to speak the truth as it was.

Representations had been shown me that some danger was approaching, and that I must prepare for it. I must write out the things God had given me in order to prepare for it.

I did not read Living Temple, though I had it in my library. At last my son said to me, "Mother, you ought to read at least some parts of the book, that you may see whether they are in harmony with the light that God has given you." He sat down beside me, and we read the paragraphs to which he referred. When we had finished I turned to him and said, "These are the very sentiments against which I was bidden to speak in warning at the very beginning of my public work. When I first left the State of Maine, it was to go through Vermont and Massachusetts, to bear a testimony against these sentiments. Living Temple contains the Alpha of these theories. The Omega would follow in a little while. I tremble for our people. These beautiful representations are similar to the temptation that the enemy brought to Adam and Eve in Eden.

When but a girl I went to New Hampshire to bear warning against these same doctrines. There was a man by the name of Billings and another by the name of Bennet who were preaching a higher spirituality. I was asked to meet these men, and I did so, giving them the light that God had given me. In the meeting a great distress came upon me. I was taken off in vision. The men began to triumph, thinking that things were going their way. When I got up to bear my testimony, they began to shout. I stopped and did not say a word until they had finished. Then I went on and told them plainly where the doctrines they were advocating would lead to.

I met these same doctrines in Dorchester, Mass., where for a time I made my home. In one meeting held there a man arose and after making a confession, said, "I have listened today to the testimony of Ellen Harmon, and I feel as if I had been partaking of the richest feast ever set before me." In the past this man had been a model of piety, but these seductive theories came before him--theories teaching that men and women could live above all sin--and he accepted them. What was the result? He left his wife and children and went to live with another woman.

I was at this time nothing but a girl, and I said, "Why am I left to bear this testimony?" Said the one in whose house I was staying, "God knows why. The men advocating these doctrines have a strong influence as being very pious men, and if we were to say anything against them, they would put us in prison. But you are a minor, and they cannot touch you."

We met these theories again in Topsham, Maine. A brother there, who had accepted them, was very sick, and he wanted me to pray for him. I said, "I cannot pray for you so long as you and these sisters are so free with one another." He sent for Elder James White, who, when he came, asked him, "What are you going to do?" "Do!" he said, "Do you ask what I am going to do? I am going to cut loose from all these evils. I am going to take my stand in harmony with what Sister Ellen Harmon has been presenting to me. I accept what she has said as the word of the Lord." Thus the company with which he was connected was broken up. And many more such companies were broken up by the light that God gave me.

Thus I worked and suffered in my girlhood. And all through my life I have had the same errors to meet, though not always in the same form. In Living Temple the assertion is made that God is in the flower, in the leaf, in the sinner. But God does not live in the sinner. The Word declares that He abides only in the hearts of those who love Him and do righteousness. God does not abide in the heart of the sinner; it is the enemy who abides there.

There are some things upon which we must reason, and there are other things that we must not discuss. In regard to God--what He is and where He is--silence is eloquence. When you are tempted to speak of what God is, keep silence, because as surely as you begin to speak of this, you will disparage Him.

Our ministers must be very careful not to enter into controversy in regard to the personality of God. This is a subject that they are not to touch. It is a mystery, and the enemy will surely lead astray those who enter into it. We know that Christ came in person to reveal God to the world. God is a person and Christ is a person. Christ is spoken of in the Word as "the brightness of His Father's glory, and the express image of His person."

I was forbidden to talk with Dr. Kellogg on this subject, because it is not a subject to be talked about. And I was instructed that certain sentiments in Living Temple were the Alpha of a long list of deceptive theories.

These sentiments have had an effect on our people everywhere. Some think it strange that I write, "Do not send your children to Battle Creek." I was instructed in regard to the danger of the worldly influence in Battle Creek. I have written hundreds of pages regarding the danger of having so large a sanitarium, and of calling so many young people together in one place. The young people in Battle Creek are in danger. They will come in contact with error. Years ago I did not think that they would meet these errors right in the Sanitarium; but when Living Temple came out, and some of our ministers told me that there was in it nothing but what I had been teaching all my life, I saw how great the danger was. I saw that blindness had fallen upon some who had long known the truth. I pray that the Lord will open the eyes of these ministers, that they may see the differences between light and darkness, and between truth and error.

In a representation which passed before me, I saw a certain work being done by medical missionary workers. Our ministering brethren were looking on, watching what was being done, but they did not seem to understand. The foundation of our faith, which was established by so much prayer, such earnest searching of the Scriptures, was being taken down, pillar by pillar. Our faith was to have nothing to rest upon--the sanctuary was gone, the atonement was gone. I realized that something must be done.

The battle nearly killed me. I saw what was coming in, and I saw that our brethren were blind. They did not realize the danger. Our young people, especially, were in danger. They delighted in the beautiful representation--God in the flower, God in the leaf, God in the tree. But if God be in these things, why not worship them?

The reason I have published anything in regard to the medical missionary work, was that the errors that were coming in must be met. I did not design to meet them, but in the visions of the night I saw a large ship far out at sea. Suddenly the man on the lookout cried, "Iceberg ahead!" Without hesitation the command rang out, "Meet it." The engines were put on at full force, and the vessel crashed into the iceberg. There was a tremendous shock, and the ship quivered from stem to stern; but she rebounded from the shock unhurt, and went safely on her way. After seeing this representation. I knew what work I must do. I knew that I must meet the errors that were coming in among us.

I have been hoping that there would be a thorough reformation, that the principles for which we fought in my girlhood, and which were brought out in the power of the Holy Spirit, would be maintained. Night after night in our early experience our brethren studied out the truths which we now hold. When they came to something that they could not understand, they would get down on their knees, and would remain there for hours sometimes. Sometimes the sun would rise before they would give up the struggle. At times, when they said, "We can do nothing more," the power of God would come upon me, I would be taken off in vision, and instruction would be given me. Then I could explain what they could not understand. I would read the Scriptures to them, never looking at the printed page. Thus light was given in regard to Christ, His mission, and His priesthood, and the great points of our faith were firmly established.

But during this period of our experience, my mind was locked to an understanding of the Scriptures. It was one of the greatest sorrows of my life. Thus it was every point of our faith was established in harmony with the Word of God.

At this time I was living in the house of Father Andrews. He was helpless with rheumatism, and was constantly in great suffering. I knelt by his side and, laying my hands on his head, asked Jesus to make him whole. The power of God came upon him and he walked back and forth across the room, praising the Lord.

Soon after this I was instructed by the Lord that I should no longer mourn in regard to my inability to understand the Scriptures. God unlocked my mind and ever since, whenever I read His Word, a flood of light comes into my mind.

Thus the work went on and we were shown where we must stand. Do you wonder that I have something to say when I see the pillars of our faith beginning to be moved? Seductive theories are being taught in such a way that we shall not recognize them unless we have clear spiritual discernment. I will stand firmly with everyone who will stand for the truth. But I do not want our young people to flock into Battle Creek. They would better not go there. Anyone who can be so utterly deceived as to place the misleading sentiments contained in Living Temple before our people, cannot be trusted as a teacher of the youth until he is converted.

I have the tenderest sympathy for the physicians associated with Dr. Kellogg. But I have no sympathy for their failure to pass over the mistakes that they see made by Dr. Kellogg, saying nothing about them. God will hold them accountable for letting matters go without saying, "Doctor, you did not do right that time." The poor man has loaded himself down until the enemy finds him a very easy prey. Unless he changes his course, and takes an entirely different course, he will be lost to the cause of God. And his associate physicians will be guilty before God unless they take their position and stand free from every error.

I have lain awake night after night, studying how I could help Dr. Kellogg. His father and mother, before they died, begged me not to give him up, but to stand by him till the last. I said, "I will try, if he will listen to me." I have spent nearly whole nights in prayer for him. Week after week I have not slept till twelve o'clock, and then for weeks I have not been able to sleep past twelve o'clock. I wrote constantly, until my left eye gave out. And at last my brain became so weary that I could not use it. My son would come up to my room and ask if he might read some letters that had come. "No, Willie," I would say, "not a word." I was in this condition for several weeks. Just before Willie left home last winter for Washington, I saw that his eyes were troubling him, and I offered to read some manuscripts to him. This brought on the old trouble. After Willie had gone, I had to give up entirely for a time. I felt that I was worn out. My brain had ceased to work. My mental suffering was intense. I had a great deal of pain at the base of the brain. I knew that for a time my mind was at a standstill.

Willie expected me to go to Washington in the spring, but it seemed to me that I could not go. I got up one morning and it seemed to me as if I had come to the place where I could not go another step. I said, "Lord, if it is Thy will for me to go into the grave, take away my life, but do not take away my life and allow me still to live." Over and over again I offered this prayer, and all at once I seemed to be shut in by a canopy of light. Every particle of pain had left my head, and the next day I wrote twenty pages before dinner.

I feared that when I started for Washington, the difficulty would come on again, but it did not. I wrote something every day during my stay in Washington, and spoke three times. Every time I entered the pulpit it was in fear and trembling, but the Lord sustained me and helped me.

My brethren, the Lord calls for unity, for oneness. We are to be one in the faith. I want to tell you that when the gospel ministers and the medical missionary workers are not united, there is placed on our churches the worst evil that can be placed there. Our medical missionaries ought to be interested in the work of our conferences, and our conference workers ought to be as much interested in the work of our medical missionaries.

It is time that we stood upon a united platform. But we cannot unite with Dr. Kellogg until he stands where he can be a safe leader of the flock of God. Until he stands in this position, we have no right to sustain him.

I have taken my position, brethren. I am not going to enter into controversy over anything that may be presented. Last night I woke at ten o'clock and remained awake for several hours. During that time the whole matter was laid open before me, and I was instructed that I must bear the testimony given me and then leave matters with the Lord. It is not my work to try to make people believe the message given me. When the assertion is made, "Someone has told her," I am to make no response. On that point the conflict is over for me. I shall tell you the truth as it is in Jesus. And when anyone comes to me to know about this thing or that thing, I shall point them to the One who has said, "Come unto Me, all ye that labour and are heavy laden, and I will give you rest. Take My yoke upon you, and learn of Me; for I am meek and lowly in heart: and ye shall find rest unto your souls. For My yoke is easy, and My burden is light." (Matthew 11:28-30)[37]

---

[37] Ms. 46, 1904; MR 900.1

Chapter 38

Instruction to Sanitarium and Restaurant Workers

"Cry aloud, spare not, lift up thy voice like a trumpet, and show My people their transgression, and the house of Jacob their sins. Yet they seek Me daily, and delight to know My ways, as a nation that did righteousness, and forsook not the ordinance of their God: they ask of Me the ordinances of justice; they take delight in approaching to God. Wherefore have we fasted, say they, and Thou seest not? wherefore have we afflicted our soul, and thou takest no knowledge?" (Isaiah 58:1-3)

The people here mentioned are represented as bringing a charge against God. They have been active in observing the outward forms of worship, and they complain because God does not acknowledge their works, and because He does not answer their prayers. But the Lord charges them with neglecting His work and refusing to follow His way.

"Behold," He says, "in the day of your fast ye find pleasure, and exact all your labours. Behold, ye fast for strife and debate, and to smite with the fist of wickedness: ye shall not fast as ye do this day, to make your voice to be heard on high." (Verses 3 and 4)

It is possible for us to be deceived in regard to our relation to God. We are not to reproach our Maker if we do not see everything worked out just as we desire. Let us rather examine ourselves to see if we are keeping His words.

In contrast with the worship offered Him by this people, God places the work that He desires them to perform. (Isaiah 58:5-7 quoted)

Here is a work for every individual. Christ's followers are to relieve the necessities of humanity wherever they see suffering or oppression. They are ever to be ready to speak a word in season to him that is weary.

We have a work to do for others. We cannot afford to live merely for ourselves. We are to represent the great Medical Missionary, who came to our world to seek and save that which was lost. When we do the work to which God calls us, we are assured of His blessing.

Chapter 39

A Divine Prescription

"Then shall thy light break forth as the morning, and thine health shall spring forth speedily." The great Physician will care for those who carry on the work that He did when He was in our world. Are you sick? Here is a prescription that will restore you to health. As you forget yourself, and take an unselfish interest in those around you, the mighty Healer will acknowledge your work and give you strength beyond your expectations. "Then shall thy light break forth as the morning, and thine health shall spring forth speedily: and thy righteousness shall go before thee; the glory of the Lord shall be thy rereward" (Verse 8). Who is our righteousness? The Lord Jesus Christ. Let us study the record of His life on this earth. Let us carry out the principles in our everyday life that He has given for us to follow. Then His righteousness will go before us, and His glory will be our rearward. Here is the prescription for every soul to accept.

"What shall I do that I may inherit eternal life? (Mark 10:17), asked the lawyer of Christ. "What is written in the law? how readest thou?" the Saviour said. The lawyer answered, "Thou shalt love the Lord thy God with all thy heart, and with all thy soul, and with all thy strength, and with all thy mind; and thy neighbor as thyself," and Christ replied, "Thou hast answered right: this do, and thou shalt live." (Luke 10:26-28) Those who will obey these two great principles will have the constant blessing of God.

Chapter 40

How to Receive an Answer to Our Prayers

"Then shalt thou call, and the Lord shall answer; thou shalt cry, and He shall say, Here I am" (Isaiah 58:9). Do you feel that your prayers are unanswered? Then do as Christ directs you. In His word He has declared it; by His Spirit He testifies to it. Will you follow the directions? Will you relieve the necessities of those around you? Will you work in behalf of the oppressed? Will you practice the life of Christ in seeking to save the souls ready to perish? In such work you will have the comfort of the grace of God in rich measure.

(Isaiah 58:9-11 quoted) I thank the Lord with heart and soul and voice for this assurance. When in trouble you may not always feel the assurance of help, but you can always say, The Lord has said it, and I will trust in Him. (Verse 12, quoted)

These words outline our work. We are to repair the breach that has been made in the law of God, to exalt the downtrodden fourth commandment. We are to point out the right path, which has been lost sight of. A false sabbath has been exalted in the place of the seventh-day Sabbath of Jehovah, and many have lost their bearings. By vigilance and faithfulness in following the true path, we are to direct them all to the right path. (Verses 13, 14 quoted)

"Not finding thine own pleasure, nor speaking thine own words." Then whose words will you speak? The very words that Christ has given to comfort, to encourage, to bless, to lift up those that are bowed down. God has given you a mind, that you may speak words to help others. Do not feed it with trash. Do not injure it by the use of tobacco or alcohol. None of us have any too much mind, and we should do our utmost to improve that which we have. We cannot afford to allow the mind to be dominated by evil for one moment, for thus we might lose an opportunity to speak a word in season to some soul ready to perish. The responsibility of winning souls to Christ rests upon us, and we must work for their salvation. We are not to speak our own words, working for our own personal benefit; we are to study how best to relieve the suffering and the oppressed, how best to help the needy and distressed.

Then shalt thou delight thyself in the Lord." He is your power, your health, your life, and your salvation. Trust in Him every moment. Pray to Him, and ask Him to keep you in your going out and your coming in. Ask Him to preserve your soul that it shall not be beguiled by the enemy.

Chapter 41

Light Reading

I ask you to put away from your homes all light reading. Do not fill the house with magazines, so that when one comes in the first thing he picks up is a magazine. The Lord has nothing to do with such reading. It fills the mind with trash. Those who indulge in it are bringing to the foundation wood, hay, and stubble. It is a sin in the sight of God to give the mind to such reading, for He claims our thoughts. We are to serve Him with the mind. In the Bible you will find reading that will be food to the soul. We have no time to spend in light reading. Let us study what saith the Word of God. Let us find out from the Scriptures what are the conditions of salvation.

Have you become acquainted with your neighbors, that you may tell them of the truth? Take your Bible and call on them. Read them some of those passages of Scripture that are the most comforting. Show them that you have an interest in their eternal welfare. God wants you to help them to place their minds in a right channel.

In the Word of God the truth in regard to the observance of the Lord's Sabbath is plainly stated. But the world is in ignorance of God's requirements. Shall it be that when you meet your neighbors in the day of judgment, they will charge you with neglect, saying, "You knew of these things, why did you not tell us?"

May God Help us to realize that our words are a talent more precious than gold and silver. May He help us to speak only words of comfort and consolation.

Remember that a large number of angels were cast out of heaven because of rebellion. These angels are continually striving to turn into wrong channels the minds of those who are seeking to obey the Lord. But if you will walk in the path of obedience to God's requirements, He will watch over you and guard you from evil. He will strengthen you and cause you to ride upon the high places of the earth.

Chapter 42

Light on Health Reform

Nearly forty years ago [1865] the Lord opened up before us the principles of health reform. At that time I was very weak physically. Sometimes I would faint away two or three times a day, and I thought as many today think, that flesh-meat was the only food that would keep up my strength. But in mercy the Lord showed me that flesh-meat is not necessary to maintain strength, and that it is not the best food.

Since that time increased light upon health reform has been given. In grains, fruits, vegetables, and nuts are to be found all the food elements that we need. If we will come to the Lord in simplicity of mind, He will teach us how to prepare wholesome food free from the taint of flesh-meat.

One-time Dr. Trall said to me, "I must tell you that you put forth too much strength when you stand before the people. If you continue to do as you are doing you cannot live over three years, and I do not know that you can live three months." I had with me a copy of the book, How to Live, and I asked Dr. Trall if he would read the book. He replied that he would, and I let him take it. A few days afterward he said to me, "Mrs. White, where did you get your instruction in medical science?" I replied that I had received it by revelation from God. As he handed the book back to me, he said, "That book is filled with truth. I hope it may have a wide circulation." Dr. Trall was an unbeliever, and he used often to speak against our ministers, but he would never say one word against Mrs. White. He is now dead, and I, whom he thought could live only a short time, have been preserved all these years. I shall soon be seventy-eight years old. I have placed myself in the hands of God, and He has sustained me, enabling me to bear my testimony in many parts of the world.

Chapter 43

Early Experience

When the State Fair was held in Battle Creek, our people took with them onto the ground three or four cooking stoves and demonstrated how good meals might be prepared without the use of flesh-meat. We were told that we set the best table on the ground. Whenever large gatherings are held, it is your privilege to devise plans whereby you can provide those who attend with wholesome food, and thus educate them in the matter of the most simple and healthful diet.

In our early experiences the Lord gave us favor with the people, and we had many wonderful opportunities to demonstrate what could be done through the principles of health reform to restore to health those whose cases had been pronounced hopeless. At one time the wife of the high school teacher in Battle Creek was thrown from a sleigh and seriously injured. We took her into our house, which was close by, and cared for her. The doctor called, and when he saw what we were doing, he said, "You are doing the very best that can be done. I leave the case with you." She recovered. Some years afterward she came to my house, bringing her husband and her little girl. She said to the child, "This is Mrs. White. You would not be here today if she had not saved my life several years ago." We knelt down together and thanked the Lord for His mercy.

The light on the subject of health reform was given by the Lord, and we are not to depart from it. The Lord has put into the minds of some a knowledge of how to prepare wholesome articles of food. But it is not His design that this knowledge shall be confined to a few. In every family there should be those who understand the science of healthful cooking.

Chapter 44

Restaurant Work

Light was also given that in the cities there would be opportunity to do a work similar to that which we did on the Battle Creek fairgrounds. In harmony with this light, hygienic restaurants have been established. But there is grave danger that our restaurant workers will become so imbued with the spirit of commercialism that they will fail to impart the light which the people need. Our restaurants bring us in contact with many people, but if we allow our minds to be engrossed with the thought of financial profit, we shall fail to fulfill the purpose of God. He would have us take advantage of every opportunity to present the truth that is to save men and women from eternal death.

I have tried to ascertain how many souls have been converted to the truth as a result of the restaurant work here in Los Angeles. Some may have been saved, but many more might be converted to God if every effort were made to conduct the work in God's order, and to let light shine into the pathway of others.

I would say to the workers connected with the restaurant, "Do not continue to work as you have been working. Seek to make the restaurant a means of communicating to others the light of present truth. For this purpose only have our restaurants been established."

The food work must not be so enlarged that it will call for the talent that should be put to use in the ministry, or in other lines of evangelistic work. There is danger that the restaurant work will employ those who are needed to take an active part in house-to-house labor and in various lines of missionary work. Some who have been held in the restaurant should have been engaged in helping Elder Simpson in his efforts to present the truth.

The workers in the Los Angeles restaurant and the members of the Los Angeles church need to be thoroughly converted. To everyone has been given the talent of intellect. Have you received power to prevail with God? "As many as received Him, to them gave He power to become the sons of God, even to them that believe on His name." (John 1:12)

We should put forth greater efforts to teach the people the truths of health reform. At every camp meeting an effort should be made to demonstrate what can be done in providing an appetizing, wholesome diet from grains, fruits, nuts, and vegetables. In every place where new companies are brought into the truth, instruction should be given in the science of preparing wholesome food. Workers should be chosen who can labor from house to house in an educational campaign.

You prepare food for those who come to the restaurant for meals, but what efforts are you putting forth to teach them the commandments of God, and point them to the path of life? The restaurant should be a place where a holy influence is exerted. Do not give your patrons merely the newspapers to read. Let them have the publications that are filled with truth. Endeavor to become acquainted with those with whom you are brought in contact. Lead them on to inquire in regard to the truth, and then have ready some tract or book that will answer their question. In this way seeds of truth may be sown, and the time will come when some of it will spring up into life eternal.

Heavenly angels are waiting to cooperate with those who work on the side of truth and righteousness. The enemy of souls is working diligently to bring in his so-called science that will make of God and of Christ a nonentity. His delusions are flooding the world, but we cannot conceive of what will be in the future.

Chapter 45

Sanitarium Work in Southern California

We are so thankful that God has opened the way for us to secure such favorable locations for our institutions in Southern California. He brought first to our notice the buildings now occupied by the Fernando School. When someone wrote and told me of the buildings that were offered for sale at such reasonable prices, I replied, "Lose no time in securing the property." The instruction given was obeyed, and for two or three years a school has been conducted there. God calls upon you to take a greater interest in this school than you have taken in the past.

The Lord has wonderfully opened up the way for us to establish sanitariums. These institutions should be centers of education. They should be conducted by men and women who have the fear of God in their hearts and who can speak words in season, bringing to troubled souls the comfort of the grace of God. This is the work that should be done in every sanitarium.

For a long time we have desired to see a work begun in Redlands. Now, in the providence of God we have come into possession of Loma Linda. This will give us an influence in Redlands and Riverside, enabling us to find openings for the proclamation of present truth. This beautiful property was offered to us at a very low price. It is completely furnished. We have only to take possession. We trust that our people will rally to the support of this institution, that it may not be burdened with a large interest-bearing debt.

Chapter 46

A Reform Needed

At this time, when Satan is rallying his forces, shall the people of God lay off the armor, and go to sleep? Shall we do nothing, or shall we remember that there is One who says, "All power is given unto me in heaven and in earth. Go ye therefore, and teach all nations, baptizing them in the name of the Father, and of the Son, and of the Holy Ghost: Teaching them to observe all things whatsoever I have commanded you: and, lo, I am with you alway, even unto the end of the world." (Matthew 28:19, 20)

Many have so little faith in God that He is unable to work for them. Elder Simpson has labored diligently and faithfully in Los Angeles, and the Lord has given him success. But his success would have been far greater had the church rallied to his support, had every member been consecrated to God. Some have thought that Elder Simpson should labor for the church. The church members should rather have assisted Elder Simpson by going to their neighbors and telling them of the truth, inviting them to attend the meetings.

There is now a large number of believers in Los Angeles. Many of these should be fitting themselves to work for the Master, that the truth may go forth as a lamp that burneth. Read the fifty-eighth chapter of Isaiah. Read it over many times, and you will receive a deeper impression each time.

I have always felt a deep interest in the work in Southern California. For more than twenty years this part of the State has been represented to me as an important field. Our people should be ready to meet those who come and go, and speak to them the words of life. They should scatter the publications containing present truth. The Lord will do great things for those who cooperate with Him.[38]

---

[38] Ms. 27, 1906; MR 900.2.

Chapter 47

Lessons from the Fifteenth of Romans

[Sermon preached by E. G. White at the Congregational Church, which was being temporarily used by the Oakland SDA Church, 18th and Market Streets, Oakland, California, on Sabbath afternoon, October 20, 1906]

In the fifteenth of Romans the apostle Paul declares: "We then that are strong ought to bear the infirmities of the weak, and not to please ourselves. Let every one of us please his neighbor for his good to edification. For even Christ pleased not Himself; but, as it is written, The reproaches of them that reproached thee fell on Me." (Verses 1-3)

Mark especially the words, "The reproaches of them that reproached thee fell on Me." Oh, that these words might sink deep into the heart of every one of you who think you are doing God's service while finding fault with others. This is the weakness, the besetting sin, of many in this congregation, and our great desire is that you shall get rid of this evil before the Lord gets rid of you. The reproaches with which we reproach the servants of the Lord, fall upon Christ Himself.

"For whatsoever things were written aforetime were written for our learning, that we through patience and comfort of the scriptures might have hope." (Verse 4)

We want to be Bible Christians. We want to come right to the Word, and to carry out this Word in every particular. Then we shall know that Jesus Christ is our efficiency, our healer, our strength, our frontguard, and our rearward. Then we shall have that help and that power which God alone can give to us.

God desires that His commandment-keeping people shall stand on vantage ground. He desires that they shall stand before Him without fault. In order to do this, they must perfect holy characters through the merits of Christ. They must look unto Jesus, the author and finisher of their faith. As they become changed into His image, the salvation of God will be revealed through them, and unbelievers will be converted. Unbelievers will see and understand that God's Word means something to those who claim to believe it.

"Now the God of patience and consolation grant you to be likeminded one toward another according to Christ Jesus." (Verse 5) Why? That we shall be of half a dozen different minds, or of a great variety of minds? Oh, no. The apostle exhorts you to be "likeminded one toward another according to Christ Jesus: that ye may with one mind and one mouth glorify God, even the father of our Lord Jesus Christ. Wherefore receive ye one another, as Christ also received us to the glory of God." (Verses 5-7)

What does this injunction entail? It places us under obligation to God. It leaves us in a position where we shall understand that we are amenable to God. It leads us to realize that when the Holy Spirit is abiding in our hearts and working through us, we shall love one another, in the place of feeling that we must show animosity toward one another.

My dear brethren and sisters, God is not pleased with your spirit of criticism and fault-finding. We must humble our hearts daily before God, and seek for a new conversion, that we may be brought into right relationship with Jesus Christ. Those who are striving to keep the commandments of God ought to be in harmony, and to show a spirit of humility and love. God is not in any of the differences that are so apparent. He does not inspire words of fault-finding. He is now calling upon us to humble ourselves under the hand of the Almighty, in order that He may lift us up.

The apostle continues: (Verses 8 and 9, quoted)

God's people are to stand as lights in the world. They are to realize that upon them rests the solemn responsibility of reflecting rays of light upon the pathway of those who are not keeping the commandments of God. Christ Himself has declared, "Ye are the light of the world." (Matthew 5:14) We are to seek to be lightbearers.

And when the light of divine truth shines forth with distinctness from the words and works of God's children, will there be seen any quarreling, any backbiting, among the lightbearers? The world will see no dissension in the lives of those from whom the light of heaven is shed abroad. Brethren and sisters, as you let your light shine before men, they will "see your good works, and glorify your Father which is in heaven." A precious influence will go forth as the result of these good works, that will bring salvation to those who behold it. God desires that we shall keep our light constantly shining.

(Romans 15:8-10, quoted)

In this our day, we see the Gentiles beginning to rejoice with the Jews. There are converted Jews who are now laboring in Boston and in various other cities, in behalf of their own people. The Jews are coming into the ranks of God's chosen followers, and are being numbered with the Israel of God in these closing days. Thus some of the Jews will once more be reinstated with the people of God, and the blessing of the Lord will rest upon them richly, if they will come into the position of rejoicing that is represented in the Scripture, "And again He saith, Rejoice, ye Gentiles, with His people." The apostle continues, (Verses 11-13, quoted)

In the name of whom were you baptized? You went down into the water in the name of the three great Worthies in heaven--the Father, the Son, and the Holy Ghost. In the name of the Father, and of the Son, and of the Holy Ghost you were buried with Christ in baptism; and you were raised up out of the water to live in newness of life. You were to have a new life. You were to live unto God; you were not to live unto yourself, and keep yourself under your own supervision for fear someone would touch you and hurt you.

My brethren and sisters, keep the mind fixed on Jesus. Keep the heart uplifted in prayer to God. Behold Jesus and what He endured and suffered for us in order that we might have that life which measures with the life of God. How can any of us wear our nerves on the outside, ready to break forth into disaffection if every movement made by someone else is not in exact accordance with our ideas? All this super-sensitiveness is to be put away.

In the night season God has revealed to me the spiritual condition of the church members living in Oakland and the nearby cities. A large standard was raised up at a time when many were complaining and finding fault and speaking to the detriment of one another; and this standard was turned around until it appeared before them as a great looking glass, from the face of which everyone that looked saw himself with all his faults and sins. The whole erring company, convicted of the sinfulness of their course, prostrated themselves before God and immediately began to confess their own wrong-doing; and, oh, what a scene of repentance and confession there was! A most wonderful cleansing of the camp followed, and the mighty power of God was revealed.

I shall never be satisfied until just such an experience comes into the church here in Oakland and in San Francisco. We want to see the salvation of our God. We want the truth to go forth with mighty power; and why, oh why, do we continue to stand in the way? Why do we grieve the Holy Spirit of God? Why do we put Him to open shame by carrying with us our selfish, unconverted dispositions, and yet all the while claiming to be Christians? God grant that every one of us may have clear eyesight to discern what we can do by looking unto Jesus and by realizing how our course must appear in His sight and how He must regard envy and strife. God help us to put away our individual defects of character. We want to see the power of God revealed in this community. If it were not for this, I should not leave my home and come down here to speak to you so often. But night after night I cannot sleep more than a few hours; and often, in the hours of the night, I find myself sitting up in bed, praying to God in behalf of those who do not realize their spiritual condition; and then I arise and walk the room, and say, O Lord, set Thy people in order, before it shall be everlastingly too late.

Oftentimes during the seasons of intercession, when the burden rests heavily, my heart is drawn out with great longing, and the tears start from my eyes, and I wring my hands before God, because I know there are souls in peril in the churches at Oakland and nearby places--souls who, in their condition of mind, know no more regarding how they stand before God than they would know had they never professed religion.

Brethren and sisters, it is time now that we were looking unto Jesus to see whether we are reflecting His image. It is time now that we put away everything that will grieve the Holy Spirit of God--divisions, dissensions, fault-finding, incriminations. God wants us to come to the light, that our light may shine forth in good works. Let the praise of God be in heart and voice.

"And again he saith, Rejoice, ye Gentiles, with His people. And again, Praise the Lord, all ye Gentiles; and laud Him, all ye people."

This is what we want to do when we are assembled in God's house. Let us cherish a spirit of gratitude and thanksgiving. We want our faces shining, reflecting the glory of God. We want to pray a great deal more than we talk regarding the faults of others. We want to be on our knees before God, and to come into communion and fellowship with Christ Jesus.

"And again, Esaias saith, There shall be a root of Jesse, and He that shall rise to reign over the Gentiles; in Him shall the Gentiles trust. Now the God of hope fill you with all joy and peace."

Here we are. As children of God, we claim to be brought under the direct leadings of the Spirit of God. Is the Holy Spirit among us? Are we moving under its guidance? If not, do not persist in dishonoring God, but come humbly before Him, and have heart and mind renovated, and the thoughts brought into unison with Christ Jesus. Then you can rejoice; then you can praise the Lord; then you can shout His praises with joyfulness.

Those who have been baptized can claim the help of the three great Worthies of heaven to keep them from falling, and to reveal through them a character that is after the divine similitude. This is what we claim to be--followers of Jesus. We must be molded and fashioned in accordance with the divine pattern; and if you have lost your Christlikeness, my brethren and sisters, you can never, never come into communion with God again until you are reconverted and rebaptized. You want to repent and to be rebaptized, and to come into the love and communion and harmony of Christ. Then you will have spiritual discernment which will enable you to see those things that are above, where Christ sitteth at the right hand of God. There is enough to contemplate regarding heavenly things, to fill every heart and mind, every congregation that is in the land, with rejoicing and praise and thanksgiving to God.

"Now the God of hope fill you with all joy and peace in believing, that ye may abound in hope, through the power of the Holy Ghost." If this were your condition, sinners would be converted.

As you arose from the watery grave at the time of your baptism, you professed to be dead, and declared that your life was changed--hid with Christ in God. You claimed to be dead to sin and cleansed from your hereditary and cultivated traits of evil. In going forward in the rite of baptism, you pledged yourselves before God to remain dead to sin. Your mouth was to remain a sanctified mouth, your tongue a converted tongue. You were to speak of God's goodness, and to praise His holy name. Thus you were to be a great help and blessing to the church.

The apostle continues, "And I myself also am persuaded of you, my brethren, that ye also are full of goodness, filled with all knowledge, able also to admonish one another." (Verse 14)

We may make mistakes, and we may have to "admonish one another." But there has come into the churches at Oakland and the surrounding community a spirit of backbiting, of faultfinding and evil-speaking, which demonstrates that you are not converted. Words are uttered that never should pass the lips of a Christian. My brethren and sisters, when you have nothing better to speak of than something about the faults of others, remember that "silence is eloquence." Cease to dwell upon the shortcomings of others. Keep the tongue sanctified unto God. Refrain from saying anything that might detract from the influence of another; for by indulging in these words of criticism, you blaspheme God's holy name as verily as you would were you to swear. I am instructed to present these things before you, that you may see how you dishonor the name of Christ Jesus. (Verses 15, 16, quoted)

Here is where the work of the Holy Ghost comes in, after your baptism. You are baptized in the name of the Father, of the Son, and of the Holy Ghost. You are raised up out of the water to live henceforth in newness of life--to live a new life. You are born unto God, and you stand under the sanction and the power of the three holiest Beings in heaven, who are able to keep you from falling. You are to reveal that you are dead to sin; your life is hid with Christ in God. Hidden "with Christ in God"--wonderful transformation. This is a most precious promise. When I feel oppressed and hardly know how to relate myself toward the work that God has given me to do, I just call upon the three great Worthies, and say: You know I cannot do this work in my own strength. You must work in me, and by me, and through me, sanctifying my tongue, sanctifying my spirit, sanctifying my words, and bringing me into a position where my spirit shall be susceptible to the movings of the Holy Spirit of God upon my mind and character. And this is the prayer that every one of us may offer.

Oh, I am so afraid that the next judgment of God will come upon Oakland and San Francisco again, before you are ready! But if you come to the Lord, if those of you who profess to be His commandment-keeping people will come to Him and humble your hearts before Him, your ignorance may pass away.

The church members in this community who are not in harmony with God and with their brethren, are carrying a great load of ignorance. This is a certain hindrance to their efforts to perfect a character through the gracious power of truth upon the human soul. They do not know that they are ignorant, but they are. God desires that every one of us shall be susceptible to the influence of the Holy Spirit, by which we shall be fashioned into the likeness of the divine.

There remains now only a little while in which we can work to save our own souls and the souls of others; and we want all the powers that God has given us cleansed and sanctified. We want to clear the path for every working agency, in order that they may not be impeded as they try to advance. We want to come into working order, and into perfect unity with one another.

Let us, in tenderness, "admonish one another," and seek to help one another. Let us pray with one another, and put away everything that would keep us from entering into and following that narrow path that leads upward to heaven. This path is narrow, it is true, and because of its narrowness, "few there be that find it." We cannot afford to leave the path that leads to life everlasting. We cannot afford to make any mistake in this matter. If you mistake your way, and disease comes upon you suddenly, and you die without truly repenting of your cruel spirit which has been a hindrance to many souls, there is no hope in your case.

God calls upon us to come into harmony with the divine pattern. He calls upon us, while it is called Today, to repent and be reconverted; and then His Spirit will dwell in us richly, and there will be transformations of character little dreamed of. As His Spirit works with your spirit, there will be manifest a saving grace by which we shall be deeply convicted of the wonderful transformation that is taking place in your character. Others will notice it, and be influenced thereby. Thus a constant and progressive work will be going on in the church. Oh, my dear brethren and sisters, let us all come into line. We cannot afford to be out of line now--it is too late in the day.

Again, we read: "I have therefore whereof I may glory through Jesus Christ in those things which pertain to God." (Verse 17)

"Whereof I may glory through Jesus Christ." This is the manner in which we may glory. And as transformation of character takes place, through repentance and confession and reconversion and rebaptism, you will glory through Jesus Christ "in those things which pertain to God," not in the things that pertain to your own personal, selfish interests. (Verse 18, quoted)

Oh, that every soul in this congregation would consent to humble his own heart before God! Oh, that every soul in this room would be reconverted Oh, that every soul would prostrate himself before God, and yield self unreservedly, and solemnly vow that with Heaven's help he would henceforth keep his lips from all guile, and sanctified; that he would keep the life and the course of action sanctified; that soul, body, and spirit should ever be sanctified unto the Lord. If thorough work were done, what a missionary company we should have with which to work these cities! Oh, what numbers we could have to send into places where the people have never heard the third angel's message!

Some talk of going to far-off countries as missionaries; and this is well, if the Lord so directs. A brother under conviction of sin once said, "I want to be converted, that I may go out to the heathen to help them." "Why," said I, "begin at home; become right with God where you are; put away your sins, and be a home missionary." If we cannot be missionaries at home, we can never expect to do good in another field. All about us there are heathen. Only a few miles from where you live, there are poor people who have never heard of the Seventh-day Adventists and the third angel's message; they know but little regarding the sacredness of God's law.

How true this is of San Francisco and of Oakland, and of all the lesser places nearby! I beg of you, brethren and sisters, in the name of the Lord Jesus Christ, to be converted, that you may go to work for those who are living within easy reach. As you go forth in humility and faith, the impression made on heart and mind will be such as will lead those who accept the truth to begin humbly. They will not regard themselves as full fledged, capable of depending on their own strength; but they will sit at the feet of Jesus with meekness and lowliness of heart, to learn of Him. When the truth is spoken by God's servants, those new converts will receive it into good and honest hearts, and it will abide. Thus they will steadily increase in knowledge and understanding.

As you engage heartily in this work, the converting power of God will be revealed. Your own hearts will be softened and subdued under the influence of the Holy Spirit. Christ is watching you. He is the One who has paid so great a price for your salvation. He greatly desires to bring to God all for whom He has sacrificed so much. He desires that they shall learn how to be obedient and heavenly-minded. In this world we are to prepare for a home in the city that hath foundations, whose builder and maker is God.

In order to prepare for entrance into this beautiful city, we must now be clothed with the wedding garment--with the robe of Christ's righteousness. We must stand before Him without spot or wrinkle or any such things. You have not been appointed to talk about others' faults. While probation still lingers, every soul ought to be washing his own robe of character, and preparing for translation.

It is our privilege now, in this world, to be workers together with God. But first of all, we must be reconverted. Only when the brain-power and the talent of speech are sanctified, are we fitted for service.

During the past few weeks you have been highly favored with opportunities for Bible study. None can realize how heavily the burden rested upon me when I saw the important work that must be speedily done in California. And when Brother S. N. Haskell and his wife, about this time, were looking first at one place and then at another, with a view of visiting several places before returning to Nashville, where they seemed to think they must labor again, I wrote to them, You have a message to bear in southern California and in other portions of California, and I beg of you to come West soon. I am so thankful that they came. Now that they are here, I greatly desire that their work shall not be impeded in any wise. I want that you should clear the King's highway. And do not be afraid of the converting power of God. Be not afraid of His truth coming into the formation of your own individual character. If this work should tear your character to pieces, it can bring it together in a wholeness that is sanctified. We greatly need to humble the soul before God and before Christ Jesus, and so relate ourselves toward our maker and toward one another, that we shall be brought into unity of action.

We read further: "I have therefore whereof I may glory through Jesus Christ in those things which pertain to God." (Verse 17) "In those things"--you see where the glory is. It is not in self-exaltation; it is not in one's telling of his faultless character; it is in humbling one's self before God. Then you shall represent in your own life the life of Christ.

Says the apostle: "For I will not dare to speak of any of those things which Christ hath not wrought by me, to make the Gentiles obedient, by word and deed." (Verse 18) "Wrought by me." How did God work through Paul? Through a multitude of revelations whereby he might "make the Gentiles obedient." Paul had many wonderful visions. He saw that which could not be described by mortal man, and concerning these visions he remained nearly silent; but, nevertheless, God "wrought" through His servant by the abundance of His revelations, to accompany Paul's preaching with a power that could not be withstood. So thoroughly was Paul's faith substantiated by these visions that his message was ever "Yea and Amen." He could not think of consenting to say "Nay" when he had formerly said "Yea." His words were established by a weight of evidence that was immovable.

(Verses 18-26, quoted)

Paul had been gathering up money for the poor at Jerusalem, in order that the way might be opened before him to preach the truth. In Jerusalem there were many who believed not that Jesus had been raised from the dead and was indeed the living Son of the Most High God. Paul desired to reach this class, and so he brought in these contributions in order to open the way.

Respecting this contribution, Paul declared of the Gentiles: (Verses 27, 28, quoted)

Go where we may, everywhere there is work to be done. We need a fitting up for this work, and we need especially to guard against having a tongue that is sanctified to Satan. The tongue that God has given is to be used to glorify Him in speech. Unless it is, we shall be standing directly in the way of God's work in this world, and the judgments of heaven will surely fall upon us. But we hope that we shall see of the salvation of God in a much larger degree than we have yet seen it. Paul continues: (Verses 29-31, quoted)

As Paul goes to Judea to bear the message of the gospel of Christ to those who were opposing the idea of Jesus' being the Saviour of the world, he wanted the Christian Gentiles to strive together with him in their prayers to God. How much better is this than to talk about the faults of one another! Brethren and sisters, when you are talking with one another, and someone begins to speak about the sins of someone else, listen not. Tell him that you must refuse to hear, for this is not your line of work. Instead of entering into a conversation that tends to tear down, try to speak a word of encouragement. Your talent of speech is to be sanctified unto God; it is to be cleansed from everything like faultfinding. Let us strive together with God's appointed workers in prayer to the Lord that He shall protect them and bless them, and that they may be "delivered from them that do not believe." Thus the way will be opened for the reception of the gospel. (Verses 32, 33, quoted)

These words that I have been reading to you this afternoon are the words of the Bible in regard to your duty and my own duty. And I greatly desire that you shall learn to guard the door of your lips lest you speak unadvisedly. I used to say to my children, as they were leaving home in the morning: "Now, children, you are going out for the day's work. Remember that you are to guard your tongue. Speak not one word that will provoke a wrong act. If you fail, then when we meet at family worship during the evening hour, we shall talk the matter over and make it right with God. You see, children, kind words never cause you any pain and sorrow. Speak kindly, tenderly to one another, and see what a refreshing, what a blessing, comes to your own heart. But if you begin to contend one with another, then passions arise, and you have to strive with all your might to retain control over yourself. Be brave, be true."

And at eventide, when the children would gather together before going to bed, we would talk over the happenings of the day. Possibly during the day one of the children had said, "Mother, someone has done thus and so to me." I had replied that when we all came together in the evening we could talk it over. When evening came, they had all had time for reflection, and they did not feel inclined to bring charges against one another. They would say, "Mother, I have done thus and so," and the tears would start from their eyes, as they would add, "I feel as if I would like to have you ask the Lord to forgive me. I believe He will." And then we would bow in prayer and confess the sins of the day, and pray for forgiveness. After confessing their wrongdoings, these little fellows would soon fall asleep.

But when a child hears an older person constantly talking about the faults of someone else, he in turn is imbued with the same spirit of faultfinding and criticism. The seeds of contention are being sown. Oh, how can professed Christians indulge in such a work! Two nights before I left my home, I was charged, during the visions of the night, to tell the congregation that I should meet at Oakland on the Sabbath, that the wicked words coming from their lips regarding the supposed faults of God's servants who are doing the very best they can to spread the truth and to advance His work, are all written in the heavenly books of record. Unless those who speak these words repent, they will at last find themselves outside the city of God. God will not allow a quarrelsome person to enter into the heavenly city.

After my visit to Oakland two weeks ago, I was sick for a whole week. I carried a very heavy burden, but I felt that if duty seemed plain for me to go down again, God would give me strength to speak to you.

I feel an intense interest regarding every faultfinder, for I know that a quarrelsome disposition will never find entrance into the city of God. Quarrel with yourself, but with no one else, and then be converted. Confess your sins right here where you are, before you return to your homes. With words of confession, humble your hearts before God.

When you are tempted to speak unadvisedly, be on guard. If someone else approaches you with words of criticism regarding one of God's children, turn a deaf ear to every such word. If you are spoken to harshly, never retaliate. Utter not a word. When under provocation, remember that "silence is eloquence." Silence is the greatest rebuke that you can possibly give a faultfinder or one whose temper is irritated. Keep your eye fixed on Jesus. Keep your eye on the One who never finds fault with you, only to lay before you perils from which He would deliver you.

There is a great work to be done, and many are unready to engage in sacred service. The judgments of God are soon coming upon all our cities, and I desire that we shall all be prepared. I greatly desire that we shall confess our sins, and be converted. If any of you desire to have your hearts softened and broken before God, it is best for you to clear the King's highway this afternoon, without delay. It is best to prepare the heart for the reception of the Holy Spirit, that it may have free course in the entire being. It is best that you should open the door of the soul-temple, and let the Saviour come in. "Behold, I stand at the door, and knock," the Saviour says; "If any man hear My voice, and open the door, I will come in to him, and will sup with him, and he with Me." (Revelation 3:20)

We ought to long with all the heart for a thorough reconversion, that the truth may be enthroned in heart and mind, and that we may, by the aid of the Holy Spirit, be prepared to present the third angel's message before others who need it so much. Now is our opportunity; now is our chance. May God help us, that we may be converted.

Dear brethren and sisters, if there are any of you that desire to say anything this afternoon, be free. Are you ready to rededicate yourselves to God? Christ is ready; He is waiting, watching, longing. Angels are in this room. Wicked angels are here, and holy angels are here. Which side shall gain the victory over your heart here today, my brother, my sister? These are the hours of the Sabbath; you cannot spend them any better than by clearing the King's highway. Remove the root of bitterness from your heart. Do not break off the top of it. Root it out lest, springing up again, many shall be defiled. You cannot afford to be content with half-hearted work. Dig it out by the roots, and then God will help you to be reconverted.

Elder S. N. Haskell speaking: Perhaps some would like to bear testimony. If we could see the interest that heaven is taking at the present time in our behalf, if we would realize what is going on above, there is not one of us that would rest satisfied before we knew that we had a clean record on high.

The Lord is anxious to save us. He is anxious that everything separating us from Him should be put away, that our hearts may beat in unison with heaven. It is time to be in harmony with God. Let us spend a little while in clearing the King's highway. If we have been indulging in the sin of telling others' faults, let us confess it before the Lord and before our brethren, When probation ends it will come suddenly, unexpectedly--at a time when we are least expecting it. But we can have a clean record in heaven today, and know that God accepts us; and finally, if faithful, we shall be gathered into the kingdom of heaven.

(Several testimonies were borne by various members of the congregation; but the response was not so hearty as might have been expected after such an appeal had been made. The testimonies were more or less indefinite, with, however, a few exceptions. The break that seemed necessary in order that the spirit of confession might come in, was not made. It seemed as if the powers of darkness were striving for the mastery. It was at this juncture that the prayer was offered by Sister White.)

Mrs. E. G. White: I should like to pray. (Praying) Our heavenly Father, we come to Thee this evening, as our only Refuge, as our only Helper, as the only One who can save us from ourselves. Oh, my heavenly Father, Thou hast heard the words that I have tried to say to this people this afternoon. And I ask Thee, Lord, that Thou wouldst make the impression. Thou alone canst break the iron bands of the heart. Thou alone canst cause the blind eyes to discern what sin is. Thou alone canst impress the understanding with a realization of the character that every soul must have and reveal in this world before he can be prepared for translation into the family of heaven. Oh, my Father, my Father, the blindness, the terrible blindness, that comes over the people, that they do not discern what manner of character Thou canst accept and what Thou wilt be compelled to reject! We ask Thee, Lord, that Thou wouldst work upon minds and hearts. Oh, that Thou wouldst impress upon all the terrible nature of sin, and how Thou dost regard sin.

Oh, my Father, my Father, Thou didst so love the world that Thou gavest Thine only beloved Son to die a shameful death, that the world through Him might have everlasting life! Thou hast given the human family here below the privilege of educating themselves in right-doing, that they may be prepared to unite with the sinless family above, and dwell forevermore in Thy kingdom. We see the opportunities and the privileges that are passing by, and yet there are hearts that are becoming more and still more hardened, less and still less sensitive. Oh, we pray Thee, for the sake of Jesus Christ who has borne the stripes, who has suffered the agonies of the crucifixion to make it possible for every soul that lives to unite with the family of God--oh, we pray, my Saviour, we pray Thee to break up this hardness of heart! I pray Thee to melt and subdue the soul.

I pray Thee, my heavenly Father, that Thou wouldst flash light upon the people here, that they may obey the call. If they repent not, Thou wilt have to say to them, "How canst thou come in hither, not having on the wedding garment?" It is the wedding garment of Christ's righteousness that must be put on. Oh, Lord, I ask Thee to have compassion upon human minds in this congregation! I pray Thee, Lord, that they may not go on hardening their hearts any longer. I pray Thee that this awful manifestation of self may be broken up. I pray Thee that self may be crucified, and that self may die, in order that there may be a reconversion in the midst of us, and that souls may be brought to humble themselves before Thee, and to be reconverted.

My Father, my Father, for Christ's sake, let Thy Spirit impress the minds of those who are in this house, and may they clear the King's highway, and prepare the way for Thee to come to work with human minds. Help them to remove the stumbling-blocks out of the way, and to take themselves out of the way. They are standing directly in Thy way; and oh, impress their hearts so fully, so sensibly, that they will repent, repent, repent, and be converted, before it shall be everlastingly too late!

Oh God, the word is about to be pronounced: "He that is unjust, let him be unjust still: and he which is filthy, let him be filthy still: and he that is righteous, let him be righteous still: and he that is holy, let him be holy still." Awful words to hear, to those that are unready!

Wilt Thou, Lord, break up this coldness, this iciness, this frozen-heartedness! Oh, give them no rest, day nor night, until they see the necessity of transformation of character; until they see the necessity of clearing the King's highway.

My heavenly Father, we come to Thee as Thy little children. Thou hast called us little children, and I pray Thee that we may become little children. Oh Lord, Thou didst say to Thy disciples, when they were seeking to be first, that those who seek to be the first shall be the last of all. Help us to humble our souls before God. Help our hard hearts to repent.

My Father, my Father, I present before Thee the merits of our Redeemer, Thy Son Jesus, who suffered the awful agonies of the cross to redeem the race. I plead with Thee that Thou wouldst break up the fallow ground of the heart, in order that the seeds of truth may become fastened in the mind and spring up and bear the best kind of fruit, to the glory of God. We cannot endure the thought that of the large number who are in this congregation, many at last may say that "the harvest is past, the summer is ended," the final proffers of salvation have been made, and my soul is not saved! What an awful acknowledgment this would be! Break, I pray Thee, break the minds of the congregation, so that every one of us may seek Thee with all the heart, as we go out from this house, in order that we may carry with us the impression of the Spirit of God. Help, oh, help us to be converted, that the light of heaven may come into our minds and our souls, and that we may have something to say in honor of Jesus, to glorify His name upon the earth.

Oh, heavenly Father, I ask Thee that the angel of the Lord before whom Joshua the high priest is represented as standing while the enemy accuses the sinner of his defiled garments--may this angel vouchsafe his presence unto us this afternoon. Thou didst turn to Satan, and say, "The Lord rebuke Thee, O Satan; even the Lord that hath chosen Jerusalem rebuke thee; is not this a brand plucked out of the fire?" And to those who accused the sinner, the angel said, "Take away the filthy garments from him. And unto him he said, Behold, I have caused thine iniquity to pass from thee, and I will clothe thee with change of raiment." And he added: "Let them set a fair mitre upon his head. So they set a fair miter upon his head, and clothed him with garments. And the angel of the Lord stood by."

Satan is trying to fix upon every one that he can influence, all the discouragement possible. Lord, I pray Thee, let the baptism of the Holy Spirit come into this congregation. I pray Thee, for Christ's sake, to sweep back the mist and the cloud that Satan interposes here. He is here; his followers are here; there are those here who are listening to his words; and I ask Thee, Lord, to break the spell; I ask Thee that there may be such marked consecration before God, that Christ can say, "I will clothe thee with change of raiment."

Oh God, we want raiment without a spot; we want garments without a stain; we want a preparation to do a grand, a great, a holy work that must be done. We pray Thee that Thou wouldst work mightily, so that the salvation of God shall be revealed. Thou hast a whole heaven of blessing that Thou art waiting to pour out upon a people who are ready to receive it, and use it. Oh, all heaven is full of Thy graciousness and Thy pardon, which we may receive abundantly if we will only come to Thee and repent and be converted.

My Lord and my God, I ask Thee to carry through the reformation that is to be done in this place, and the reformation that is to be done in the different meeting-places in this community. Let the salvation of God be revealed. My Saviour, my Saviour, Thou art inviting: Thou art waiting for them to come, so that Thou canst say, "Thy sins be forgiven thee; go, and sin no more." May the healing power of God come upon body and soul. My Father, my Father, I ask Thee for Christ's sake to come into the midst of us, and break the terrible power of darkness, and let souls go free, and Thy blessed name shall have all the glory. Amen.

As the congregation arose, Sister White said: "Let us sing, 'Jesus Lover of My Soul.' Sing it with all your heart."

Benediction.[39]

---

[39] MR 900.25

Chapter 48

Lessons From the Visions of Ezekiel

Part One: Exhortation to Faithfulness--In visions of the night I seemed to be speaking with great earnestness before an assembly of people. A heavy burden was upon my soul. I was presenting before those gathered together the message of the prophet Ezekiel regarding the duties of the Lord's watchmen

(Ezekiel 33:1-11 quoted)

The prophet had by the command of God ceased from prophesying to the Jews just at the time when the news came that Jerusalem was invaded and siege laid to her. In the twenty-fourth chapter Ezekiel records the representation that was given to him of the punishment that would come upon all who would refuse the word of the Lord. The people were removed from Jerusalem and punished by death and captivity. No lot was to fall upon it to determine who should be saved and who destroyed.

(Ezekiel 24:6, 7, 9, 10, 12-24 quoted)

I am instructed to present these words before those who have had light and evidence, but who have walked directly contrary to the light. The Lord will make the punishment of those who will not receive His admonitions and warnings as broad as the wrong has been. The purposes of those who have tried to cover their wrong while they have secretly worked against the purposes of God will be fully revealed. Truth will be vindicated. God will make manifest that He is God.

There is a spirit of wickedness at work in the church that is striving at every opportunity to make void the law of God. While the Lord may not punish unto death those who have carried their rebellion to great lengths, the light will never again shine with such convincing power upon the stubborn opposers of truth. Sufficient evidence is given to every soul regarding what is truth and what is error. But the deceptive power of evil upon some is so great that they will not receive the evidence and respond to it by repentance.

A long-continued resistance of truth will harden the most impressionable heart. Those who reject the Spirit of truth place themselves under the control of a spirit that is opposed to the word and work of God. For a time they may continue to teach some phases of the truth, but their refusal to accept all the light God sends will after a time place them where they will do the work of a false watchman.

The interests of the cause of present truth demand that those who profess to stand on the Lord's side shall bring into exercise all their powers to vindicate the advent message, the most important message that will ever come to the world. For those who stand as representatives of present truth to use time and energy now in attempting to answer the questions of the doubting ones, will be an unwise use of their time. It will not remove the doubts. The burden of our work now is not to labor for those who, although they have had abundant light and evidence, still continue on the unbelieving side. God bids us give our time and strength to the work of preaching to the people the messages that stirred men and women in 1843 and 1844.

We are now to labor unceasingly to get the truth before Jew and Gentile. Instead of going over and over the same ground to establish the faith of those who should never have accepted a doubt regarding the third angel's message, let our efforts be given to making known the truth to those who have never heard it. God calls upon us to make known to all men the truths that have made us what we are-- Seventh-day Adventists.

God is speaking to His people today as He spoke to Israel through Moses, saying, "Who is on the Lord's side?" My brethren, take your position where God bids you. Leave alone those who, after light has been repeatedly given them, have taken a stand on the opposite side. You are not to spend precious time in repeating to them what they already know and thus lose your opportunities of entering new fields with the message of present truth. Take up the work which has been given us. With the Word of God as your message, stand on the platform of truth and proclaim the soon coming of Christ. Truth, eternal truth, will prevail.

For more than half a century the different points of present truth have been questioned and opposed. New theories have been advanced as truth, which were not truth, and the Spirit of God revealed their error. As the great pillars of our faith have been presented, the Holy Spirit has borne witness to them, and especially is this so regarding the truths of the sanctuary question. Over and over again the Holy Spirit has in a marked manner endorsed the preaching of this doctrine. But today, as in the past, some will be led to form new theories and to deny the truths upon which the Spirit of God has placed His approval.

Any man who seeks to present theories which would lead us from the light that has come to us on the ministration in the heavenly sanctuary should not be accepted as a teacher. A true understanding of the sanctuary question means much to us as a people. When we were earnestly seeking the Lord for light on that question, light came. In vision I was given such a view of the heavenly sanctuary and the ministration connection with the Holy Place, that for many days I could not speak of it.

I know from the light that God has given me that there should be a revival of the messages that have been given in the past, because men will seek to bring in new theories and will try to prove that these theories are Scriptural, whereas they are error which if allowed a place will undermine faith in the truth. We are not to accept these suppositions and pass them along as truth. No, no. We must not move from the platform of truth on which we have been established.

There will always be those who are seeking for something new and who stretch and strain the Word of God to make it support their ideas and theories. Let us, brethren, take the things that God has given us, and which His Spirit has taught us is truth, and believe them, leaving alone those theories which His Spirit has not endorsed.

Part Two: Warning Against Rebellion--Ezekiel again writes: (Ezekiel 28:1-26, quoted)

The first sinner was one whom God had greatly exalted. He is represented under the figure of the prince of Tyrus flourishing in might and magnificence. Little by little Satan came to indulge the desire for self-exaltation. The Scripture says: "Thine heart was lifted up because of thy beauty; thou hast corrupted thy wisdom by reason of thy brightness." "Thou hast said in thine heart ... I will exalt my throne above the stars of God. ... I will be like the Most High." (Isaiah 14:13, 14) Though all His glory was from God, this mighty angel came to regard it as pertaining to himself. Not content with his position, though honored above the heavenly host, he ventured to covet homage due alone to the Creator. Instead of seeking to make God supreme in the affections and allegiance of all created beings, it was his endeavor to secure their service and loyalty to himself. And coveting the glory with which the infinite Father has invested His Son, this prince of angels aspired to power that was the prerogative of Christ alone.

To the very close of the controversy in heaven, the great usurper continued to justify himself. When it was announced that with all his sympathizers he must be expelled from the abodes of bliss, then the rebel leader boldly avowed his contempt for the Creator's law. He denounced the divine statutes as a restriction of their liberty, and declared that it was his purpose to secure the abolition of law. With one accord, Satan and his host threw the blame of their rebellion wholly upon Christ, declaring that if they had not been reproved, they would never have rebelled.

Satan's rebellion was to be a lesson to the universe through all coming ages, a perpetual testimony to the nature and terrible results of sin. The working out of Satan's rule, its effects upon both men and angels, would show what must be the fruit of setting aside the divine authority. It would testify that with the existence of God's government and His law is bound up the well-being of all the creatures He has made. Thus the history of this terrible experiment of rebellion was to be a perpetual safeguard to all holy intelligences, to prevent them from being deceived as to the nature of transgression, to save them from committing sin, and suffering its punishment.

At any moment God can withdraw from the impenitent the tokens of His wonderful mercy and love. Oh, that human agencies might consider what will be the sure result of their ingratitude to Him and of their disregard of the infinite Gift of Christ to our world! If they continue to love transgression more than obedience, the present blessings and the great mercy of God that they now enjoy, but do not appreciate, will finally become the occasion of their eternal ruin. When it is too late for them to see and to understand that which they have slighted as a thing of naught, they will know what it means to be without God, without hope. Then they will realize what they have lost by choosing to be disloyal to God and to stand in rebellion to His commandments.

In His great mercy, God has spoken words of encouragement to the children of men. To all who repent and turn to Him, He offers abundant pardon. Repentance for sin is the firstfruits of the working of the Holy Spirit in the life. It is the only process by which infinite purity reflects the image of Christ in His redeemed subjects. In Christ all fullness dwells. He teaches us to count all things but loss for the excellency of the knowledge of Christ Jesus our Lord. This knowledge is the highest science that any man can reach. It is the sum of all true science. "This is life eternal." Christ declared, "that they might know thee the only true God, and Jesus Christ, whom thou hast sent." (John 17:3)

The time has come when the righteous should understand that God's judgments are to fall on all who transgress His law, and that those who walk humbly with Him will triumph with holy gladness. As Jehovah is holy, He requires His people to be holy, pure, undefiled; for without holiness no man shall see the Lord. Those who worship Him in sincerity and truth will be accepted by Him. If church members will put away all self-worship, and will receive in their hearts the love for God and for one another that filled Christ's heart, our heavenly Father will constantly manifest His power through them. Let His people be drawn together with the cords of divine love. Then the world will recognize the miracle-working power of God, and will acknowledge that He is the Strength and the Helper of His commandment-keeping people.[40]

---

[40] Manuscript 125, 1907, Written from Sanitarium, Calif., July 4, 1907; designated "to be read in Battle Creek, Oakland, Chicago, and other large churches"; MR 900.21.

Chapter 49

Lessons From the Experiences of Pentecost

[Sermon by Mrs. E. G. White at Lodi, California May 9, 1908]

(Acts 2:1-11, quoted)

At this time there was in Jerusalem a great religious festival, and God used His disciples on this occasion to give to the multitudes assembled there the message of the risen Saviour.

In preparation for this important work, the disciples had for several days been together, confessing their sins and praying for the Holy Spirit. Jesus had told them that they were not to depart from Jerusalem until they had received the promise of the Father. "Ye shall receive power," He had told them, "after that the Holy Ghost is come upon you: and ye shall be witnesses unto me both in Jerusalem, and in all Judea, and in Samaria, and unto the uttermost part of the earth." (Acts 1:8) The second chapter of Acts records the experiences that came to the disciples when they received the Holy Ghost.

Some who heard the disciples tried to say something that would counteract the influence of their preaching. (Acts 2:12-21, quoted)

If this prophecy of Joel met a partial fulfillment in the days of the apostles, we are living in a time when it is to be even more evidently manifest to the people of God. He will so bestow His Spirit upon His people that they will become a light amid the moral darkness; and great light will be reflected in all parts of the world. O that our faith might be increased, that the Lord might work mightily with His people.

We all need the Holy Spirit. Our ministers need it. Our medical and educational institutions and our churches need it. We need a thorough, living experience in the work of the Lord.

We thank the Lord that here at this meeting there has been seen some of the moving of the Spirit of God, and that some of these young people and children have been given a desire to obtain an experience in religious things. I was glad, as I saw them coming forward the other day, that they were not living in wicked cities such as San Francisco and Oakland, but that they are here in the country, where they may be kept free from evil associations and many of the temptations that come with life in the cities.

"It shall come to pass, that whosoever shall call on the name of the Lord shall be saved." This a comforting promise. Can we grasp it by faith? Shall we not by our actions show that we appreciate the rich provisions of the Word of God?

Peter continues, "Ye men of Israel, hear these words; Jesus of Nazareth, a man approved of God among you by miracles and wonders and signs, which God did by him in the midst of you, as ye yourselves also know: Him, being delivered by the determinate counsel and foreknowledge of God, ye have taken, and by wicked hands have crucified and slain." (Verses 22, 23)

It took courage to bear this straight testimony. This courage and boldness in speaking the truth had come in answer to the united prayer of the disciples, while they had been together in the upper chamber.

Peter then speaks of the resurrection of Jesus: (Verses 24-27, quoted)

Thank God, we all have a hope that reaches to the grave. When we die, we do not go immediately to heaven. But if the Lord calls us to die, and we have been faithful in His service, we may lie down with the expectation that when Christ comes to raise the dead, we shall hear His voice and be brought out of our graves. Our flesh may rest in hope. When the righteous shall come forth from their graves, what a rejoicing there will be! (Verses 32-39, quoted)

These promises are for our children as well as for us. We can bring them to Christ. It will require great watchfulness on the part of parents, but if they are faithful they may keep their children from being spoiled by the vanity and the corruptions that are in the world.

"And with many other words did he testify and exhort, saying, Save yourselves from this untoward generation." (Verse 40)

This exhortation has a special application to us. We are living in the generation concerning which it is said, "As the days of Noe were, so shall also the coming of the Son of man be. For as in the days that were before the flood, they were eating and drinking, marrying and giving in marriage." (Matthew 24:37, 38) If any of us are to be among the overcomers, we must be diligent to keep ourselves free from the corruptions of the age.

(Acts 2:41, 42, quoted)

The Holy Spirit has not been diminished since the days of Pentecost. It will be given today to every soul that will seek for it. The Lord is willing to send His Holy

Spirit into all our institutions. We want a spirit of prayer. Let us take hold of God by living faith. Let us believe that He will do all that He says He will do, and let us prepare our hearts to receive what He has promised for us.

In many places we have established our educational institutions. Our schools and our sanitariums are to reach a high standard. The Bible is to be made the great educational book. It is the Book of books, that gives us a knowledge of Him whom to know aright is life eternal. It is to be made the foundation of all true education.

We are not to aim for a lower standard than that which Christ has laid out for His people. But there are many things included in what is commonly called a higher education, that we do not need. John the Baptist received a training for his life work, not in the schools of the rabbis, but in the wilderness, alone with God and His Word. As he prayed, the Scriptures were opened before him in a wonderful manner. And today God is just as willing to instruct those who will humbly seek for that wisdom which cometh from above.

We need experienced workers in the cause of God. It is not necessary that they all know several languages, but they do all need an experience in the things of God. Some who go to foreign countries will need to learn a language, but all need not spend time in learning languages that they will never use. We have not time to spend years in studying subjects that will be of no practical value. We are not to think that we must climb to the highest rounds of knowledge on every science. Time is short, and we must labor earnestly to save souls. If we will take the Word of God, and study it diligently and prayerfully, we will find the light and the knowledge that we need.

In our sanitariums, we advocate the use of simple remedies. We discourage the use of drugs, for they poison the current of the blood. In these institutions sensible instruction should be given [on] how to eat, how to drink, how to dress, and how to live so that the health may be preserved.

Before there were any sanitariums amongst us, my husband and I began work in medical missionary lines. We would bring to our house cases that had been given up by the physicians to die. When we knew not what to do for them we would pray to God most earnestly, and He always sent His blessing. He is the mighty Healer, and He worked with us. We never had time or opportunity to take a medical course, but we had success as we moved out in the fear of God and sought Him for wisdom at every step. This gave us courage in the Lord.

Thus we combined prayer and labor. We used the simple water treatments, and then tried to fasten the eyes of the patients on the Great Healer. We told them what

He could do for them. If we can inspire the patients with hope, this is greatly to their advantage. We want all that have any part to act in our sanitariums to have a firm grasp on the power of the Infinite. We believe in Him and in the power of His Word. When we do our best for the recovery of the sick, we may then look for Him to be with us, that we may see of His salvation. We put too little confidence in the power of the Hand that rules the world.

The Lord instructed us that we should have a place were the sick might come, and be treated in a rational way. In harmony with this instruction the sanitarium at Battle Creek was built. Now we have many of these medical institutions, and the Lord is blessing their work.

We believe in the living God and in the simplicity of true godliness. It is important that those who are treating the sick shall have a living connection with the Source of all life and healing.

Somehow, we often seem to carry on our meetings in a tame, lifeless way. We need a revival of the Spirit of God. Every one is to work out his own salvation with fear and trembling. If you will all plant your feet upon the living Word of God, believing it and acting in harmony with it, confessing your sins in all humility and following Christ, we shall see among us more of the working of His mighty power.

Let us prepare for that life which measures with the life of God. We have not before us the prospect of lying in our graves. Some of us may be translated without tasting of death. Who will not deny themselves in order that they may help to send the truth where it will be received? We have now but a very little time in which we can work, so let us deny ourselves in every way possible that we may give the light of truth to all that can be reached. Every penny that we will invest in this work will be returned to us with large interest.

Let us take hold in faith. Let us pray. Let us believe. Let us act, and the Lord will encourage and strengthen us in the way. I want to see the salvation of God revealed in this meeting. He has power to give us. There is no lack of power on His part, but there is a lack of faith and of humility on the part of His people. Many of us would not know how to use that power if we were to receive it. Let us learn of the great Teacher, what it means to walk in humility, as Christ walked in humility.[41]

---

[41] Ms. 49, 1908; MR 900.19.

Chapter 50

I Am the True Vine

[A sermon based on John 15, preached on Sabbath, October 16, 1909, at San Jose, California]

"I am the true Vine, and My Father is the Husbandman. Every branch in Me that beareth not fruit He taketh away; and every branch that beareth fruit, He purgeth it, that it may bring forth more fruit." (John 15:1-2)

Jesus is speaking of the fruitless Christian, the professing believer, who, because he does not comply with the conditions of discipleship, departs more and more from Christ. He does not in his life bear the fruits of righteousness; he does not copy the life of Christ. But the true follower of Christ can have no lower standard than His perfect life.

"And every branch that beareth fruit, He purgeth it, that it may bring forth more fruit." "He purgeth it." Christ suffers trial to come upon His followers that they may be led to seek the Lord more earnestly. Then when trials come, do not think that the Lord is your enemy. He purges for a reason. He does not want you to be discouraged, but He would prove you, to see if you will be true to Him and will conduct yourselves circumspectly under every circumstance. He does not want to drive you away, but to drive you nearer to the Lord. In God is the Christian's only hope in time of perplexity.

Do not talk to others about your trials, for they have enough of their own to bear, and our human friends cannot always understand. It is your privilege to go to One who will always understand, because His life on earth was one of constant trial and perplexity, borne without failure and sin.

"Abide in Me," Christ says, "and I in you. As the branch cannot bear fruit of itself, except it abide in the vine; no more can ye, except ye abide in Me" (John 15:4). Christ would not tell us this if it were impossible for us to abide in Him. He shows us the possibility and the importance of a close relation with Himself. "He that abideth in Me, and I in him, the same bringeth forth much fruit: for without Me ye can do nothing." (John 15:5)

What is the "much fruit" that we must bear? It is fruit of a heavenly nature, the result of lives sanctified by the Holy Spirit of God. When we abide in Christ, and Christ abides in us, we shall be men and women of prayer, of truth, men and women who carry themselves circumspectly before God and before the world. Daily we shall draw from Christ the strength we need to work the works of God. This is what the world needs--a manifestation of the power of truth in Christian characters. What we need is faith in the Word of God, and with true faith we shall have the living witness that our ways please God. Of what worth is religion to us if when we approach God we cannot have the evidence in ourselves that He hears and answers prayer?

"Without Me," He says, "ye can do nothing." Then let us press close to the bleeding side of Christ. In Him our humanity is provided for. In Him we may become partakers of the divine nature, and overcome the corruption that is in the world through lust.

"If a man abide not in Me, he is cast forth as a branch, and is withered; and men gather them, and cast them into the fire, and they are burned. If ye abide in Me, and My words abide in you, ye shall ask what ye will, and it shall be done unto you. Herein is My Father glorified, that ye bear much fruit; so shall ye be My disciples." (John 15:6-9)

It is not enough that now and then you offer a prayer, and now and then deal righteously. You are to have the attributes of an abiding Christ working out in your life constantly. How many of us have this experience? Yet we may have it, and having it, we will be the happiest people on the face of the earth. With Christ's word abiding in us, we shall give evidence that we have wholly received Him who in His humanity lived a sinless life. In the strength of divinity we shall overcome every tendency to evil.

But if men abide not in Christ, "they are cast forth as a branch," and are withered. Man may make great claims to piety, but if in his business transactions he does not reveal that the Holy Spirit of God is governing words and actions, he had far better make no profession. Christ's life and death does not avail for him who chooses to do as he pleases, who follows his own imaginations and carries out on his own way and will.

"As the Father hath loved me, so have I loved you: continue ye in my love. If ye keep my commandments, ye shall abide in my love; even as I have kept my Father's commandments, and abide in His love." (John 15:9, 10) Let us thank God that this is our privilege. Though we are sent out into the world, we can keep before us the example of the pattern Man, and in His strength carry out the principles of overcoming. It is only the overcoming Christian who will reach the kingdom of heaven. May God help us in this matter, is my prayer. Let us see that we keep His commandments in all our dealings with one another. When we not only talk, but live our religion, we shall show that we are branches of the living vine.

"These things have I spoken unto you," the Saviour continued, "that My joy might remain in you, and that your joy might be full." (John 15:11) I think there was something said when the disciples heard that. Do you not think that if we had that full joy, we would do as we did when we first felt the sanctifying power of God upon our hearts? When we were looking for the coming of the Lord in the early days of this message, we would praise Him in our prayers and in our conversation. There was not one particle of fanaticism among those who truly loved the Lord and were seeking His glory.

True religion does not demand great bodily demonstrations such as some of you have had the misfortune to witness here. These are no evidence of the presence of the Spirit of God. In 1843 and 1844 we were called to meet just such fanaticism. Men would say, I have the Holy Spirit of God, and they would come into the meeting and roll just like a hoop. Because some would not receive this as evidence of the working of the Spirit of God, they were looked upon as wicked people. The Lord sent me into the midst of this fanaticism though I was not more than sixteen years of age. Some would come to me and ask, Why do you not join with them? I said, I have another Leader than this, One who is meek and lowly in heart, One who made no such demonstrations as you are making here, nor such boasts. These demonstrations are not of Christ, but of the devil.

Every particle of selfishness is to be purged from the character. We are to show the difference between the lovers of pleasure and the world, and the lovers of Jesus. "This is My commandment, That ye love one another, as I have loved you. Greater love hath no man than this, that a man lay down his life for his friends. Ye are My friends, if ye do whatsoever I command you." (John 15:12-14)

All that was communicated to Him by His Father, Christ makes known to His followers. "Henceforth I call you not servants;" He says, "for the servant knoweth not what His Lord doeth: but I have called you friends; for all things that I have heard of My Father I have made known unto you" (John 15:15). How was this done? By words merely? No; by character; by the daily life. It was thus that Christ represented His Father. My brethren and sisters, let us make it known that we are branches of the living vine in that we represent the character of Christ. By a life of fruitbearing we are to make known the truth of the Word. You may profess a religion that is as high as the heavens; but unless you do the commandments of

God, you are certainly not recommending the love of Christ to the world.

"If the world hate you, ye know that it hated Me before it hated you. If ye were of the world, the world would love his own: but because ye are not of the world, but I have chosen you out of the world, therefore the world hateth you. Remember the word that I said unto you, The servant is not greater than his lord. If they have persecuted Me, they will also persecute you; if they have kept my saying, they will keep yours also. But all these things will they do unto you for My name's sake, because they know not Him that sent Me." (John 15:18-21)

"If I had not come and spoken unto them, they had not had sin: but now they have no cloke for their sin. He that hateth Me hateth My Father also. If I had not done among them the works which none other man did, they had not had sin: but now have they both seen and hated both Me and My Father. But this cometh to pass, that the word might be fulfilled that is written in their law, They hated Me without a cause. But when the Comforter is come, whom I will send unto you from the Father, even the Spirit of truth, which proceedeth from the Father, He shall testify of Me: And ye also shall bear witness, because ye have been with Me from the beginning." (John 15:22-27)

The difference between the character of Christ and the character of other men of His day was everywhere apparent, and because of this difference the world hated Him. It hated Him for His goodness and His strict integrity. And Christ declared that those who manifest the same attributes would be likewise hated. As we near the end of time this hatred for the followers of Christ will be more and more manifest.

Christ took humanity and bore the hatred of the world that He might show men and women that they could live without sin, that their words, their actions, their spirit might be sanctified to God. We can be perfect Christians if we will manifest this power in our lives. When the light of heaven rests upon us continually we shall represent Christ. It was the righteousness revealed in His life that distinguished Christ from the world and called forth its hatred.

We are nearing the close of this earth's history. Let us ever remember that there is a heaven to win and a hell to shun. There are some among us who refuse to purify their souls by obedience to the truth, and they bring forward their sophistries to show that those who adhere strictly to a thus saith the Lord are altogether too particular. They seek to divert the mind from purity and truth and holiness and the development of Christian character; but such souls stand on Satan's side of the question.

Shall those who refuse to be converted, who reject the right of entrance through the gates into the city, charge God with severity and harshness? The result of allowing one sinner to enter heaven would be a second rebellion, and God cannot permit another. All who enter the heavenly city must be sanctified through the grace of God. Their weaknesses must be brought into such relation to truth that truth shall be their strongest point of character. Only those who have kept the truth--kept it in practice--can enter through the gates into the city of God.

The words of Christ are spoken for His people in all ages--for us upon whom the ends of the world are come. The test that will come to us will be upon the commandments of God. Only as we become partakers of the divine nature shall we learn to overcome. I pray that none in this congregation may lightly regard this great privilege, but that each may be a living branch of the true vine, bearing fruit to the glory of God.

In the life of Christ a perfect pattern has been given to every child of humanity. From infancy to manhood the life of Christ was perfect, teaching us that in everything we should seek perfection. To His work at His father's bench He brought the same principle. Some would laugh at Him for the pains He would take, but He would not be turned from His purpose to bring out of that which was imperfect something that would stand the test of proving.

And in His spiritual as in His temporal life Christ was perfect. Did He not have temptations? We know that He did. We know that temptation came to Him in every form. He knew what trial was. He spent whole nights in prayer to His Father. He wrestled with the powers of darkness until He overcame. And how fully the glory of the Father was revealed through Him!

Should we not honor the One who gave His Son to a life of trial and reproach for us? In giving His Son to a life of suffering God would teach us that because we suffer we have no reason to feel that we are not children of God, and thus lose faith in Him. When we are in trouble, let us think of this. If we would have more faith, we would see more of the glory of God than we do.

I think of the children in our families. Are we teaching them to live so that the gates of the city of God will be opened to them? Let fathers and mothers feel the solemn obligation resting upon them to teach their children the way of the Lord in kindness and tenderness and love. The mother should be the first teacher of her child. Parents, be kind and gentle with your children, and they will learn gentleness. Let us demonstrate in our homes that we are Christians. I value as worthless that profession that is not carried out in the home life in kindness and forbearance and love. Let us seek to form characters after the divine similitude. Let us maintain a living connection with heaven.

Consider the blessed reward in the kingdom of God awaiting those who in this life seek for the divine similitude. There there will be no more trial, no more affliction or pain or death. There we shall receive the crown of the overcomer and the harp of gold. Not for a few short years, but from everlasting to everlasting, we shall live to sing the song of praise to the Lamb. Will you engage in the effort to win these eternal blessings? Will you give your hearts unreservedly to God? He wants you. He stands ready to accept you, ready to forgive when you repent and turn from your sins. You may fail again and again, but again and again He will forgive if you truly repent, and He will bring you off more than conqueror at last through Him who has loved you and washed you in His own blood.[42]

---

[42] Manuscript 97, 1909; MR 900.47.

HARD TO FIND BOOKS AVAILABLE ON AMAZON

In Spanish versión also available

(EVERY BOOK IN BIG PRINT UNIQUE EDITION)

1. The Two Babylons (Big Print Edition) Hislop, $29.99.
2. The Book of Jesus Martyrs John Foxe, $29.99.
3. Daniel Uriah Smith, $22.99.
4. Revelation Uriah Smith, $27.99.
5. Thoughts from the Mount of Blessing with study guide, $19.99.
6. War of the Jews Flavius Josephus, $29.99.
7. Final Time Events Ellen White, $21.99.
8. Country Living Ellen White, $8.99
9. The Sanctified Life with study guide, $12.99.

BOOKS THAT WILL COMING SOON

1. Daniel: An Exhaustive Commentary of Ellen White.
2. Revelation: An Exhaustive Commentary of Ellen White.
3. The Third Angels Message, Alonzo T. Jones.
4. Genesis: An Exhaustive Commentary of Ellen White.
5. Steps to Christ with a study guide, Ellen White.
6. Last Day Events with a study guide, Ellen White.
7. Country living with a study guide, Ellen White.
8. Daniel and Revelation, Stephen N. Haskell.
9. Steps to Christ Word Search, Ellen White.
10. Healthful Living, Ellen White.

AND MORE…

Contact us for good bulk discounts and specials

kalhelministries21@gmail.com

www.ingramcontent.com/pod-product-compliance
Lightning Source LLC
Chambersburg PA
CBHW080858010526
44118CB00015B/2191